Pathways to Success in Higher Education

HIGHER EDUCATION RESEARCH AND POLICY (HERP)

VOLUME 7

The *Higher Education Research and Policy* (HERP) series is intended to present both research-oriented and policy-oriented studies of higher education systems in transition, especially from comparative international perspectives. Higher education systems worldwide are currently under multi-layered pressures to transform their funding and governance structures in rapidly changing environments. The series intends to explore the impact of such wider social and economic processes as globalization, internationalization and Europeanization on higher education institutions, and is focused on such issues as the changing relationships between the university and the state, the changing academic profession, changes in public funding and university governance, the emergent public/private dynamics in higher education, the consequences of educational expansion, education as public/private goods, and the impact of changing demographics on national systems. Its audience includes higher education researchers and higher education policy analysts, university managers and administrators, as well as national policymakers and the staff of international organizations involved in higher education policymaking

PETER LANG
EDITION

Gabriella Pusztai

Pathways to Success in Higher Education

Rethinking the Social Capital Theory
in the Light of Institutional Diversity

PETER LANG
EDITION

Bibliographic Information published by the Deutsche Nationalbibliothek
The Deutsche Nationalbibliothek lists this publication in the Deutsche Nationalbibliografie; detailed bibliographic data is available in the internet at http://dnb.d-nb.de.

This publication was supported by the European Union
and the State of Hungary, co-financed by the European Social Fund
in the framework of the TÁMOP-4.2.4.A/ 2-11/1-2012-0001
'National Excellence Program'.

Library of Congress Cataloging-in-Publication Data
Pusztai, Gabriella.
 Pathways to success in higher education : rethinking the social capital
theory in the light of institutional diversity / Gabriella Pusztai.
   pages cm – (Higher education research and policy, ISSN 2193-7613 ;
volume 7)
 Includes bibliographical references.
 ISBN 978-3-631-66426-1
 1. College students–Social networks–Europe, Eastern–Cross-cultural studies. 2. Socialization–Europe, Eastern–Cross-cultural studies. 3. Education, Higher–Social aspects–Europe, Eastern–Cross-cultural studies. I. Title.
 LC192.4.P87 2015
 378.1'980947--dc23
                       2015012300

ISSN 2193-7613
ISBN 978-3-631-66426-1 (Print)
E-ISBN 978-3-653-05577-1 (E-Book)
DOI 10.3726/ 978-3-653-05577-1

© Peter Lang GmbH
Internationaler Verlag der Wissenschaften
Frankfurt am Main 2015

This publication has been peer reviewed.

www.peterlang.com

Contents

Introduction

The most important feature of the transformation of higher education in the modern age is expansion. Having begun after World War II, this phenomenon is still being driven by ever increasing social demand. Along with the growth of student participation, the institutional system has diversified – with regional differences – into individual hierarchies of institutional types, sectors and branches of study (Teichler 2008, Zgaga et al. 2014). As the number of students has grown, the organisational complexity within educational institutions has also been increasing. The social demand for higher education is likely to increase further. It is questionable whether this will lead to greater social mobility or not, how the socially diverse student population will be distributed among different regions and institutions, whether a restructured curriculum will favour certain social groups and indeed who will learn what from whom in higher education.

The weak point of the literature analysing the consequences of the expansion is that students are left in the background and the tendency is for researchers to give an increasingly schematic picture of them (Altbach 2009). Even though student representatives were given a say in institutional decision-making owing to the democratisation of higher education after World War II, and new interest groups such as women and minorities have appeared in the system, students are still represented by only a limited amount of statistical data in the specialist discourse. Analyses focus on the behaviour of the macro-level actors of the multi-dimensional and multi-actor force field of educational politics. Priority is given to investigations into organisational aspects, i.e. the network of organisations. Today's researchers are occupied with the spectacular measures taken within the framework of international and national higher educational politics. The issues and changing principles of control and financing have drawn such intense professional attention that they have overshadowed the cultural changes that have been taking place inside the student population and left them almost unnoticed, deprived as they are of any ringing declarations. Even students' mobility between the cycles of courses and among regions has generated some interest only because of its relevance to the structural changes within the institutional system. Is it possible that students and their communities are no longer relevant actors in the world of higher education?

According to a model constructed in the 1980s for the international comparison of higher education systems, the higher education policies of a particular country are determined by the balance of power regarding the expectations formed by three major centres of power (Clark 1983), namely the academic oligarchy, state bureaucracy and market subsystems. Each of them has their own binary code, for the implementation of which they hold the institutions of the higher education system accountable. In the 1990s, critics of this model drew attention to a shift in the value system of the state towards a role that is more sensitive to the logic of the market, holds institutions accountable and evaluates them. They also pointed out that the academic value system had given way to the dominance of administrative-managerial logic (Neave 1998) and that the model can be applied to post-socialist systems only with certain limitations (Tomusk 1997). Since the turn of the millennium, the description of the impact mechanism, usually defined at a national level, has been expanded in the regional and international context because of increasingly specific expectations, which may be different from the expectations formulated at the national level (Hrubos 2010). The other reason why Clark's model had to be reworked was that previously the centres of power representing different value systems had only included organisational bodies, although the presence of collective interest groups and individual actors also had to be reckoned with (Chen–Barnett 2000, Marginson–Rhoades 2002). Besides, education researchers recommended that it would be advisable to carry out policy analyses at local or institutional levels and to explore prevailing tendencies among students in the local social and cultural milieu (Altbach 2009).

Although student groups do have a major role in negotiating institutional circumstances, researchers still seem to attach little importance to the analysis of their views and relationship networks. The literature has a rather pragmatic, simplified and dualistic image of students: they are looked upon as either customers or products. Both views are related to market-controlled higher education. According to a popular view in the sociology of economy, students are one of the stakeholders with an interest in higher education; they are an interest group influencing its operation, actors controlling their life courses through mainly independent and rational decisions. The logic of their choices is controlled by the invisible hand of the market and those who do not base their choice of institution on efficiency are punished. Others argue that national and global governments – making reference to individuals' freedom of choice and students' interests – use students for their own purposes to achieve change (Neave 1998) and refer to them as consumers, since this kind of owner's individualism is in harmony with the economic dogmas of higher education politics. However, critics warn that although students are called consumers, owing to the patterns of power in the social, historical and economic context they are in a somewhat subordinate position because in a sociological sense they are not adults in full possession of decision-making abilities, do not make rational choices and have deficient and asymmetrical information. Moreover, the conditions of competition are not clear because of the different ways of financing one's studies and the socially selective nature of public education and entrance into higher education (Amaral 2008).

The industrial model claims that students as products become the subject matter of research the moment – having come off the conveyer belt – they are released into the labour market. Accordingly, the institution is taken into account only as a production site of standardised technology. Research that uses this approach usually focuses on the short-term convertibility of the student's degree on the labour market. There are remarkable empirical findings in this field; it has been concluded that the transition between studying and starting work has become longer, and, moreover, the proportion of students who are intent on starting work has decreased, a phenomenon the background to which is yet to be explored (Teichler 2007.....). A different student image has been adopted by the model which compares students to patients in health institutions. Accordingly, the function of higher education is to provide "treatment" for students' diagnoses as established at the beginning of the institutional process. This approach, which concentrates on the institutional impact of higher education, is close to our method of research.

The results presented in this volume are the conclusions of our research in which we analysed the transformations in the paradigm of students' socialisation in a changing educational context and their impact on the success of student careers. Over the past decades higher education researchers' approaches have been shaped by one-directional and linear reconstruction models of student socialisation. More than half a century ago, the structuralist-functionalist interpretation defined student socialisation as a process during which students learn to live within the frameworks offered and prescribed by the institution, and, as a result, newcomers are integrated into the world of higher education. It looked upon organisational role acquisition as a largely asymmetrical process: under the influence of organisational norms and enforced by sanctions a "ready-made" student is produced, who will sell well on the labour market later. Most documents of educational politics and technical literature on the macro-level phenomena in higher education still reflect this schematic and uniform view. Conflict theory, which also takes a reconstructional view of socialisation, proves the reconstruction of the habitus formed by the social status of one's family of origin – and thereby the reproduction of social status – by means of a critical study of higher education socialisation. Both models presuppose a uniform pattern of academic socialisation and treat the student population as if it were the same in every institution, sector and country. In this way, their image of students becomes not only uniform but also one-dimensional. The active interactional model of student socialisation extends the characteristics of social learning in groups to include the entire student socialisation process. Owing to the interactions between newcomers and other members of the higher education community the social construction of student culture is a continuous process operating in the different cycles of study at different institutions and locations. This model looks upon the role of students and the culture of the campus as a joint product. The dispositions of local communities surrounding students (family, peer group, public education environment) all exert a strong influence even at the anticipatory stage of higher education socialisation.

Apart from active and constructive individual participation, the interpretation of student socialisation as a process and the dialogue regarding institutional impacts, a further essential new element of the development of the models is the realisation of the interdependent and reflected character of influences within and outside institutions, which has helped the revision of earlier socialisation theories. This new interpretation also has various pedagogical consequences; for example collaborative methods can gain ground and the range of the institution's relevant activities will widen with relationship building, dialogues, interactions, group learning and extracurricular and leisure activities.

The reason why student development within the institution has become a current question again in Central and Eastern Europe is because, owing to the unexpectedly large-scale expansion after the recent political transition, the homogeneous social composition of the student population suddenly diversified with the appearance of lower status and ethnic minority students and mothers with young children (Forray 2003, Pusztai 2004, Forray–Kozma 2008, Engler 2010). The umbrella term for these new groups in higher education is *non-traditional students* (Harper–Quaye 2009). Some researchers believe that the collapse of a unified student culture is due to their appearance (Altbach 2009). In our view, the cultural pluralism of society as reflected in the institutional context has also played a part in the replacement of a common higher education culture with a blend of the sometimes clashing constructions of reality found in diverse interpretive communities.

What students regard as the purpose of their studies and success is rooted in their everyday interactions and the events of their social life, and it is worded in the language they create and use among themselves. From this perspective, real higher education worlds come into life in the way students "talk them into life" in the university canteen or the dorms (Berger–Luckmann 1998). If we are to learn a little more about the world of higher education, we need insights into dominant interpretations among students and we have to know in what kind of interpretive communities they develop their world views (Fish 1980, Burr 1995). At the moment, Central and Eastern Europe are undergoing the very same transformations that were detected by the more sensitive overseas researchers back in the 1960s. Instead of the stimulating power of purposefulness and achievement-orientation, students have begun to be guided by peer influences in their attempts to find their way within the system (Riesman 1983). That is to say, students primarily learn from their peers. Above all, they learn about the relevant questions and the valid answers to them, and besides – or instead of – Mertonian de jure rules they also internalise de facto rules (Becher 1989). To students, it is the peer group that sets the agenda; the need to meet expectations and the sensors – tuned to receive signals from others and thus encouraging conformity (Riesman 1983:81) – are more influential factors than the "compass" of one's inner conscious self and aspirations to perform well (Riesman 1983:76). Therefore, the primacy of the traditional intrinsic goals and values of higher education is called into question, and individuals are classified as autonomous, anomic or norm-breaking in relation to the "peer group jury's" expectations (Riesman 1983: 130). We are convinced that students in our region do shape the profile of higher education much more actively than education politicians, heads of institutions and university lecturers would think. Each student relationship network provides a context of behaviour, which is much more likely to leave a mark than any bold curriculum or innovative education method.

As student relationship networks produce common contextual interpretations, we find it crucial to understand what kind of social constellations come about in higher education, and whether they can be viewed as a campus culture that is made up of students' views and value systems and is perceivably present over a certain period of time. The main focus of our interest is what kind of relationships serve as resources in the higher education context that can best help students' advancement. In our opinion, students' relationships (in both formal and content aspects) and relationship networks lend features to the society of an institution, a faculty or a campus which play at least as important a role in their university careers as individual social status, the structural conditions of the institution and all the planned effect mechanisms put together.

In the expanded and differentiated higher education system there are regularities similar to those in public education. There is a comprehensive higher education system under development, in which growing emphasis is given to the responsibility of higher education for social integration and the inclusion of new student groups. Therefore, further research is necessary on the factors compensating the effects of social status, residential environment and region, which – according to research on public education – are able to modify the process of social reproduction.

The increased public interest in higher education as well as competition for the decreasing amount of resources has called attention to the problem of the comparability of institutions with respect to performance and productivity. High priority is given to how much progress students make during their years of study and how the institution contributes to student learning outcomes. This is an extremely important question, given the internal diversity of institutions and of the entire institutional system and the increasing heterogeneity of the student population (Teichler 2008). Neither the ranking of universities nor even their multi-ranking (although the latter method has attempted to correct the shortcomings of ranking), are able to grasp the pedagogical productivity of institutions with a high proportion of non-traditional students. Several homogeneous and closed groups can develop from non-traditional students on campuses, especially in the peripheral border regions of Central and Eastern Europe. Student communities in institutions of differing status and prestige may change or even disregard the declared goals and standards of higher education institutions, thereby putting into operation goal interpretations and norms that differ completely from what has originally been planned; something which will have an impact on student outcomes as well (Bloch 2008).

The study of institutional impact has been given a new impetus by the growing proportion of drop-out students and the need to tackle regional and local problems of youth unemployment in our region. Initially, institutional impact was attributed to the structural features of institutions, such as size and selectivity, but it has now become clear that those factors only have an indirect impact. However, some social scientists claim that institutional impact does not exist in itself, since apparent differences in achievement are caused by differences in social status hidden behind the distribution of students among institutions and faculties (Bourdieu 1988, Berger 2000). Others think it is obvious that institutions and faculties do not only differ from one another regarding social composition but also regarding their contribution to shaping students' initial knowledge, skills and value systems during the years of study (Banta- Pike 2012).

Research into the institutional contribution to students' progress has made it clear that it is not primarily the structural and infrastructural conditions of an institution of higher education that effectively support the success of a student. Instead, it is the interactional force field offered by the institution that backs up the progress of the students (Pascarella-Terenzini 2005). When the success of students is explained, the related literature focuses on the differences in the cultural and economic resources of the students concerned, and relatively little attention is paid to the network of interpersonal connections and cooperation in the framework of which the objectives of the students and their images of the profession would be well worth analysing. Tinto (1993) believes that the student's integration into the society of an institution is a major predictor of the success of the individual. In his comprehensive model he analysed the students' involvement and participation in their learning and social systems. Tinto claims that integration into these systems largely influences the performance of a student, so much so that the student may finally become detached from their bonds to the outside world. As a result of integration, and because of frequent interaction, students will conform to the forces attracting them to the higher education institution. In his theory, students will be integrated into the system to the degree to which they are able to share the norms and values of their peers and to the degree that they are able to meet the formal and informal requirements of the institution. As students' integration improves, so does their commitment to the objective of their studies (profession) and to the institution. All these have a positive effect on their performance, whereas the lack of integration may lead to their marginalization, departure to another institution or to dropout. Non-traditional students do not have any inherited experience from parents and, what is more, in an underdeveloped region, their local environment and social status draw them away from the institution (Hurtado 2007, Harper-Quaye 2009, Pusztai 2011).

Tinto's theory has been criticized because he assumes that normative congruence will take place as a result of structural integration but that this will lead to the acculturation of non-traditional students who come from a social background different from that of the dominant group. Integration is impeded by cultural distance as well as by the fact that large institutions are not really favourable environments for real student communities. The theory of integration into the formal and informal structures of the campus is, with certain refinements, acceptable to us. As a result of our previous research findings, we give priority to the effects of informal ties (Pusztai 2009, 2011). While in Tinto's interaction model it is the network of interpersonal links that forges students into a community, in Coleman's functional community concept shared values accomplish the same result and maintain integration. In our theory, a strong bond to an element of the institutional network constitutes a source of social capital. In our assumption it has a more powerful influence on students' careers than a less intensive bond to a wide range of open networks (Coleman-Hoffer 1987, Pusztai 2011).

Although the characteristics of the relationship structures among young people within institutions of education has already been studied, the theory of social capital has been applied mainly in public education research. The concept of social capital has long been avoided by studies on higher education students even though the problems arising in higher education in the last two decades have all been similar to the education sociological problems of secondary education at the time of its great expansion in the middle of the last century, and many accumulated research findings deal with student context and relationship systems. Problems that used to be characteristic of public education such as equal access to education for groups of different social status, demographic and ethnic composition, the chance of achieving a successful performance and the need to decrease attrition have also emerged in higher education during the past two decades and it was in connection with the above issues that the idea of social capital was mentioned (Kim-Schneider 2005, Perna-Titus 2005, Altbach 2009). The concept of social capital as referred to by that name sneaked into higher education research via the economic approach to the study of academic success and peer impact. However, the authors of those papers did not manage to identify themselves with the essence of Coleman's theory (Sacerdote 2001, Arcidiacono–Nicholson 2005, Winston–Zimmermann 2004).

In our research we concluded that students' careers are distinctively and measurably influenced by the social experiences they obtain during their years in compulsory and higher education, the contact they have with dominant socialising agents existing at the institution and a supporting and inspiring working and learning environment. During our previous research on the effects of network resources on students' academic careers we found that with regard to learning outcomes, Bourdieusian reproductional determinedness, which is beneficial to students with a favourable social background, does not manifest itself equally but depends on the school context. In our monograph entitled School and Community (2004, in Hungarian) we highlighted the explanatory power of Colemanian social capital, a concept little known in Central and Eastern European education research at that time but which, in the Anglo-Saxon sociology of education, was at the beginning of its significant career in studies on the comparison of school sectors in public education. Later, in an analysis of the role of extra-familiar relationships in the social rise of Gypsy/Roma intellectuals, we pointed out that bonds with teachers can become extremely important resources, requiring extraordinary preparedness, a sense of mission and a completely transformed role image on the part of the teacher. In our monograph Social capital and the School (2009, in Hungarian) we examined the direct effect of institutional resources on academic careers and their long-term effect on young people's life strategies. The most important empirical achievement of this work was that, drawing on the growing amount of international research and debate on the subject and taking a firm stand on the interpretation of social capital as a concept of educational sociology, we made an attempt at a comparative test of the theories of reproduction and social capital. Not only did we try to remain faithful to the theoretical roots, we also made efforts to define the possibilities and limitations of measurement. In order that Central and Eastern European interpretations of the theory could be presented, we participated in the development of the indicators of social capital and the creation of reliable and valid instruments for its measurement among higher education students. Our findings, presented in the work From the Invisible Hand to Friendly Hands (Pusztai 2011, in Hungarian), show that the individual's academic career is decisively influenced by the student community

14

living together in the various institutional units, together with their views on the purpose of studies, the norms to adhere to during one's studies, optional activities and the circle of people they rely on. Under certain circumstances this influence is able to overcome the influence of the student population of a higher socioeconomic status.

This volume consists of studies on the development of the use of institutional social capital as a concept in higher education research. What we can conclude from these papers is that both public- and higher education research have followed the same path: in the beginning, the lifting effect institutions had on individual achievement was attributed to structural factors. Only after accurate analysis did it turn out that better student achievement was not due to the traits of the educational system, the sector or the type of institution, but to the internal features of the institution, and the special traits of the context. Both public and higher education research have finally found that what makes the difference in institutional impact is primarily the society of the institution, the relationships of those who cooperate within the same organisational framework and the institutional culture they create.

International discourse on education politics pays considerable attention to the efficiency of schools, colleges and universities. The three papers in the first chapter attempt to identify those factors of institutional social capital that support student success. This topic needs elaboration because Coleman's original concept of social capital is used in different and often ambiguous meanings or is even misunderstood. The first study gives a summary of our present knowledge regarding how social capital influences student success and whether schools and colleges can increase the chance of social integration through their institutional impact. We point out the differences between theories using the same concepts but forming separate paradigms that can even serve as bases for alternative hypotheses in empirical research. Our paper argues for the application of the concept of social capital as a theory of mobility and offers an alternative interpretational framework by raising the question of institutional impact.

The second paper in the first chapter looks at the reasons for the differences in student achievement from a comparative perspective in order to challenge earlier explanations, which did not attach much significance to institutional impact. We compare students from the different sectors of the Hungarian, Romanian and Ukrainian school systems with regard to what institutional factors influence their academic careers. A comparative study became necessary because in previous studies it had been revealed that denominational schools had a favourable influence on the school careers of students with disadvantageous backgrounds, but later it became apparent that the sectoral impact may not be the same in every school system. Learning outcome was measured with a summarising index that included aspects such as taking on extra academic work and planning one's future higher education studies. As our research showed that sector impact was influenced by school relationship networks, we wanted to know whether the institutional factors supporting success were the same or different in state and denominational schools in Central Europe.

The third paper in the first chapter searches for indicators of school context effect, and going beyond individual student traits it includes in the analysis the attributes of school contexts as independent factors. It focuses on the structures and contents of students' relationships at school. We carried out analyses based on individual students and tried to represent contextual effects with the attributes of aggregate students groups. According to the results, there is significant divergence among the characteristics of school context, which are able to create more or less added value.

Given that in mass higher education the concept of student success is even less clearly defined than in public education, the second chapter searches for indicators and explanations of higher education student success. The first paper in the second chapter examines the university-age population as to whether they need similar or different supporting factors to be able to enter higher education, get a degree and find a job. There are arguments that confidence in being able to find an optimal job can be listed alongside the tried and tested outcome indicators. We presumed that differences in students' achievement in higher education can also be explained by the social network theory: more isolated young people have limited aspirations and opportunities.

The second paper in the second chapter reacts to the Bologna process. When searching for outcome indicators we have found that after the introduction of the multi-cycle system, the crossing point between bachelor and master's studies became a crucial point of selection. Intention to continue one's studies was viewed as an obvious outcome indicator by education sociological research, but it is no longer self-evident in restructured higher education, since the need to continue one's studies may only be a sign of the poor marketability of bachelor degrees. The paper analyses data on full-time bachelor students who were the first to enter two-cycle higher education and points out that both going on to master's level and finding employment can be outcome indicators. In many cases, similar institutional factors may lead to either option.

In the third paper of the second chapter we first summarised our investigation into the origins and alternatives of student success, constructions popular in higher education research. Following this we introduced a complex indicator that opens up new possibilities to diagnose success, and we compared the individual components and the complex indicators of student success. We finally examined the correlation between student success and institutional, demographic and social background variables.

Since the 1960s several authors have observed that what actually happens in institutions of higher education is different from what education politicians, heads of institutions and faculty have planned. The question, first raised by overseas researchers and later by researchers in Europe as well, is how a higher education institution can exert a stronger influence on students. The third chapter presents the diversity and resources of the institutional environment in higher education. In the first paper of the third chapter we analyse researchers' theories on the effects of the social milieu of higher education institutions and present our own idea about how the theory of social capital can be applied in campus settings. Among the theories that might function as interpretative frameworks for the campus impact research findings available on the subject, the most influential are student involvement theory (Astin 1993), student integration theory (Tinto 1993), the theory of institutional habitus (Tierney 2001), and Coleman's concept of social capital (Coleman 1988). We strongly advise that further thought should be given to these and they should be widely used in research.

We hold the view that an individual's success in higher education depends on what kind of interpretive community they are embedded in. In our previous research we pointed out that religious student groups contribute to the formation of distinctively novel patterns of socialisation within the institution, which is a good reason to pay attention to this aspect of student diversity as well. The fundamentally mono-confessional blocks of Europe have been replaced by the broadest and most manifold multi-confessional belt in Central and Eastern Europe. Ethnic and confessional factors are interrelated in multi-confessional and multi-ethnic states and religiosity is stronger in those regions where confessional affiliation functions as a central component of identity. An important question for the education researcher is whether religion-based communities support or hinder young people's higher education careers. In the second paper of the third chapter we examine in what ways membership of on-campus and out-of-campus religious student groups affects students' academic and social integration as well as their academic success.

The final paper of the third chapter shows the diversity of campus environments. The current trends in higher education largely consist of homogenisation at both national and international levels, while at the same time we are also witnessing major structural, programme and reputational diversification in Central and Eastern Europe. The institutions within a country and their units within an institution are now largely different, but the system is not only arranged into a hierarchical order in terms of gradual differences, as the compilers of various lists of colleges and universities tend to believe, but also presents serious nominal differences, which necessitate an urgent examination of regional and institutional differences. While previously we concentrated primarily on the heterogeneity of the relational and cultural integration of the students, in this paper we discuss as factors those elements of the institutional environment that exert a more or less powerful attraction on the individual. We intend to find out where institutional impact is rooted and how it is measured most effectively. In the study an attempt is made to survey the roots of institutional impact and its dimensions. Subsequently, we examine how institutional impact influences students, and finally we provide a portrait of typical institution types in a cross-border higher educational region.

Our research was conducted in higher education institutions in Hungary, Romania and Ukraine. We used three international databases for our analyses: "Secondary School Students' Plans for Higher Education" (2006, N=1,446), "The Role of Tertiary Education in Social and Economic Transformation" data for full time bachelor (2008, N=1,399) and master (2010, N=602) students, as well as "Higher Education for Social Cohesion Cooperative Research and Development in a Cross-border Area." (2012, N=2,728). Besides these, we used the results of the most recent wave of a research project entitled "Hungarian Youth 2012" (N=8,000).

How context matters in education

Social capital in educational research: interpretations

Abstract

The international discourse on education politics pays considerable attention to the efficiency of schools, colleges and universities. This study gives a summary of our present knowledge regarding how social capital influences student success and whether schools and colleges can increase the chance of social integration through their institutional impact. We point out the differences between theories using the same concepts but forming separate paradigms that can even serve as bases for alternative hypotheses in empirical research. We can state that the application of the theory about how social capital compensates for reproductional determinants can give new impetus to education research and offers an alternative interpretational framework by raising the question of institutional impact.

Several Theories for One Concept

The concept of social capital is rooted in the sociology of education, and has been widely interpreted in literature. Owing to the multitude of theorists, definitions and empirical research, we intend to restrict our overview to that line of the theory which is relevant to the world of education and which can be regarded as a starting point in education research. The concept of capital, having originated in economics, was extended to denote any means capable of producing profit as early as the 19th century and was used in that sense in the works of such classic figures of social science as Durkheim, Weber and Simmel (Durkheim 2014, Weber 2001, Simmel 1949). It was Hanifan in 1916 who first wrote about the impact on school achievement of belonging to a community, using the umbrella term social capital to mean all the goodwill, fellowship and mutual sympathy around the society of a school and the social intercourse among a group of individuals and families living at the same location, which might offer a solution to individualisation, fragmentation, the integration of immigrants and the general loss of trust after World War I. As a follower of Dewey, Hanifan may have borrowed the term from him. Social capital was also used by Marx's contemporaries to mean the wealth produced by workers which remains in society's possession after consumption, i.e. the common profit yielded by common goods. Dewey, in contrast, used it for the spiritual wealth accumulated by humanity. In his view, schools were centres of communal education and community building. He emphasised the importance of establishing relationships based on empathy and cooperation during school work, which might bridge social divides. That was how he tried to find an answer to the problems mentioned above, such as the devastating influence of big companies, resulting in the destruction of the individual. Facing macro-level tendencies that were endangering democracy, he regarded local democracy as the way out, since he looked upon society as an alliance of members realising democracy through their interactions in communities created by educational institutions. His train of thought bears obvious resemblance to Tocqueville's views, adapted to the world of education (Pusztai 2009).

The discourse of social sciences in the 1950–60s referred to traditional relationships as phenomena decelerating modernisation (Lenski 1961). Even rational choice theory took relationships into account as factors diminishing the costs of exchange, but it overestimated related obligations and underestimated the benefits. Settlement sociologists and economists had already pointed out the lasting and significant influence of relationships, and followers of the Chicago school repeatedly referred to local neighbourhoods as resources or, for that matter, regressive forces. Bourdieu used the term social capital in one of his studies in the early 1970s, highlighting its class-specific nature, namely that relationships provide the proletariat "with a safety net against misery, bad fortune, loneliness and squalor" (Bourdieu and Passeron 1977:262) and the upper classes with connections that are "indispensable for economic and cultural capital to yield the highest possible profit" (Bourdieu and Passeron 1977:263). Loury, an economist critical of the excessively individualistic interpretation of human capital, also created a definition at the end of the 1970s. By the term social capital he understood all the resources coming from one's family and environment that are incorporated in one's human capital, but, like Bourdieu, he treated them as fully individual resources (Loury 1977, Coleman 1990:300, Carbonaro 1998).

The real milestone in the history of the concept occurred in the late 1980s, when two detailed analyses were written almost simultaneously (Bourdieu 1986, Coleman 1987). On the surface the two theories might even be confused, although their difference and the fact that the two authors very rarely referred to each other suggest the different roots and parallel development of the two theories (Coleman 1990:300). The concept was further developed after the 1990s by Putnam, whose main focus was on social capital generated by civil society.

Both Bordieu and Coleman based their theories on the functional value of social capital. This is how Bordieu's theory of reproduction (bearing the influence of Weber as well as Marx) defines capital: "capital is labour accumulated in its materialized form or its 'incorporated,' embodied form", a means of producing profit or reproducing itself, which, "when appropriated on a private basis by agents or groups of agents, enables them to appropriate social energy in the form of reified or living labour" (Bourdieu 1986: 241). His wording evokes the labour theory of value used by Marx. Social structure in his interpretation means an essentially vertical hierarchy, although the structuring forces operate in multiple dimensions: society is structured by the unequal distribution of economic capital, which is "directly and immediately convertible into money" (Bourdieu 1986:242), cultural capital, available on the educational market or "social capital, made up of social obligations or connections" (Bourdieu 1986:242). Bourdieu thinks the efficiency of social capital does not approach that of economic or cultural capital as the economy is one of the dominant fields of modern society. Conversions of the different capital types ultimately result in unambiguous and long-lasting conditions, because the distribution of every type of capital is rooted in the unequal possession of economic capital. The large-scale conversion of economic capital into cultural capital is a response to the challenge of modernisation, and in his view the education system legitimises the reproduction of cultural capital in an efficient way.

Bordieu's theory denies the possibility of individual choice, because he holds the view that every action and all behaviour is the result of unconscious obedience to structural forces. School success is the result of the conversion of family cultural capital, whether it is available in the form of different qualifications, possessed cultural goods, erudition or sophisticated behaviour. The amount of cultural capital determines educational investment strategies in the sense that different social classes develop special types of habitus, comprising, among other things, permanent attitudes to the future, career and school. Such attitudes are, for example, one's attitude to the knowledge offered by the school and willingness to take part in education. That is to say, in Bordieu's opinion cognitive factors are manifestations of reconversion strategies that follow from the social position of the family (Bourdieu 1977), and they are even more permanently reproductive than the social status determined by qualifications and occupation (Róbert 1987).

Coleman, on the other hand, -influenced by the theory of human capital, social exchange theory and rational action theory- made an attempt at a synthesis of all three (Schultz 1971, Homans 1958, Becker 1994). In his view, the behaviour of the social system has to be discussed at the macro level, whereas the concept of purpose orientation has to be interpreted at the level of individuals. The foundation of his theory is purposive action aimed at satisfying individual needs. As this theory looks upon society as consisting of individuals and their relationships, objectives and interests can also be attributed to individual or communal actors; therefore social phenomena can be regarded as the effects of their decisions. Coleman tried to create a theory which as well as accepting the principle of rational, purposive action, emphasises the role and modifying effect of the specific social context, since processes aimed at satisfying individual needs take place in a social setting. This was the theoretical background to his interpretation of the processes taking place at schools and he claimed that an individual students' choice of school and their achievements do not exclusively depend on their position in the vertical social structure and purely individual choices, because those factors are heavily modified by the impact of social connections on individual decisions.

In Coleman's system there are also three types of capital which more or less correspond to Bordieu's categories, but in the discussion of their origin exchange is more emphatic than exploitation. What he calls physical capital is roughly equal to economic capital. Human capital, which "is created by changes in persons that bring about skills and capabilities that make them able to act in new ways" (Coleman 1988:17), corresponds to cultural capital; the third category is social capital, which exists in interpersonal relations. A crucial difference between the two theories is that the accumulation of social capital in the Colemanian sense does not lead to the exploitation of other people. Coleman's capitals are also convertible, but in his view it is social and not economic capital that is best convertible into human capital. Social capital in Bourdieu's theory is an attribute of conflicting individuals (Bourdieu 1986), while in Coleman's it is that of actors cooperating in the system of social exchange (Coleman 1990).

Bourdieu lays great emphasis on the mechanisms of the formation and maintenance of relationship networks, the so called institutionalisation rites. The groups that have been formed through relationships have closed boundaries, and the entrance of new members might pose a danger to them because it changes the system of legitimate exchanges in the network, thereby undermining the existing hierarchy. Coleman does not give much thought to the formation of relationship networks. His distinction between value-based and functional communities reveals his conviction that social capital is above all kept alive by living relationships, that is to say, –as in Durkheim's concept of social integration– a minimal number of exchanges is necessary for trust to be maintained, norms to function, and sanctions to be taken, i.e. for social capital to produce an effect. It is primarily the family, neighbourhood communities, voluntary organisations and religious communities that meet the above requirement (Durkheim 1997). Coleman finds both the formal, organisational and the informal instances of maintaining relations effective.

In Bourdieu's view the use of relationships is that they increase the individual's creditability and recognition, so the value of connections is provided by the connected individuals' characteristics. An individual's central values are well-known and acknowledged, so the amount of social capital in their possession depends on the amount of capital possessed by those they are connected to. In contrast, according to Coleman, value lies in the characteristics of the relationship structure (its stability, closed nature, density, attitude to norms), and the most precious resource of capital is the cohesion of a relationship network, when an individual's friends are also in close connection to one another.

In Bourdieu's theory the individual's actions are determined by social class and personal interest, whereas in Coleman's view the individual is characterised by rational actions modified under the influence of the relationship structure. An important difference is the judgement regarding the deliberate or involuntary nature of any kind of profiting from the relationships. According to Bourdieu, access to potential relational resources is the result of investment strategies, for which it is necessary to have knowledge of the structure, functioning and utilisation of networks. In Coleman's theory social networks are not formed in order to produce social capital but to serve other purposes, for example as charity organisations or religious communities. Their normative-regulatory function is only a side product; therefore investment and return do not appear as the outcomes of purposive action but are so called externalities. Besides, efforts and connections do not bring immediate benefits but result in much more profit in the future when –seemingly wasted– resources spent on maintaining connections start to yield a return. This phenomenon is of key relevance to our topic.

Bourdieu states that social capital has to be reproduced again and again, and the permanent maintenance of connections (attending exclusive cultural and social events, visiting select organisations, residential areas and schools, etc.) demands a lot of time and money. Still, investment yields profit and even exerts a multiplying effect on the capital currently available. Bourdieu thinks in terms of a hierarchically constructed field, where the distribution of the possession of connections is unequal. The more economic capital is invested in social capital, the more income it yields, and therefore the major investors can concentrate the entire social capital and become the representatives or delegates of the people connected by the network. The situation carries the possibility that representatives might use their power against the group, a phenomenon which Bourdieu calls the embezzlement of social capital.

Coleman does not discuss the hierarchy within relationship structures, but instead emphasises that they provide group members with access to the kind of goods which would not be accessible individually, so a well-functioning structure makes it easier for individuals to attain their goals. By abandoning the structure, individuals may do the others harm as they break the chain of information, trust and social control. Yet we cannot speak of exploitation, as the person leaving the network also does harm to him or herself. Coleman also points out certain positional differences within a group, e.g. in hierarchically structured big families or in a traditional rural milieu, but he emphasises that in closed relationship networks norms limiting self-interest and sanctioning selfish behaviour are well adhered to.

On the whole, there is an essential difference between the two theories of social capital owing to their different theoretical roots, namely rational and functional action theory on the one hand, and field theory, bearing the traces of Marx's class theory, on the other. The two theories can be juxtaposed as alternative hypotheses (Pusztai 2004, 2009).

When interpreting social capital, Putnam (2004) picks up Coleman's thread, his main interest, however, being focused on norms and trust. He looks upon certain relationship patterns as depositories of their prevalence. In his perception the inner solidarity of dense, local, multiple networks has been replaced by relationships based on egocentric, loose ties, which has led to the general decrease of social capital. Decreasing social capital can result in a growing number of phenomena that are harmful to the community: not only crime and political passivity but also truancy and school vandalism.

He also agrees with Coleman about the fact that very close and cohesive relationships can form the foundation of a community that creates social capital, and if such relationships are present to a large extent, they provide society with immunity against the breaching of norms. In addition, he detects the loosening of neighbourhood, friendship and family ties as well as a decline in traditional voluntary participation in organisations (clubs and religious organisations). His research data show that there is also a decline in trust in the entire society, that is to say, people help others only if their favour is returned immediately. He attributes this negative tendency to the joint influence of economic competition, the weakening of the family, geographical mobility, technical development and social policy measures. In contrast, civil participation, and voluntary and religious group membership enhance trust and, as a result, altruism. By applying this concept to education research, one can make distinctions among school organisations according to the extent of trust and its influence on academic success (Bryk and Schneider 2002).

As far as the present use of the term social capital is concerned, besides being the subject of a vast amount of literature, it has crossed the borders of science and become a popular slogan of international organisations. Since the millennium, several international publications have expressed a demand that apart from passing down knowledge and culture, schools should develop and strengthen social capital. Moreover, it has been referred to as a precondition of economic competitiveness (Field 2005).

An interesting feature of the history of the concept's reception in Central Europe is that it has become outstandingly successful in the sociology of economics and health, associated with the names of Putnam and Fukuyama rather than Coleman and Bourdieu (Kopp and Skrabski 2003, Orbán and

Szántó 2005, Skrabski et al. 2004). It has even been suggested that the term social capital is too empty and vague to serve as an umbrella term for resources provided by relationship networks. The sociology of economics prefers the concepts network capital or relational capital. Those, however, are primarily used for relational resources established or maintained in order to gain profit and exploit those outside the relationship network, while authors who focus on relationships based on sympathy rather than scheming usually insist on the term social capital (Sík 2005, Pusztai 2009). It was around the millennium that the concept appeared in educational research, where most references were made to Bourdieu's theory (Gordos 2000). The boom in the use of Coleman's concept of social capital in Hungarian sociology of education started with investigations into the forms of social capital in the family, but the analysis failed to detect the impact of social capital (Róbert 2001). It was during our survey on the academic achievement of students of denominational secondary schools that we found empirical evidence that membership of a religious community and the density of practising students explained the discrepancies in students' ambitions to enter higher education (Pusztai & Verdes 2002, Pusztai 2005). They were also very influential factors in avoiding drug use and developing a more tolerant attitude towards outside groups (Pusztai 2004). The second half of the decade was the first time our research had focused on the identification of the possible sources, manifestations and effects of intra- and intergenerational social capital in school communities, and we drew intersectoral and international comparisons (Pusztai 2007). We also highlighted that the capacity to generate social capital is an important property of an educational institution. We have been conducting research on the emergence of institutional social capital in higher education since 2010 (Pusztai 2011).

Types of Social Capital Utilised in Education

Some authors claim that social capital inheres in the formal aspect of relationships, others claim that it is rooted in their content. The formal approach interprets social capital in relation to the number and density of a student's relationships in the family, neighbourhood and school and whether the relationships point into or out of the networks, whereas the content approach focuses on the characteristics, strength, duration and emotional intensity of relationships.

The content dimension of social capital is relevant when students are surrounded by a strong interpretive community, and the network shares a common cognitive system, representations and interpretations, world view and language use. The most important pillars of a common cognitive system are mutuality, trust, shared norms and commitment to participation in the life of the community. These values are acquired by individuals during their up-bringing. The social units involved (family, settlement, region, religious and ethnic community) and the extent to which the cognitive system is a shared one differ according to culture and school system.

Social capital draws attention to interpersonal relationship structures as resources and it is impossible to come to valid conclusions unless one examines students in the school context (in their relations to teaching staff, classmates, schoolmates) (Lee 2002). Therefore research relies on the approach, findings and methodology of (structural) relationship network analysis. In this method, based on the sociometric tradition, actors are primarily characterised by their relationships and only secondarily by their attributes. Hence, individuals are illustratively called nodes. When it comes to the description of relationship networks, the boundaries between them are of utmost importance. In so called a priori networks such as school classes or university groups the boundaries also exist in reality. In spite of being separate populations, these communities also reach outside into ever wider circles. Boundaries, on the other hand, can be established by the analysts themselves, forming occupational, demographic or ecological aggregates (Reagans and Zuckerman 2001, Angelusz and Tardos 2001) for comparison.

Social relations have multiple layers: one can distinguish between individual, organisational, communal, social and global levels. Relationships can be analysed within a class or school or among schools belonging to the same administrative body or region. As relationship analysis is primarily interested in interpersonal relations and looks upon them as a major characteristic of the individual, research usually focuses on either one particular type of relationship such as friendship (Albert and Dávid 1999), or the exploration of all the relationships within a particular community (Angelusz and Tardos 2001).

Relationships, or ties, offer for analysis many qualities whose significance goes beyond themselves. These include their existence, the density of their patterns, their relative or absolute importance to the individual, their simplex or multiplex function, the homogeneity of the connected individuals (homophily based on status or role in the organisation, heterophily), the type of relationship (classmate, relative, friend) and their strength or emotional intensity. Granovetter (1983) claims the strength of relationships is determined by the total amount of time, emotion and intimacy invested in them. Strength is in fact the most debated aspect, as one of its dimensions, interactional properties, includes not only the frequency of interactions but also the degree of emotions, something which is very difficult to measure. Besides, one also has to take into consideration the morphological patterns of relationships. According to the literature, multiplex relationships functioning simultaneously in several contexts and relationship types have proved to

28

be stronger than single-function ones. The direction of relationships is also an important subject of analysis as the relationship network is strengthened by reciprocity as well.

Granovetter (1973) refers to acquaintance-level relationships as weak ties and according to his hypothesis they play a more significant role than strong ones. He argues that a closed friendship circle is unsuitable for channelling outside information as its members are too much alike and less likely to serve as channels of useful information from outside, whereas weak ties are capable of bridging wide social gaps. Society is made up of an endless network of networks involving people who are in a so-called bridge role joining networks and channelling up-to-date information; an example of this is students who transfer achievement-oriented norms from religious communities into the classroom (Lin 2001, Pusztai 2009, 2011). Isolation may keep students in an unfavourable social position, for example students of a vocational school who have no friends from outside the school are less likely to venture a school-leaving exam than their peers who have friends from grammar schools (Coleman 1961).

The Functions of Social Capital at School

It is a crucial question whether we should regard social capital as a general theory of mobility or a compensational theory complementing the theory of reproduction. Another issue for debate is if there is a related division of function among the particular types of relationship, i.e. if weak and strong ties have a general or differential impact on students.

It has been found that the main factors that mediate between the structures of relationships and students' school achievement are the nature of role systems and language use; and research has established the efficiency of open role systems within the family (Bernstein 1971). Individuals who lack weak ties cluster together in fragmented and isolated relationship networks that are separated on a geographical and ethnic basis (Lin 2001). Our survey among Roma intellectuals also led to the conclusion that the acquaintances made after the family had moved away from the gypsy settlement or the father had gained employment enhanced aspirations to continue studies (Pusztai 2004b, Kozma et al. 2005). Undoubtedly, the advantage of weak ties is that individuals are able to meet several expectations at a time without losing their integrity; moreover, it is precisely with the help of weak ties that they are able to keep their complex identities, as has been pointed out in analyses of highly achieving minority schoolchildren (Antrop-González et al. 2003). Higher education students produced the same result in our survey: those who held an outside job or were involved in a civil community performed better than their peers (Pusztai 2011). The analysis of the impact of different relationship types on academic success revealed that weak ties helped young people make better decisions regarding their higher education through counselling and conveying information, and better school grades were due to weak ties at school, non-family relationships and the higher proportion of non-ethnic people in the relationship network (Stanton-Salazar and Dornbusch 1995).Other researchers believe all relationship types generate some social capital, but micro-level contacts limited to a close circle are of primary importance (Coleman 1987). The advantages of the unity of relationships in terms of content and form are the most apparent in what Coleman called closures, in which every single member of the network knows all the others and special cohesion is provided by the commonly accepted norms (Coleman 1988, 1990). Our survey of denominational secondary school students showed that mutual trust and shared norms served as a protective shield against deviant behaviour, and norms prescribing high achievement encouraged students to achieve even better (Pusztai 2005). Norms, however, cannot always fulfil their task of reducing negative influences from outside. There are certain age groups that also need a closed intergenerational structure so that norms can function steadily. Coleman's term "intergenerational closure" refers to a complex structure in which parents, teachers and children who are connected to one another form a closed structure with all their relationships outside the family. This provides more effective control, there is a joint monitoring of the younger generation's behaviour, and decisions receive outside confirmation not only in school matters but also in free-time activities (Carbonaro 1998). According to Morgan and Sorensen (1999) closure is a property of the community, so they treat it as a school-level phenomenon. We demonstrated the efficiency of such closures among students of Hungarian denominational schools, where students who otherwise had poor relationship networks but belonged to the denominational school community, which abounded in strong ties, enjoyed the same benefits as their peers who were strongly embedded in relationship networks (Pusztai 2005).

In the debate about the efficiency of weak versus strong ties there have been attempts at a reconciliation of the two opposing views to develop a common theory. Putnam distinguishes between bonding and bridging relationships but points out that the ability to establish bonding relationships that provide cohesion for small communities can predict willingness to establish bridging relationships (Putnam 2004). According to the structural hole theory, the presence of social capital is perceptible where there are individuals mediating between networks that are otherwise not connected (Burt 2000). Bridging the structural hole between the boundaries of networks is beneficial to the dissemination of information, which, in Burt's interpretation, also includes norms. He thinks networks are the most useful when there is information flowing through them. As information spreads better within a group than among groups, the basis of social capital is participation in the division of information. The more opportunities one has to mediate between relationship networks, the more social capital one has. That is partly why students who are in regular extracurricular communication with their teachers or lecturers are more successful than their peers (Pusztai 2005, 2009, 2011). The ideal proportion of members in possession of new information necessary to benefit the entire community is a matter of debate. The problem leads to the dilemma Coleman first discussed in his 1966 report, namely what proportion of students from various social strata and cultural groups there should be at integrated schools (Coleman 1966).

In Burt's view it is also necessary to differentiate between the most effective forms of social capital with respect to age. Since in closed networks information spreads rapidly, safely and without distortions, this is the relationship type that best promotes the development of young people in search of their identity. At that age redundancy is especially supportive because it helps incorporate norms. Similarly, the validity of trust is different in open and closed networks as it involves more risk in the former than in the latter, where norms and sanctions are consistent, therefore a closed network serves the purposes of the school better. Burt thinks there is no major contradiction between the two opposing source theories, and he refers to Granovetter (1985), who emphasised that the perception of effective sanctions is instrumental in the development of trust since it is less possible to deceive others or spread false information in a dense network. In his view there is also asymmetry with respect to social status: weaker networks and serving as a bridge is an advantage to those who have plenty of certain kinds of resources, whereas dense networks provide social capital against falling behind and are helpful in regeneration. High achievement requires both a high degree of closeness of the group and many non-redundant relationships outside the group; all other combinations are less effective (Burt 1990). Another example of the different strengths of the influence of strong and weak ties was our survey of schools with students from unfavourable social backgrounds, of which the ones that were measured as more successful had more cooperative teaching staff (Bacskai 2013).

Another debated issue is whether social capital is unevenly distributed in society according to its vertical or horizontal structure. One opinion is represented by Granovetter (1983) and Lin (2000), who claim that the activation and investment of capital increases individuals' or communities' chances of desired advancement. They define social capital as the investment and use of resources rooted in interpersonal relationships in the hope of profit. Low-status individuals are embedded in networks where resources are scarce, so inequalities among different social strata are visible in social as well as human capital. Resource-rich networks are typical of high status individuals, because their networks are rich in resources in the quantitative sense as well, and are more extensive and socially more heterogeneous. Lin's opinion is close to Bourdieu's view in that a higher position on the social scale means a better position in the network with better connections. Low-status people can only cross the boundaries of social strata under special circumstances, for example if they happen to find a patron such as a well-to-do relative or a school integrating a wide range of social layers, a finding is supported by our own research on Roma graduates (Pusztai 2004b).

The opposite opinion is held by Coleman, who claims that social segmentation on the basis of norms excludes selection on the basis of social status. Church communities are relationship networks whose members come together on the basis of internalised norms, so homophily is present in the networks only with respect to those norms, whereas –unlike other relationship networks– socially they are heterophilic i.e. relationships span boundaries of social status. An example of such networks are school communities formed around denominational schools, referred to by Coleman (Coleman and Hoffer 1987) and Dijskra (2006), who presented the advantages of the pillared Dutch institutional system with respect to social heterogeneity. Intersectoral comparisons in Hungary also showed that the composition of denominational secondary schools was more heterogeneous in terms of their students' social status (Pusztai 2009b).

Deviations in social capital may be due not only to gradual but also to nominal differences. Inequality between the sexes follows from the differences between men's and women's social networks. Several surveys have detected the difference: males' networks are dominated by weak ties, while females' by strong ones (Albert and Dávid 1999, Lin 2000). In the course of our research among secondary school students we have also observed the sex-based differences between networks (Fényes and Pusztai 2006). A popular theme of social capital related research is the comparison of the resources of ethnic groups living together. Most of the data show that attachment to a minority community has an unfavourable impact on school career, but there are discrepancies according to the origin of the coexistence, the homogeneity of the ethnic group's social status and integration strategies (Sanders 2002, Portes and Sensenbrenner 1993). We have conducted research on Central European institutions of national minorities where students closely attached to the indigenous minority group make considerable extra investments of time and money for the sake of their successful academic careers (Pusztai 2009, 2011).

Key "Outsiders" in the Creation of Social Capital at School

Actors from outside the school who still have a significant influence on one's school achievement usually come from the family, friendship circles, groups of contemporaries, the neighbourhood and groups based on voluntary membership. Although our present study aims at an exploration of institutional social capital, for several reasons it is essential to take into account the resources of capital coming from outside. First, research has revealed that family social capital has a direct impact on achievement (Coleman 1988). Second, the types of relationship one is engaged in and one's willingness to bond are stable throughout one's life and the patterns of relationship networks formed at school resemble the relationship patterns within the family (Pusztai 2009). Furthermore, the sum total of social capital coming from families can be regarded as a characteristic of the school (Pusztai 2005).

Below, we will give a review of the form and quality of family social capital, as well as the kinds of help (advice, information, norms) it can provide (Astone et al. 1999). Coleman primarily draws attention to the structure of the family, the indicators of which are the number of parents and the number of children per parent. The formal variants which are -compared to the ideal of closure- lacking in capital are presented in graphic figures and ratios, which are numerical expressions of the consequences of the distribution of finite resources (Coleman 1997). With their help it is possible to calculate the amount of family social capital, allowing for the type and size of family, the number of generations, the parent types and the number of siblings and the members' differences in age and qualification (Róbert 2001). We think it is misleading to count social capital in the material sense; what ratios and graphs let us conclude is the chance of a successful transmission of values: the two-parent model gives more support, control and information as well as better access to family resources, whereas in a single-parent family the parent-child ratio is not necessarily worse, but parental control is less secure and norms are more vulnerable. In two-parent families the realisation of consistent norms depends on the strength and stability of the parents' relationship (Bukodi 2002). If one of the parents is often missing, it can lead to a break or absence of love in the relationship network (Meier 1999). European research has also demonstrated that single-parent family structure has a definitely negative impact on children's school achievement (Dronkers and Róbert 2004). That there is more to family structure than what can be explained by a mathematic-economic model is reinforced by several research findings suggesting that restructured families still remain inadequately structured in terms of social capital (Astone and McLanah 1991). However, education research in Central Europe does not seem to pay enough attention to the appearance of family structures in school environments and their influence on achievement.

There had been instances of investigation into parental presence and absence before the theory of social capital came about, but usually they were simply treated as indicators of missing parental income (Blau and Duncan

1967). The other form of family social capital is the communicative content of socialisation. Several of its properties, such as the frequency, content and channels of interaction have an influence on the amount of social capital. Looking at parent-child communication one can estimate the period with the highest risk of failure at school, and conversations about school can be predictive of its avoidance (Jimerson et al. 1997, Pusztai 2009). Research has supported Coleman's assumption that without remarkable interaction parents' high physical and social capital cannot be utilised, which is an evidence of the fact that parent-child interaction has an important compensatory power (Meier 1999, Teachman et al. 1996). It is highly probable that students who communicate regularly with their parents and are involved in joint activities with them are more successful (Parcel and Dufur 2001, Pusztai 2009).

Although literature on relationship networks has proved the priority of fathers' connections when it comes to finding employment (Granovetter 1983), research on school success has shown the dominance of the mother in the family. Her presence and activity is usually the most discussed aspect of family interactions. This issue already sparked a debate after the publication of Coleman's first theoretical model. He found a very high return rate of the attention invested in children among mothers who did not work outside the home or full time, whereas the human capital of very highly qualified mothers who worked outside their homes did not seem to yield such a good return (which is why he was criticised by some feminist authors). Our research on Roma graduates in Hungary has confirmed the positive influence of uneducated, sometimes even illiterate mothers who still exercise close control over their children's home study (Pusztai 2004b). All this should be seen not only in the light of the simple economic model of time input, it should also be noted that individuals forgoing their self-interest produce other, cognitive benefits of social capital: esteem, the reinforcement of communal cohesion and reciprocity (Pusztai 2009). This variable, however, has not been the focus of much research; it has rather been replaced with the mother's expectation of the child's going to college (Ainsworth 2002, Antrop-González and Garrett 2003). Besides, the equal importance of the presence of both parents is supported by the fact that frequent extra work done by either the mother or the father can lead to students' behavioural problems and undermine their verbal skills (Parcel and Dufur 2001).

It was also the theory of social capital that brought siblings into focus in the sociology of education. Coleman (1988) regarded the number of siblings as a formal indicator of social capital, trying to use them as predictors of the amount of parental attention and care per student. Although not entirely consistent with his theoretical foundation, he regarded siblings as actors dividing parental resources such as time, material wealth, attention

34

and emotions (Parcel and Dufur 2001). However, research on the correlation between the number of children and academic career has shown that resources somehow multiply rather than fragment in families, just as in the sample of female postgraduate students, whose achievement –contrary to expectations– was not diminished by a higher number of children (Engler 2013, 2014). The original discussion of the concept of social capital did not raise the issue that a large family structure might also be useful as students can have access to more social capital through their close and confidential relationships and shared norms with a number of children, which also makes it possible to spread useful information concerning school. A higher number of siblings in denominational schools and their quite usual attendance at the same school might be helpful in the reinforcement of school norms and the consolidation of trust between the school and the family (Pusztai 2004, 2009).

The impact of siblings is still an open question, but it seems that younger siblings can benefit from the strength of the family's relationship network (Meier 1999). Hungarian analysts have observed higher school achievement on the part of extreme position (eldest or youngest) children, which partly supports the competitive approach. Apart from the fact that siblings' education can correct the influence of parents' education upwards or downwards, it seems to be proven that a sibling with a lower education has a very strong negative impact and the impact of siblings is asymmetrical with respect to sex (women's school careers are more strongly influenced by their siblings' education) (Róbert 2001). Although the above survey suggests that in terms of school achievement an only child is in a more favourable position, when it comes to relationships, children from big families manage to develop a smoother teacher-student relationship (Meier 1999) and make friends more easily in their teens. In the latter respect, researchers have noted that children without siblings tend to have difficulties establishing relationships (Diósi 2000).

As regards friendship as a source of social capital outside the family, Coleman seemed to ignore it as his database did not contain any relevant data. As a special kind of relationship, friendship has the following main properties: a friendship-based relationship network is usually quite small and consists of chosen relationships; it is grounded in trust and results in solidarity, and it works permanently and reliably without formalised frameworks (Albert and Dávid 1999, Utasi 2002). Like strong relationships in general, friendship is essentially homogamous and mostly includes relationships of endogamous origin. It necessitates a certain degree of vicinity or overlap of vertical and horizontal positions and cultural orientations and it may have instrumental and emotional functions as well. The size and composition of one's friendship circle varies according to one's age, sex and social status. Research has shown that individuals who are involved in other strong relationships are more likely to have friendships, that is to say, strong and intense family ties promote the formation of strong friendships (Utasi 2002). Among the various aspects of friendship it is worth examining one's disposition towards making friends, the circle from which friends are found, the number of friends, views on friendship, prevalent norms in the friendship circle and the influence of all of this on school achievement. Apart from this, as young people gain more benefit from a context that has a more homogeneous value and norm system, special attention should be paid to how the friendship circle's accepted norms and values relate to the culture of the school. It is generally known that badly-achieving friends have a negative influence on their peers, and well-achieving friends have a positive one (McEwan 2004). In our research, we have been permanently monitoring how religious friends influence academic success, and our findings show a strongly supportive influence among students of denominational schools and also a definitely positive influence in higher education (Pusztai 2004, 2011).

Traditional literature on the sociology of education uses the term peer group instead of friends, meaning a group of adolescents who are in regular interaction with one another. Peer groups are thought to coincide more or less with a student's immediate social environment at school or at the place of residence. The answer to the question of why the influence of peer groups is so strong is borrowed from social psychology (Coleman 1961). There is no complete consensus on the particular age when peer group influence is the greatest. The conditions under which group norms support the realisation of school norms is crucial to school success. In Coleman's view, chances are the highest in the case of non-religiously based and religiously based private schools. Students' membership in a religious community supplies them with the kind of transitive relationships that allow even those who are not directly connected to support one another, and if young people make their friends in that same circle, their relationships will have a multiplex nature. Coleman's findings confirm that belonging to a religious circle of friends creates such a unity of form and content that the resulting social capital decreases attrition and increases the chance of becoming more successful (Coleman and Hoffer 1987, Pusztai 2004, 2007). In non-denominational schools similar support can be derived from other voluntarily formed relationship networks.

The interpretation of the residential environment as a relationship network is an area of interest in common with the ecology of education. As this approach pays special attention to the powerful impact of the social context on the individual's actions, related analyses traditionally present a microsociety with aggregate data (averages and ratios). The social composition of a residential environment is measured by indicators such as the unemployment rate or the proportion of people with university degrees in a settlement or a district.

Its economic position is characterised by the proportion of the population on low income or social welfare, while its cultural context by ethnic and denominational ratios. In Central Europe the significance of the above factors is very great because of regional differences, and the consequently different experiences have a remarkable impact on young people's vision of the future and academic motivation (Ceglédi–Nyüsti 2012, Garami 2013).

Although national politics encourages geographical mobility, a family's intergenerational embeddedness and the amount of social capital at a young person's disposal largely depends on the stability of their places of residence. Morenoff claims that intergenerational stability at a place of residence has a favourable impact on one's studies through the mutual exchange of material and cognitive goods, the informal social control of young people and other mutual support (Morenoff et al. 1999). Moving house, in Coleman's opinion, is harmful to social capital as relationships are broken. It is paradoxical that immobile families' relationship networks are more cohesive as they draw support from their connections in the neighbourhood and the stability of their residence. At the same time, however, depending on family structure, the children's age, the density of relationships within the family and the new environment, moving house and the consequent dissolution of old relationships might well have a favourable impact on academic achievement (Humke and Schaefer 1995, Meier 1999).

Sandefur's explanation is close to Bourdieu's interpretation of social capital: people who move convert their economic capital into social by placing their children in a more favourable environment and trying to establish more valuable relationships at the new location. As regards family strategies on moving, it can be observed that high-income families move more except for during the crucial periods of their children's development (Sandefur and Laumann 1998). It is as a result of teenage identity crises that moving house or changing schools have a more negative impact in one's adolescence (Meier 1999). In today's Hungary, research on the impact of moving on children's school achievement has become urgent because of the large-scale migration for employment following the country's European integration. Further investigation is also needed into the impact of the migration of ambitious Roma families on their local communities with families who are still undecided about supporting their children's education. Embeddedness in local relationship networks can also be ended by commuting or living at student hostels, but the influence of the two is different, as in the former case students might end up belonging nowhere, while the latter may offer stable relationship structures. This question leads us into the world of schools and student hostels and throws light upon the differences between the official and familiar character of institutions' self-identification.

Membership in a religious community, one of the most widespread forms of voluntary organisation membership is looked upon as a special type of relationship. That is what Coleman used as an example to illustrate the idea that the functioning of social capital is the latent aspect of an existing culture. It is a relationship network whose members undoubtedly facilitate one another's actions. Much research has found a connection between the social capital accessible through religious practice and the success of minority students (Antrop-González and Garrett 2003, Lauglo 2010, Hallinan-Kubitschek 2012). Listed among the cognitive consequences of relationships within a religious community are positive attitudes, values and good behaviour, which all support school success and protect against demoralising behaviour patterns (Coleman and Hoffer 1987, Carbonaro 1998, Muller and Ellison 2001). Doing sports can also serve as a safety net for young people, because apart from its health benefits, belonging to a sporting community helps students consciously formulate their goals in life and do persistent work (Kovács 2014).

Key "Insiders" in the Creation of Social Capital at School

According to sociological education research based on the theory of reproduction, the success of one's educational career is essentially determined by one's family background, and schools are hardly able to modify that predictable path. However, the relationship-network based approach has brought schools back into sociological education analyses. Having analysed the relationships that count as possible sources of social capital, we can classify them according to whether they exist among people of similar or different positions, among co-workers at the school or among outside participants. Similar-position relationships are those among students, among teachers and among parents; different-position relationships are those between teachers and students, teachers and parents and students and their parents (the latter has already been discussed among family relationships). Coleman does not claim that any of them has an exclusive role in enhancing academic success, but while further developing his hypothesis, he has devoted several analyses to this issue.

This issue, along with the characteristics and actions of the individuals involved, has been extensively dealt with in psychology, pedagogy, the sociology of education and management theory. Nowadays growing attention is paid to the composition of the teaching staff as part of the composition of the school as well as to their capacity to create social capital (Gamarnikow and Green 2009, Campbell 2009, Minckler 2011, 2013, Hargreaves and Fullan 2012, Bacskai 2013, Fullan 2014).

All school populations have a kind of comprehensive quality that is made up of a certain aspect of the population's homogeneity or heterogeneity. Most often this is the students' social or ethnic composition, but the composition of the teaching staff is also an important characteristic. The most common criteria used to describe the composition of the teaching staff are data on demographic features, qualifications, work experience and professional dedication. The composition of the teaching staff can be shaped by selection on the part of the leadership or administrative body or by teachers' self-selection according to ethnic, cultural, ideological or professional criteria and social structure. Some research has shown that an unfavourable make-up of the student population is accompanied by a disadvantageous composition of the teaching staff: teachers in such schools are less qualified and devoted, pedagogically less flexible and show higher turnover (Nye et al 2004, Varga 2009, Horn 2010, Montt 2011). The accumulation of all this may hinder the emergence of social capital among them.

Social capital in the teaching staff can be thought of as a structural property based on the frequency of teachers' cooperation and their joint activities on the one hand, and the dimension of shared values on the other. Several research results confirm the positive effect of teachers' cooperation on student success (Fenzel and O'Brennan 2007, Goddard and Goddard 2007, Liu and Wang 2008, Cohen et al. 2009, McMahon 2009), and others have pointed out that intergenerational interactions at school enhance achievement very effectively (Pusztai (2004). According to Dronkers and Róbert (2004), Bryk et al. (1992) and Leana (2006, 2010), it is "the culture of trust" that facilitates the fruitful transmission of teachers' human capital and it is a lack of trust and the large-scale turnover of teachers that can undermine the teaching staff's social capital, which is so much needed when a new teacher has to be integrated (Bryk, et al. 1999, Kardos et al. 2001). The impact of teachers' intragenerational capital resources –which can even compensate for deficiencies in individual human capital– seems to be more powerful in schools whose population is dominated by those at the lower end of the social scale (Malone 2009, Bagley 2009, Bacskai 2013).

During the conceptualisation and measurement of teachers' social capital the question of the school leader's role in its generation and consolidation was raised (Otero et al. 2000, Bryk and Schneider 2002, Bryk et al. 2010, Minckler 2011, 2013). There is an ever-growing consensus on the issue that a leader has a considerable impact on the generation of social capital at school, but at the same time, the reverse is true as well: invested with power, directors can easily destroy the teaching staff's social capital. That is why the change of school principals is a critical moment; however, it might also occur that the professional community, equipped with high social capital, turns against the principal (Youngs & King 2002). The influence of a leader cannot be perceived directly but manifests itself through the teaching staff. In Leithwood's model school leadership can influence students' achievement by rational, emotional and organisational means as well as through families. In the first three cases the influence of the leadership is completed by that of the teaching staff. School leaders' tasks do not only include setting objectives, requirements and methods, but also establishing real partnership with teachers and families and creating a professional community (Leithwood et al. 2010). Leaders can introduce the kind of cooperational culture and methods that help teaching staff develop into a learning community (Stoll and Louis, 2007). If teachers are involved in an efficient Professional Learning Community, this also contributes to the improvement of achievement (Vescio et al. 2008, Bordás 2012). Other authors define the organisation of professional and other events as a structural dimension, but the role they attribute to it is the same (Penuel, et al. 2009). The teaching staff as a learning community have common goals, cooperate, and support one another's professional development actively and take advantage of the valuable relationships they have built up among themselves. This can only be achieved through community building, the key element of which is the involvement of the staff in joint activities organised by the leader (Minckler 2011, 2013). These activities strengthen the content aspect of social capital, because they offer teachers an opportunity to come to an agreement on and work out a common interpretation of the staff's goals (Leithwood et al. 2004, Coburn and Russell 2008, Penuel et al. 2009). Communication within the community –which is considered to be crucial to the creation of social capital– such as the re-negotiation of their mission, serves as a means of formulating and coordinating different viewpoints (Preskill et al. 2000, Bryk and Schneider 2002). The question certainly is whether the staff are only able to agree on a few values or on an entire coherent value system. Major international surveys do not provide any data on teacher's value orientation and educational value preferences, but if Coleman's hypothesis of functional community is credible, a teaching staff's consensus on their values can give students an advantage in achievement (Bacskai 2008).

Another means by which the leader of the institution can increase social capital around the school is to make parents interested, encourage their participation in school work, influence their cultural habits and develop their pedagogical skills. This can be put into practice by accustoming them to taking part in school events, organising parents' clubs or other occasions for meeting, where parents' abilities can come to the surface. Hungarian data show that a high proportion of the parents of denominational school students feel they are treated as partners by the school, and consequently they approach the institution with more trust, and are more willing to accept teachers' opinions and acknowledge their competence (Pusztai 2011).

To make matters more complicated, the role of the principal is different in the English-speaking and Continental models; in the former they are more managers, while in the latter they are teachers themselves (Lannert 2006). That may be the reason why in America academic success is found to be promoted by meetings between parents and the school leadership, building up local connections, communication with outside actors like the press or foundations, i.e. the collection of external capital (Leana 2011).

Although the teacher-student relationship is one of the most frequently examined school relations, it has not been dealt with extensively in this theoretical framework. The formal aspect of the relationship is mostly illustrated by ratios such as the teacher-student ratio or the ratio of teachers with particular traits (e.g. full time, well accepted among students, minority) within the school. Ratios are important because of the amount of attention and control per student, and in this respect it is small schools and a high teacher-student ratio that seem to be a more favourable learning environment. How ratios are judged has to do with debates still going on about the ideal school size (Morgan and Alwin 1980, Cotton 1996, Luyten et al. 2014), in which there are an infinite number of arguments for organisational and economic efficiency; nevertheless, from the point of view of social capital, merging schools into extra large institutions, in spite of having brought about favourable changes in the infrastructure of education, has produced the opposite effect regarding the creation of social cohesion. According to Putnam's (2004) theory the solution to the dilemma of size lies in building up the school structure from small cohesive units like cells, forming "schools within schools".

The use of cooperative techniques in class and the frequency and content of personal teacher-student communication is already a question of relationship quality (Antrop-González et al. 2003, Algan et al. 2013). What Lannert (2004) calls pure pedagogical effect is the increase in the aspiration of low-status students in a homogeneous school to continue their studies as a result of their good relationship with a dedicated teacher. Surveys reveal that the interest teachers generally take in students is mainly restricted to giving help with studies and assisting student organisations' work, but there is hardly any non-technical communication outside classes (Szabó and Örkény 1998, Ligeti and Márton 2003), which suggests that teacher-student relationships in most Hungarian schools are instrumental. Recent surveys have already included the extent of agreement with the teacher's behaviour, attitude and views, but the effect mechanisms of the teacher-student relationship are still unexplored (Meier 1999, Imre 2008, Pusztai 2009). The main question is what social indicators can be used to describe the group of teachers whose role interpretation includes personal care and willingness to do extra work voluntarily. Humes (2009) highlights the ethical dimension of social capital in education and claims that selflessness and giving up self-interest are basic principles in a teacher's life, but they can be realised only through the joint effort of the entire teaching staff, otherwise "spongers", who would rather spare themselves any extra effort, may destroy them. In our own research among teachers of Hungarian denominational secondary schools we have detected the presence of a willingness to do voluntary work, pay attention to students outside the classroom, enter into non-technical communication and follow their students' personal life courses (Pusztai 2004, 2009).

Since the very beginning, the theory of social capital has considered the relationship between teachers and parents as a priority. Starting from Putnam's interpretation, Bryk and Schneider demonstrated that the increase in relational trust in the school community contributes to the improvement of learning outcomes (Bryk and Schneider 2002). In order to develop an atmosphere of trust, partners have to be mutually convinced that it is really important to take into consideration one another's opinions and interests, that their partners are capable of fulfilling their roles, that they pay personal attention to one another and do their work to the best of their ability. In their view, teachers, parents and students keep monitoring one another and analysing one another's behaviour in terms of the above criteria, so if a defect is detected somewhere, it can undermine trust in the whole relationship system.

Surveys on the strength of teacher-parent relationships inquire about the frequency of meetings, and the formal or informal nature and type of communication, presuming that a multiplex relationship between parents and teaching staff improves the chance of a successful school career (Jimerson et al. 1997, Meier 1999). There are detailed questions about the frequency of the various forms of communication (participation in parents-teachers meetings, consultation hours and school events, doing voluntary work for the school, phone inquiries). The working mechanism of parental activity –in the case of voluntary activity– can increase social capital through personal awareness, mutual trust and reciprocity (Jeynes 2007, Stewart 2008). There is also an invisible element in those relationships, namely the agreement between value systems, especially educational values (Pusztai 2011b). The frequency of communication proves to be beneficial to the flow of information and the control of students' behaviour, in the first stage. Trust and generalised reciprocity are the second stage, and the third stage, provided there is agreement between educational values or, better, the entire value system, produces the consistence of norms as a benefit, which –in the present interpretational framework– is the most highly appreciated and most effective result and resource at the same time (Goldring and Phillips 2008).

The literature has raised the possibility that successful communication between highly qualified parents and teachers may also have cultural reasons.

However, those relationships display a kind of competition in pedagogical autonomy, the characteristics of which are determined by the parents' social class (Weininger and Lareau 2003). Willingness to take part in voluntary work for the school also varies according to social status (Meier 1999). Our research supports the fact that high parental status does not always contribute to the emergence of social capital (Pusztai 2009), whereas steady trust in the teacher is indispensable for low status or minority parents (Pusztai 2004b, Kozma et al. 2005). Although parents' voluntary extracurricular activity has been embraced by several branches of progressive pedagogy and its benefits are supported by sociological research into education, it is not very widespread in our region except in some primary schools, mostly alternative ones (Husen 1990, Halász and Lannert 2003).

Parents' relationship networks can come about by virtue of the school's openness and broader interpretation of its mission. A school can provide ideal support for students if parents have common views on their children's school careers (Coleman 1987). There are innumerable examples in the literature to illustrate how this works, one being when collectively planned truancy is successfully prevented by parents knowing one another. Blau pointed out as early as in the 1960s that parents' exchange of information about bringing up children may prove to be useful for attaining social status (Meier 1999), but it is still an issue of debate whether it is parents' dense and closed relationship networks within the school or their extensive, outwardly oriented ties that are more helpful to their children.

It certainly makes a great difference what constitutes the basis of an intergenerational closure around a school. The norms of a school community may also produce an effect that is depressing and limits creativity, especially as a result of the anomie caused by the peripheral social position of the school community (Portes and Landolf 1996). Back in the 1960–70s education researchers thought the dominance of middle-class students would guarantee that school norms have a positive influence on learning, but because of high attrition rates among middle-class students in the 1980s and their frequent breach of norms they had to admit that it is not sufficient to consider indicators of social status alone when planning a learning-friendly composition for the school.

Coleman compared the efficiency of local, value-based and functional school communities. He argues that the parent community of a school works as a functional community if it is able to exercise social control relying on a commonly accepted system of values and norms. The parent community of a school based on shared values, e.g. of a select private school, have a consensus only on a number of essential values, and besides, parents do not know one another very well and do not have any interactions, therefore in their everyday behaviour patterns they cannot live up to the values they have set as objectives. Parents in a functional school community often belong to the same denomination or even congregation, so they have a full set of means to help their children perform in the way expected from them by the community (Coleman and Hoffer 1987). Owing to their particular structure, those communities are capable of enforcing norms; the leadership of the school and the parents form a closure to improve the outcome of school work; parents gain some influence in school life through their voluntary activities, so they can keep an eye on their children's free-time activities as well. Some findings show that students achieve better at schools where they are in close contact with one another and parents jointly participate in school policy (Carbonaro 1999, Meier 1999). Others claim that learning outcomes are worse if parents' relationship networks are closed, because more open networks can channel new information and resources into the community (Morgan and Sorensen 1999). Another advantage of intergenerational closures around schools is that they can impose uniform sanctions, thereby setting consistent norms –so important in adolescence– for their children both inside and outside the home. That also makes it easier to lay down common requirements to help one another's children in learning (Carbonaro 1999).

The influence of the student context on school norms has been a well-known and indisputable fact since Coleman's Adolescent Society (1961): students were far more responsive to the norms set by their peers than to those set by their teachers. When he examined the structure of adolescents' interpersonal relationships at school, he detected micro-communities' filter mechanisms of values conveyed by teachers. This community activity is not disfunctional but fulfils evaluating, mediating, selective (amplifying or moderating) and initiating functions and must always be taken into account in understanding socialisation processes at school (Vastagh 2005).

Coleman's report gave a detailed account of the impact of students' relationships with classmates on academic success. As regards the differences in the academic achievement of ethnic groups, the relevant factor was not differences in financial status and provision of equipment between black and white schools, but the composition of the school's population. Coleman observed that a high proportion of middle-class classmates is beneficial, whereas if there are low-status classmates in large numbers, it has a bad impact on achievement. His other important finding is the so-called asymmetric context effect: members of different social and ethnic groups are not equally sensitive to the influence of school composition. The reason for this is that the (then) school-friendly norms of the middle-class were held by students as well as teachers, whereas in lower-status schools bad achievement is prescribed by students' prevalent norms. The author identified students supporting school achievement and those in favour of anti-school norms according to their position on the vertical social scale.

44

As far as integration at school is concerned, there is a clash between two absolutely justifiable aspirations. On the one hand: there is the parents' ambition to educate their children at a school with the best possible composition. On the other hand, the state aims at integrating various social groups by mixing students (Coleman and Hoffer 1987, Coleman 1991, Breugel 2009.) Having followed studies of Catholic schools, we have found it surprising and a real breakthrough that, given the high proportion of low-status students in those schools, they are still able to maintain a system of school norms that promote learning. Our research in today's Central Europe has made it obvious that it is impossible to draw conclusions about attitudes to school norms and learning on the basis of parents' social status alone, but further study of value systems and cultural dimensions has proved to be necessary (Pusztai 2009, 2011). So far, our results in Hungary have shown that the frequency of cohesive student relationship networks with friends practising their religion has a much more significant influence on producing student behaviour that supports school values than all other explanatory variables. This influence has appeared even more powerful than the context effect of cultural capital at school. Students who have a closed religious friendship circle –quite common in denominational schools– embody the kind of social capital in the school community that can also be relied upon by those who lack that resource themselves (Pusztai 2004, Pusztai 2005).

The efficiency of academic and communal activity

Classroom events and their influence on school success are a well documented research area, but we do not know much about extracurricular activities in that respect. After the political transition in Central Europe most extracurricular activities related to ideology-ridden community movements disappeared from schools. Later, as the education system began to lose its financial resources as a result of a series of economic crises, almost all extracurricular activities became optional, ceased to exist or were shifted to the private sector (remedial lessons, preparatory courses for higher education, study circles, camps, trips and cultural events). Yet there is no doubt that investment in those activities contributes to high achievement both at the level of individuals and the education system as a whole (Bray 2007). As they are concealed phenomena, we only know of assumption-based hypotheses about whether they exert their beneficial influence through their power to shape attitudes or enrich knowledge, and whether they are examples of the successful conversion of cultural and economic capital or the active presence of optimistic predictions for the future (Bourdieu 1977).

Students' extracurricular activities often seem to be profitable investments into social and cultural capital alike. Some hold the view that they help disadvantaged students work off their disadvantages (Antrop-González and Garrett 2003), while others do not think there is a clear correlation. Early studies did not test the impact of family background and therefore could not tell whether the co-occurrence of improving achievement and extracurricular school activities was only a coincidence. There are controversial data on the number of hours per week spent on extracurricular activities that can be best utilised by the student. However, it seems that "overburdened" students tend to do very well (Broh 2002).

Another question is whether extracurricular activities are more fruitful when they are organised by the school or financed by the parents. Some elements of these activities help make up for the defects in classroom work, or serve to complete it; another element is sports and developing physical culture, a third type is acquiring musical skills, the fourth is taking part in in school politics and the fifth is involvement in religious or charity activities. As categories of learning or community building they do not carry the same weight, but there are surprising correlations. Research has demonstrated that sport, art, scientific and other school subject-based activities have a direct positive impact on school grades and higher education admittance rates. Other extracurricular activities have an indirect positive effect: participation in school politics and voluntary work enhance students' commitment to their school, which proves to be beneficial to academic success (Meier 1999, McNeal 1999). Sport is an excellent form of extracurricular activity. Earlier, the focus of studies related to interest in school sport among adolescents was on the role of respect towards particular sports and sportspeople in the formation of various student strata or groups (Coleman 1961). In the theory of social capital we interpret the effects of sport as voluntary group membership and embeddedness in an achievement-oriented cohesive community (Pusztai et al 2012). Research has shown the positive effects of sport such as improving school grades, admittance to higher education, diminishing attrition and truancy (Kovács 2014), but it is also aware of the possible risks such as aggression, irritability, the appreciation of unfair victory and the increased risk of drugs (Broh 2002, Kovács 2014). Recent studies have focused on the social capital model apart from the traditional hypothesis of personality development, according to which sport develops skills that are, in the first place, in accordance with values of the education system such as persistence, a strong work ethic, a sensible respect for authority and, in the second place, a boost for self-confidence and ambitions for academic success. According to the group leadership hypothesis, sportspeople attain a higher rank through sport, which makes it easier for them to belong to the leading group or clique and to establish close contacts with teachers, and besides, trust and solidarity within sportspeople's social circles are above average. Sport has increased students' self-control and even among friends the number of academically purpose-oriented young people has grown. The benefits of sport are specific to social status: Broh (2002) claims it helps work off disadvantages of position, and, moreover, it even increases the success of disadvantaged students to a greater extent and is an effective means of attracting their parents into the school. Other useful extracurricular investments are learning music and membership of orchestras or theatre groups, the positive impacts of which have been proved by school grades (Broh 2002, Putnam 2004, Karasszon et al. 2013).

Extracurricular activities in Hungary show sector-specific traits: in denominational schools there is access to more of them that provide opportunities for teacher-student and student-student interactions (Pusztai 2009). We have identified three basic types of activity: optional weekly occasions for a small number of students, mass events organised by the schools and activities provided by the student hostel. In denominational schools the first type includes religious- and community-building occasions such as sport activities, while in state schools it mainly includes academic activities. As for events for the whole school community, denominational schools offer more weekend events and overnight trips than average.

The third type of extracurricular activity, offered by student hostels, is traditionally one of the priorities of denominational schools as their hostels are far more than places of accommodation for students; they are parts of the school both organisationally and pedagogically and their aim is to provide students with an environment that gives them consistent norms and equal attention around the clock. It certainly demands more preparation, voluntary work and attention from teachers and other staff (Pusztai 2009).

The answer we can give to the dilemma raised at the beginning of this chapter is that -on the basis of our research findings- academic success can be achieved in several steps (Pusztai 2009). We have found that especially in the case of students who are distanced from the culture of the school the first step to be taken is to support their integration into the school's norm system by establishing intra- and intergenerational relationships and strengthening trust through the wide range of community-building extracurricular activities offered by the school. Afterwards, it is much easier to convince them of the importance of studying and offer them complementary academic activities.

Conclusion

This study has given a summary of our present knowledge regarding how social capital influences school success and whether schools can increase the chance of social integration through their institutional impact. Of the wide range of variants of social capital theory we mapped the line that is grounded in the sociology of education and the findings of education research. We pointed out the differences between theories using the same concepts but forming separate paradigms which even serve as bases for alternative hypotheses. We were the first in Hungary to identify and carry out during our research an intersectoral and international comparison of the possible sources, realisations and effects of the intra- and intergenerational social capital that emerge at schools (Pusztai 2004, 2009). Since 2010 we have also been studying the emergence of institutional social capital in higher education (Pusztai 2011). Since in this approach it is not only individuals but also relationships who have distinctive traits that can influence student success, we studied the functions of relationships and related debates according to the main relationship types. Although the primary aim of this volume is the exploration of institutional social capital, it is essential to take stock of the resources of capital outside schools such as family, friends, peer group, neighbourhood and voluntary membership in organisations. Not only because they have a direct effect on the individual's social capital, but also because the sum total of individual social capitals becomes an institutional trait in education. Although circumstances and relationships within a school have also been studied before with special focus on a particular aspect of the structure (size of school, teaching staff, teacher-student, teacher-parent relationships), we hold the view that only the theory of social capital is capable of raising them above their particularity to reveal their essence, which gives the school context-level emergent properties. We are convinced that the success of the students at an institution is not determined by individual traits but the essential appearance of trust and shared norms among school actors.

We have very few Central European research results at our disposal about the effects of extracurricular school activities. During the past two decades those activities have fallen into the background owing partly to ideological and partly to financial reasons, but there is still much voluntary teachers' work going on below the surface in those education systems which are currently trying to find their ideal path forward. Investments in these activities enhance achievement both at the level of the individual and of the education system.

The answer to the question of what kind of extracurricular activities are needed to increase academic success is that -especially in the case of students who are distanced from the culture of the school- the first step to be taken is to support their integration into the school's norm system with activities aiding the establishment of intra- and intergenerational relationships and the development of trust in school actors (Pusztai 2011). Afterwards it is much easier to convince them of the importance of studying and offer them complementary academic activities.

Regardless of its popularity, it is still a matter of debate whether the theory of social capital can be regarded as a new theory of mobility. Nevertheless, there is no doubt that the application of the theory of how social capital compensates for reproductional determinants can give new impetus to the discourse of education research. The theory of social capital offers an alternative interpretational framework by raising the question of institutional impact and expanding educational actors' space for joint activities, opportunities and responsibilities.

Student achievement in a comparative perspective

Abstract

In previous studies it was revealed that Hungarian denominational schools favourably influence the school career of students with disadvantageous backgrounds. According to our previous results, the school density of student networks with a circle of friends practising religion influenced students' educational careers to a much greater extent than all other explanatory variables (Pusztai 2006). Therefore, this influence proved to be even stronger than that of cultural capital on school context. We pointed out that these schools reduce the inequality of cultural capital with the help of organic relationships and cohesion between parents and children in the school community. The aim of this paper is to reveal the interpretational capacity of the social capital theory in connection with the differences between students' achievements. The present study is based on data gathered in the border regions of three East-Central European countries, namely Hungary, Romania and Ukraine. We have revealed that differences do not only originate from the advantages or disadvantages deriving from social background, but according to the social capital hypothesis the form, size and composition of relationships can also explain the differences[1].

Introduction

In this study we try to establish the nature of the correlation between the sector-specific differences in school achievement and the ideological orientation of the school. Previous research showed that denominational schools were more effective (Coleman, Laarhowen et al. 1990, Dronkers 2005, Preuschoff-Weiss 2001, etc), but European research in particular had lacked any subtle sociological approach up until the turn of the millennium; indices of religiosity had not been measured and included in the analyses; only assumed variables had been used. However, studies published after the turn of the millennium started to include empirically based variables indicating religiosity. Moreover, one can also detect the aspiration to understand the effect of privatised, individualised and thus invisible religiosity on the school atmosphere and on students' school careers (Pusztai 2004, 2005, Dijkstra 2006, Standfest 2005). Most papers, however, still do not try to establish

---

1   In the present essay we rely on our paper published previously in French (Pusztai 2008).

any connection between religiosity and achievement either at the individual or at school level. In our research carried out in the last decade we have been focusing on this very question. According to our previous results the school density of student closures with a circle of friends practising religion influenced students' educational careers to a much greater extent than all other explanatory variables (Pusztai 2005). Therefore this influence proved to be even stronger than that of cultural capital on school context. Students with a closed circle of religious friends –a phenomenon typical of denominational schools in particular– provide the kind of social capital in the school community that also inspires those who lack this resource themselves.

What we have so far failed to investigate thoroughly enough are the following: (1) What are the particular features of relationship structures that bring about the above effect and to what extent do they do so? (2) How much is this phenomenon tied to denominational schools? Our present study attempts to find an answer to these questions. It is especially interesting to carry out relevant research in one of the multi-ethnic and multi-confessional regions of Central Europe, where the compact Hungarian population lives in three different countries and has three different school systems.

The impact of the school sector

A sector specific divergence of students' effectiveness was first recognized in the 1960s in the international literature of educational sociology (Greeley-Rossi 1966). Comparisons among different school sectors generally concentrate on differences among students attending institutions of different school administrative bodies; however, there have been cases where, when researching the long-term effects of schools, former denominational students of higher education have been studied (Coleman-Hoffer 1987, Wilson 1996). In our "Regional University" study (2005) we examined graduate students of higher educational institutions with Hungarian as the language of teaching, in Hungary, Romania and Ukraine. Undergraduates before their finals from six Hungarian speaking universities and colleges were surveyed (3 Hungarian, 2 Romanian and 1 Ukrainian)[2]. Students from denominational schools performed in higher education more efficiently, because these students were determined to start working after graduation, they wanted to contribute to social welfare, and as students they spent more time on self-education and acquiring knowledge than the average (Pusztai 2007).

---

2 In Hungary: the University of Debrecen, the College of Nyíregyháza and the Ferenc Kölcsey Reformed Teacher Training College; in Romania: the Partium Christian University and the Teacher Training College in Szatmárnémeti, and in Ukraine: II. Ferenc Rákóczi Hungarian College of Subcarpathia.

Other researchers have explained sector specific differences in school results and admissions to higher education explicitly by the efficiency of denominational schools (Coleman-Hoffer 1987, Gamoran 1992, Evans-Schwab 1995, Kuzniewski 1997). A group of analyses studied the frequency of school failures, including dropping out of secondary schools or changing schools, in terms of the administrative status of the school. According to these findings, the rate of students dropping out or changing schools is lower in denominational schools (Russel-Scott 2000). The findings of European researchers also showed sector specific differences in school achievement (Cuyck- Dronkers 1990, Laarhoven et al. 1990, Dronkers 1995, Dronkers et al. 1999). In an international comparison analysing PISA data, Dronkers and Róbert concluded that a special effect mechanism of denominational schools exists, which manifests its role in social mobility (Dronkers-Róbert 2006).

Different longitudinal surveys helped to research the matter more thoroughly; for example, the results of panel-surveys between 1979 and 1994 demonstrated that Catholic schools were able to provide outstanding encouragement to Afro-American and Latin-American students (Polite 1992, Grogger-Neal 2000). Besides registering sector specific divergences, the studies find a great number of creative and variable explanations. Many researchers suppose that it is the greater discipline and stricter requirements that result in higher achievement in these schools (Greeley 1982, Jensen 1986, Dronkers 1995). Others claim that some of the characteristics of children or their families can cause these differences, so they started to pay attention to the character of communities in or around the schools. Beside the structures and contents of students' and parents' relationships in and outside the family (Coleman 1988, Carbonaro 1998), new contextual variables were included in the analysis, for example the nature of parents' relationships, the school density of church-adherents (Morgan-Sorensen 1999), the regional density of church adherents, the differences in tuition fees in different schools, the availability of grants regarding time factor (Neal 1997) and the nature of dominant norms in schools (Carbonaro 1999). The other direction taken by the explanations of sector specific differences puts emphasis explicitly on the influence of students' religiousness on their school career. The influence of religiousness on the attitude to school can be approached from several directions (Pusztai 2007).

Religiosity as Social Capital Convertible into Educational Achievement

Several researchers found it reasonable to integrate religiosity into theories of capital as an explanatory variable. The concept of religious human capital summarizes the cognitive and social dimensions of religion as a resource

(Azzi and Ehrenberg 1975). Research has found that this type of capital results in better physical and spiritual health for the individual and better school achievement and it decreases the chances of being influenced by deviant behaviour (Lehrer 2005).

In the theory of social capital religiosity plays a more important role than in the theory of human capital. Coleman regards social capital as primarily a latent aspect of an existing network of relationships, the members of which facilitate one another's actions. As a result of its common norms the network is characterised by confidence and mutuality (Coleman 1988). A religious community is therefore a classic example of the resources of social capital, religious practice being predominantly a communal activity in the Colemanian sense. Although Coleman does not state it explicitly, we might interpret his theory in such a way that exclusively individual religiosity does not necessary lead to the benefits of social capital such as the prevention of deviant behaviour, good achievement, reward for meeting expectations and solidarity. It is certainly very difficult to determine the extent to which the affective and cognitive aspects of religiosity are individual and communal constructions, as the essence of Coleman's social theory is that individual ambitions and decisions are largely determined by the structure of the individual's relationships (Coleman 1990).

The concept of religious capital (Iannaccone 1998) began to crystallize during research into the causes of economic success in adulthood. Apart from the interiorisation of rites and knowledge it also involves the interiorisation of relationships. Putnam emphasized the importance of communal religious activity as an indicator of social capital (Putnam 2000). Finke (2003), however, arguing that the concept includes the relationship element in an era of modern, individualised religiosity, reintegrates all the relationship components of religion into the concept of social capital, calling the purely individual elements spiritual capital. This raises the question of whether religious norms without communal religious practice have any impact on school achievement or their positive effect is weakened. As Davie argues, we cannot speak about the decline of faith; personalism and individualism rather increase its intensity, particularly among young people, so its function as an inspiring force and a resource can be considered even more important (Davie 2002).

The majority of the literature on social capital clearly shows the significant connection between the resources of relationships and educational achievement (Ainsworth 2002). Yet there is no consensus on how independent a factor social capital is in students' school achievements. Some claim that social capital, manifesting itself as a social expectation influencing students' behaviour, is a resource independent of cultural capital (Coleman 1988, Carbonaro 1998), whereas others hold the view that social capital in itself

54

is incapable of improving academic achievement, but capable of diminishing the race- and class-dependence of the reproduction of cultural capital (McNeal 1999). Nevertheless, the theory of social capital has brought about a revolutionary renewal of approach in educational sociology, as it has drawn attention to a force able to modify the determining influence of social status which contradicts with the theory of reproduction focusing on the individual determined by social class.

Basically, religiosity can influence one's school career in two ways: partly through its ideological, cognitive and affective dimensions and partly through the value systems and norms of the communities. The ideological dimension of religion puts the individual's life into a larger context. It makes the individual responsible for his/her deeds and conscious of his/her way of living. It also leads to a future-orientated attitude, which is compatible with the value system of schools. The ritual dimension of religious practice helps to adapt to school schedules and regulations. These religious rituals are similar to school rituals, as the structure of roles is easy to follow. It is obvious when people arrive and leave, stand up and sit down, speak and remain silent and how they do these things. Religious practice becomes useful in not only considering time as orientating towards the future instead of the present, but it also helps to regulate when participants can start speaking and how events follow each other in time. Thus religious practice helps students to learn linearity and circularity in school life (Bourdieu-Passeron 1977).

Most denominations require the compulsory study of scriptures. Skills acquired through this promote effectiveness in school, because one of the indicators of school achievement is students' competence in reading and reading comprehension. By the cognitive dimensions of religiosity, religious studies give practice in studying, and students gain knowledge almost without being aware of it (Wigfield-Asher 2000). The rituals of everyday prayers and introspection contribute to critical self-evaluation and self-reflection, and encourage students to improve their behaviour and not blame teachers because of their inefficiency in studying (Lee-Schneider 2002). The consequential dimension of religiosity results in partnerships with other people, which make students respect teachers more, not disturb other students in their work and refrain from unruly, violent actions or vandalism.

A possible negative consequence is that students act as partners in competitive circumstances too, which results in weaker achievement. An additional plus, though, is that they need less control and disciplining. As a consequence, they invest more time and energy in studying, and they have a steadier and more thorough knowledge. Religious identity in a plural society can help to develop the ability to choose from among the alternatives available and to lead a more conscious life. The children of religious parents choose between religiosity and the absence of religion, but the children of atheist parents almost always become irreligious (Voas – Crockett 2005). This ability is useful in finding the best way forward in the multi-level system of education. Religion defines the whole family's way of life through religious parents: it determines free time activities and habits of cultural and financial consumption, which may promote the optimistic asceticism that is necessary for school mobility (Bourdieu-Passeron 1977). When we research the effects of religious behaviour, we rightly use the conditional mood for some types of behaviour, because their appearance is not certain, only likely – somewhat more likely in the case of religious students than non-religious ones. In Freeman's opinion (Freeman 1986), the primary effects of religiosity cannot be registered with certainty, only dominant associations reference their existence, while the secondary or indirect effects, for example those being felt through the control of the religious community, can be detected more easily.

Religious practice in the community can become efficient through clear, unambiguous prescriptive and prohibiting norms. We interpret the church community and within it group membership (which, by its nature, involves interpersonal relationships) as closures in the Colemanian sense (Muller-Ellison 2001, Pusztai 2005). Active participation in small religious communities may not only multiply the effects of the norms and attitudes enhancing success at school, but may also prevent the individual's becoming involved in their contemporaries' gangs, whose behavioural patterns are alien to those of the school. Moreover, as a result of group membership the circle of their patrons and counsellors will become intergenerational (Coleman-Hoffer 1987, Carbonaro 1998, Muller-Ellison 2001).

Arguments for the indirect effect mechanism of religiosity have been grounded in the idea that it is social capital within the family –family structure, communicational habits and attentive child-rearing– that religiosity first has a favourable influence on (Evans-Oates-Schwab 1992, Pusztai 2007). According to a possible model of the differentiated effects of religiosity within the family, parents are more likely to expect their children to go on to higher education and talk with them more about school if their religious practice is more active than average. Consequently, religious parents' children set themselves higher standards, do extra academic work more often, spend more time doing homework, are more likely to make friends with children who like studying, and are less likely to play truant or drop out (Muller-Ellison 2001).

According to our earlier findings, one of the possible transmitters of religiosity is contemporaries' and friends' group norms, which may reinforce the norms of the religious family and the school. The more homogeneous young people's value and norm systems are, the more they succeed in interiorising these norms (Pusztai 2005). Belonging to a religious community supplies young people with transitive relationships in which even those who are not directly related give support to one another. Moreover, if a young person's friends are also from that group, the relationships become even more complex. Coleman's results suggest that belonging to a religious circle of friends brings about a formal and essential unity such that the social capital it creates will decrease drop-out rates and increase the chances of becoming more effective (Coleman-Hoffer 1987). Coleman thinks this is more likely to happen in denominational schools.

Our research has posed the question whether this resource is available to all students alike, or whether there are other structures of relationships capable of functioning as a resource for those who are only loosely connected to a religious relationship network.

Impact of schools

Whereas the hypothesis on denominational schools as functional communities producing social capital has been a matter of discussion since the 1980s in American research, in Europe it received attention after the turn of the millennium, when a PISA survey showed that private schools had better results than state schools in 14 of the 17 countries[3] (Preuschoff-Weiss 2001, Dronkers-Róbert 2004).

Several researchers attribute the influence of the school to the influence of students' religiosity, but others have tried to separate the influence of the denominational school from that of individual religiosity (Coleman-Hoffer 1987, Jeynes 2002). Byrk et al. found that the stimulating force of the pedagogical dimension of religiosity is rooted in its personalism and respect for human dignity, from which it follows that all students can be developed (Bryk et al.1992). While comparisons among different school sectors generally concentrate on social status differences among students attending denominational and non-denominational schools, we started to pay attention to the character of communities in or around the schools. In former studies we revealed that Hungarian denominational schools favourably influence the school careers of students with disadvantageous backgrounds. We pointed out that these schools reduce the inequality of cultural capital with the help of organic relationships and cohesion between parents and children in the school community (Pusztai 2005).

When Dronkers (2005) first tested the theory of social capital, he grounded his hypothesis on Coleman et al.'s concept (1987) of the functional school based on shared values. In the original interpretation the value system of

---

3 Government-financed private schools in Europe are usually denominational schools.

the functional community makes up a coherent unity with a unified system of preferred values such as an individual's life in this and in the other world, a person's mission in the world, the individual's dignity irrespective of abilities or social background, paying attention to the teacher and making decent use of one's talents. These values support one another, forming an efficient and functional system for the community. Coleman emphasizes both the cohesive nature of the network (closure) and the fact that there is a general consensus on values in the school community, so he focuses on form and content alike. The existence of an intergenerational closure around the school is often not a measured but a so-called assumed variable in surveys concerning denominational students. The only thing even Coleman and Hoffer may have been certain about was that the majority of denominational students were churchgoers, from which they concluded that churchgoers living in the inner areas of big American cities were most likely to know one another. Dronkers, who insisted on Coleman's formal criteria, found that European data did not support the idea that the functional school community came into being due to parents' frequent personal interaction within the same religious community. This is because the European school system is not based on districts.

We think that as long as the majority of those belonging to a denominational school community are involved in communal religious practice, we might assume a relatively general value consensus among the members of the local church community (the network of networks) even without everybody knowing everybody else. Approaching the concept of the functional community from the content element of the structure of relationships we concluded that the unity of norms and behavioural patterns is an important element of a consistent value system. In other words, a functional community is characterised by harmony between everyday actions and religious norms. If the members do not feel the interaction between behavioural patterns and religious norms, do not stand up for their religion in their everyday lives or do not take part in the rites with real commitment, there is no real functional community. To return to the formal approach, we find it a bold hypothesis that the effectiveness of a denominational school can be explained with the density of religious students, who function as a bridge between the school community and the religious community, thereby supplying their fellow students with important and seemingly novel -under modern school circumstances- input such as discipline, respect for the teacher's dignity and conscientious work (Burt 2001). In other words, the better achievement of denominational schools may be due to the fact that students do not only mobilise their interiorised, achievement-stimulating norms for their own purposes, but they also make them available to the rest of the school community. The question is what the proportion of those spreading new information in the community should be in order for the spill-over effect of stimulating norms to reach the other students.

Research Area and Data

The present study is based on data gathered in the border regions of three Central Eastern European countries, namely Hungary, Romania and Ukraine. We surveyed students of secondary schools in Hungarian speaking institutions. Since 1920 in Romania and Ukraine there have been compact Hungarian national minorities along the Hungarian borders[4]. This border region can be characterised by traditional multi-confessionalism, a significant Protestant (Reformed church) presence and confessional tolerance: in the sample areas in Romania and Hungary almost half of the students, and in Ukraine two thirds of them belong to the Reformed church, so the proportion of Catholics is 30–50%. At the time of the political transformation, the peripheral border areas in Hungary as well as in Romania and Ukraine had an insufficient network of secondary education. The gap was filled by opening denominational schools. Denominational schools in the Central-Eastern European region had played the main role in education for centuries. The cooperation between church and state was characterised by complementarity and the sharing of tasks. After the communists came into power church schools were nationalised: first in the Sub-Carpathian area in today's Ukraine in the former Soviet Union in 1945, and then simultaneously in Hungary and in Romania in 1948. In Hungary 10 denominational schools were allowed to exist within strict limits. After the political transformation of 1989–90 several denominational schools were opened or re-established. However, in Romania and in Ukraine there was no legal way for the churches to run schools and receive financial support, because the dominant Orthodox church preferred not to run schools of general education, and other denominations were not allowed to engage in activities that were incompatible with Orthodox tradition. As a consequence, church-oriented schools are run by local authorities and foundations.

It is only in Hungary that the previously very extensive denominational school system has been reorganised at the primary level, with about 10% of students attending a denominational institution. At secondary level less than

---

4   In Ukraine the Hungarian population of 150,000 lives in a compact community along the border and also in diaspora. In Romania the number of Hungarians is 1.5 million, living in two compact areas and in diaspora. Apart from the border area, the other compact Hungarian area is in the middle of Romania in the very Eastern corner of the Carpathian basin. Until recently, religion has been one of the pillars of ethnic Hungarians' national identity.

one fifth of Hungarian-speaking students go to denominational schools in all the three countries. Naturally, the schools follow the National Curriculum of the given country. A major defect of the curricula imposed by Romanian and Ukrainian educational authorities is that ethnic Hungarians have to follow the same syllabus in their studies of the official language as native students. As a result, it becomes impossible for them to acquire a good knowledge, which excludes most secondary schools and higher education. Moreover, the Hungarian language is not appropriately respected in official transactions, either.

We conducted a survey[5] in 20 denominational and 20 non-denominational secondary schools in the border region in 2006. As we intended to examine the school careers of Hungarian students within and outside Hungary in denominational (church-run) and public secondary schools, we picked the schools to be sampled by pairing each denominational school with a non-denominational one of similar status regarding their location and the students' social position (Neuwirth 2005). Thus, the list of sample schools consisted of pairs of schools chosen in the way described above. The students included in the survey were picked from the 11th and 12th grades. The sample consisted of 1466 students. Above all, we wanted to find out by applying precise research methods whether there were any differences between the student populations, seemingly similar in status, of the two sectors.

Hypotheses

Investigating the reasons for the differences in achievement between denominational and non-denominational students we revealed that sector-specific differences do not originate from the advantages or disadvantages of social background. As we had earlier detected a strong influence of the relationships organised along religious practice on denominational students' school achievements, we went on to examine whether it was religiosity or relationship structures that exerted such a powerful influence. Our sample enabled us to have an insight into three different school systems and examine the role of denominational schools. The sector-specific differences did not always show the same tendencies in the three regions. Denominational students in the border areas of Romania, for example, turned out to do worse at school than non-denominational students in the region. This anomaly gave us a good opportunity to find out what conditions had to be satisfied in order for denominational schools to have high-achieving school-leavers. We set up two main hypotheses. Firstly, according to the social network hypothesis, we

---

5   The "Secondary school students' plans for higher education" project was supported by OTKA T-048820.

assumed that the form, size and composition of relationships could explain the differences. Therefore we compiled a questionnaire based on the findings of international research on relationship networks and previous interviews conducted in the research area in order to map all the possible relationships students had. Secondly, according to the religiosity hypothesis we presumed that the differences were directly related to religiosity, and we also took into account religious motivation and religious practice in the family, in small or large communities or individual religious practice.

Students in the Border Regions of Three Countries

According to our findings, denominational school students of the border region have an average/standard social status compared to state schools. We took the sample from schools where students have equal social status, so we compared students with more or less similar backgrounds from the denominational and non-denominational school sectors. Still, there are some minor differences. In Ukraine few qualified parents tend to send their children to denominational schools, whereas it is the other way round in Romania. Denominational students have a slightly worse financial status in Hungary compared to students in other school sectors. The number of children in families is higher in denominational schools except for in Ukraine. There are definitely more denominational students than non-denominational ones who live in student hostels in north-eastern Hungary and Ukraine.

According to some experts, denominational schools are in the vanguard of social segregation; their sole existence causes an unequal distribution of children with different socio-economic backgrounds among schools. In our research, however, non-denominational schools turned out to be socially very closed and segmented, compared to their denominational counterparts. Non-denominational students go to schools which can be classified socially into 5 different groups according to the composition of the school. At one end of the scale we find schools where the proportion of parents with degrees is only 10%, whereas at the other end this rate is over 60%. There are no such castes in denominational schools. According to our experience, if a school is organised on a cultural (e.g. ethnic or religious) basis, identification with the given culture overwrites vertical social status in recruiting students. In this way, segregation which negatively influences the capacity of the education system is less characteristic.

In order to map accurately enough the social and cultural climate in which the sampled students were brought up, we attempted to identify much subtler social categories than the usual vertical and horizontal inequalities. We tried to grasp the differences between family milieus and establish their categories by examining the variables referring to families' religious practice, parents' education and occupations, and their places of residence. As a result of our cluster analysis we established five clearly distinguishable groups.

In the individually religious lower middle-class milieu of small towns 70% of students practice their religion personally, and half of them go to church regularly and have religious friends. The value system is predominantly conservative. Fathers, who usually work as skilled workers or run their own businesses do not usually practice their religion; at most, they only pray. Mothers, who have secondary education and a personal religious practice, sometimes even turning up at church with their children, are mainly subordinate professionals or, less frequently, skilled workers.

We gave the name rural religious lower milieu to the environment characterised by definitely and strongly religious (both individually and communally), conservative parents with mainly a primary education. All family members practice their religion actively, and in addition, they are also members of small religious groups. Students have a conservative value system and they hold religion and traditions in high esteem; their religiosity is both individually and communally oriented, and their circle of friends is homogeneously religious.

The heterogeneously religious urban upper-middle milieu mostly includes intellectual or professional parents in small towns. Mothers and children practise religion personally, and every now and then they even go to church as well, but it is only mothers that might be members of small communities. Fathers may only have loose connections to a religious institution or a community. The families have a post-materialistic value system with priorities such as friendship, love, freedom, experiences and an eventful life. Less than half of the students have a religious circle of friends.

In non-religious upper milieu families in big cities highly qualified mothers and fathers mainly with secondary education refrain from both communal and personal religious practice. Nor do they encourage their children's religious involvement. Students' top value preferences are power and material values, and only a very few have religious friends.

In the non-religious worker milieu in big cities parents are workers with low qualifications and no church attendance, only some of the mothers pray, but the children's religious practice is typically more active than the parents'. Students hold material values and power in very high esteem, and they have few religious friends.

Table 1: Various family milieus in student groups, percentages

	Hungary***		Romania***		Ukraine***		
	public	church-run	public	church-run	Public	church-run	altog-ether
Small town lower middle	29.5%	34.6%	22.8%	26.0%	<u>45.9</u>%	<u>56.8</u>%	32.4%
Rural religious lower	2.3%	<u>25.0</u>%	<u>26.5</u>%	<u>31.1</u>%	15.3%	<u>33.7</u>%	18.3%
Urban upper middle	<u>12.0</u>%	<u>12.2</u>%	8.5%	3.6%	5.1%	3.2%	9.4%
Big city non-rel. upper	<u>34.1</u>%	20.1%	20.1%	11.7%	18.4%	4.2%	22.5%
Big city non-rel. worker	<u>22.1</u>%	8.1%	22.2%	<u>27.6</u>%	15.3%	2.1%	17.4%
N=	484	384	189	196	98	95	1446

Source: Secondary school students' plans for higher education (2006). The underlined figures indicate that the percentage in the given cell is higher than expected in a random distribution. Level of significance: ***= 0.000.

Looking at the representation of family milieus in the student groups we can see that certain milieus play a determining role in certain sectors. The question is what degree of representation can be considered to already dominate the atmosphere of the school and what degree of representation can still allow students with religious backgrounds to function as "bridges". The atmosphere of non-denominational schools in Hungary is essentially dominated by the two non-religious milieus, only slightly modified by the urban heterogeneous upper middle class milieu. In denominational schools it is the rural religious and the urban heterogeneous types that are over-represented, but the individually religious lower middle-class milieu also plays a significant role. As for Hungarian schools in Romania, there is not such a great difference between the sectors: it is students from low-status families with regular religious practice that dominate each sector, but there is also a large number of non-religious urban children from working-class families in the denominational sector. In the Hungarian schools of Ukraine students from the individually religious lower middle-class milieu make up the majority in both sectors, but the atmosphere of schools is also marked by the presence of students coming from traditionally religious families with lower levels of education.

Comparing the results of this survey to those of the nationwide one carried out in Hungary at the turn of the millennium, we have found that the most striking difference was that in our sample area the professedly religious intellectual family background in big cities and the religious entrepreneur family background of small towns are completely missing, while these milieus prove to be considerable driving forces in the denominational schools of Western Hungary.

Students' Religiosity in Different School Sectors

With respect to apparent religiosity, the gap between denominational and non-denominational students is the greatest in Hungary and the smallest in the border regions of Romania. As in our sample the majority of students in most of the surveyed groups have definite religious practice both at communal (more than half are weekly churchgoers) and at individual levels (two thirds pray), at the interviews we applied a list of items compiled and tested on the basis of the Albert-Ross scale, originally intended for measuring intrinsic and extrinsic religiosity (Murányi 2006). What we wanted to find out was the extent to which the religious culture surrounding the students was consistent, and how much it contributed to the birth of a functional community. The motives of communal and personal religious life were not considered dichotomies such as extrinsic vs. intrinsic, mature vs. immature religiosity, but as different kinds of religious practice or as consequences of the different motives of religious practice. On examining the 19 variables, we received such a varied picture full of interesting correlations that we started applying factor analysis to search for the latent variables that produced the peculiar patterns of the answers. As a result, we were able to distinguish between five religious motives.

The first summarising variable, including the majority of the items, was called self-oriented motivation. This mainly summarises elements related to the causes and modes of personal religious practice. The dominant aspects of religion are elements that give meaning, minimise tension and diminish contingency, and elements of all religious dimensions that can be individually experienced and are enriching for the individual such as the experience of God, the cognitive need for and the necessity of consistent behaviour. None of the statements about communal participation express the experience of sharing but rather emphasise that studying in a group is a way of increasing one's own knowledge.

What the essential variables of the second type have in common is that they focus on the correlation between communal religious practice and establishing and maintaining relationships, so we gave it the name community-oriented motivation. Apart from the motivation to establish relationships, this includes the relevant qualities of a religious community as a network of relationships; for example, the features that promote the development and survival of confidential relationships. The element shared by the variables

64

making up the third type is that they question the correlation between religiosity and its possible consequences in both directions; that is, they claim that religiosity does not influence one's decisions or the quality of one's lifestyle and vice versa. We called this type inconsistent motivation; yet it is an inconsistency rooted in strong self-confidence and not any kind of chance or misunderstanding.

The hidden motivation also contains an element of inconsistency: a contradiction between inwardly experienced and outwardly represented religiosity. The communal elements of religiosity and, most of all, its consequential dimension are defective. Inconsistency is usually explained in terms of self-defence against a hostile or even threatening environment. The fifth type of motivation is the rite-oriented one, supported with a small amount of data, yet clearly distinguishable. The motive behind religious practice is habit. The scale was developed in such a way that it should suit young people, and, although students did not have to rank the items but score them, it is a definite sign of ritualism, especially in the case of an adolescent, if someone practises their religion only because they have been taught to. Nevertheless, since religiosity fluctuates during the course of life in patterns more complicated than the frequently mentioned U-shaped curve, it is also possible that in a certain period of one's life this is the only positive indicator of religiosity (Bögre 2002). Besides, we should not ignore the fact that although the wording of the question suggests that this motive is a priority, for those who find tradition-directed behaviour important it may be only one of the motives.

We examined the presence of the above motives in our sample groups. Data show that the proportion of students with self-oriented motivation is above average in denominational schools. Their number is still smaller than that of those who pray: although the orienting, tension-easing and contingency-diminishing functions of religion meet real needs, they still do not always provide enough motivation for personal religious practice. The unique nature of denominational schools in Ukraine lies in the fact that they are boarding schools with an active communal religious life, which leads us to a conclusion that might at first sound paradoxical, namely that it is a strong community that promotes the development of a religious personality.

One third of the all the students questioned belong to the community-oriented type. In line with expectations, this motivation is more typical of denominational students in all the three sample areas, and it is the most common in Hungary. Ethnic Hungarian denominational students have proved to be not as community-oriented as denominational students in Hungary because there are more religious people in their social environments outside school: in their neighbourhoods, places of residence and among their relatives. Denominational students in Hungary do not have so many religious people around them.

More than half of the sample in Romania and of non-denominational students in Ukraine deny any correlation between religiosity and behaviour. Experiencing and accepting the conflict between religion and contradictory behaviour are symptoms of anomy, a general phenomenon in regions which have remained underdeveloped after the political transformation. The inconsistent type of motivation is the rarest among denominational students in Ukraine, for whom life in the boarding schools provides a greater security in terms of norms.

Whereas the inconsistent type questions the validity or the operational capacity of the regulating function, the main characteristic of the hidden type is the conflict between high rule consciousness and the environment with contrary values as a major external force. Such an anomic environment is present in all the sample areas, above all in Ukraine, with two thirds of the students classifiable in this category. As we see it, the phenomenon is rooted in the large-scale persecution of religious people during the Soviet era with the aim of destroying the traditions of Western Christianity and also in economic processes of dubious legal status since the 1990s. This orientation is more typical of denominational students in Romania and Hungary than their non-denominational peers. As for Ukrainian students, it is just the other way round. Their religiosity must have already surpassed this simple level.

Social Capital from Institutional Resources

As regards the relationship between parents and children, religious parents communicate with their children significantly more frequently and control them far more strongly. On average, we can state that parents in denominational schools place greater emphasis on minimising those norms that are not compatible with the norms of the family. In the early phase of studies parents more clearly limit activities that may hinder school achievement. Later, however, we can detect an aspiration towards an independent, sovereign development of the children.

We pointed out that three features of social capital building are more characteristic in denominational schools. When we analysed extracurricular school programmes on a weekly basis, it became clear that for non-denominational students schools are considered as institutions solely for the purpose of studying. Students of denominational schools refer to extracurricular activities mostly as spiritual and communal occasions. As far as school community programmes are concerned, in denominational schools one can record a higher frequency of weekend programmes and day-long excursions compared to the other sector. As for the many-sided relationships that exist between teachers and students, in this case we concentrated exclusively on personal communications focusing on private problems and plans for the future. It turned out that this personal care is one of the components of the sector effect. According to the third important experience, student hostels are not only considered as accommodation for students, but also as a framework for their education.

In connection with the relationships among students, we asked secondary students how important they think studying and achieving good marks are to their classmates. We found that both denominational and non-denominational students consider studying and good marks important, while attending school and paying attention to teachers seem to be more important for denominational students. Unlike in a previous former hypothesis, the importance of attending school or paying attention do not seem to be related to the children's intellectual background, but to their religiosity. In denominational schools the social networks, their weak and strong ties, have a dominant effect in linking parents and children to a religious circle. Relationships along the religious community with the help of social control positively influenced student achievement. The second most significant network of relationships link denominational students to well-educated people.

Explanations of educational achievement differences

As we intended to describe secondary school students' school careers, we needed indices of achievement that helped us assess students' progress at school. We introduced several variables to measure dimensions of success. We did not measure academic achievement by test scores; instead, we tried to find indices that matched our questionnaire. Using the various dimensions of achievement we created a summarising index of achievement that included aspects such as taking on extra academic work (taking language exams, participating in competitions), planning one's future academic career (higher education) and a subjective element, namely the importance attached to academic activities by the particular student. The numerical value of the index ranged from 1 to 5. The index is capable of giving a comprehensive picture as it unites past achievements, hard work, ambitions for the future, conscious preparation and favourable attitudes.

We recorded divergences in different regions: in Ukraine and in north-eastern Hungary the denominational sector effect is clearly positive, whereas in Romania this effect is not universally positive. Among the numerous differences between the two sectors we wanted to spot those particular differences that give the best explanations of students' good or bad achievements. As the dependent variable was continuous, we chose linear regression models. The individual regions were treated in separate models, because detailed analysis made it obvious that the functions of the institutions are very different in the three areas.

We always started our investigation by measuring the gross sector effect, and then went on to observe its changes after introducing the range of explanatory variables. The variables included factors that appeared to be relevant during the detailed analysis described above as well as variables commonly used in educational sociology. If a variable of our own choice turned out to be of no help, we replaced it with a more useful one, so our final model contained only relevant variables.

Since leading theories attribute achievement to families' cultural capital, we planned to include variables indicating parents' education. However, because of insufficient data we replaced them with variables referring to above average occupational status. We incorporated the data on the two parents into our model one by one, because in the above two-variable analyses they had often produced different results. The two variables appear in a dummy form and indicate an occupational status which is considered higher in its field. The influence of material wealth on school career is indeed a realistic question in the sample regions. Although part of our research shows that it does not have a stronger influence than parents' education, it is important to note that there is high unemployment in the sample areas and the additional costs of education such as transport and textbooks are also high for families that mostly live in the country. In order to get a picture of the families' financial resources, we asked students about their families' possessions rather than actual incomes, which people are usually reluctant to reveal in that region. The data are indicated with a continuous variable (1–11).

We tried to take into account various forms of social capital indices, but in several cases there was no direct effect to be observed. Parental and teacher attention, however, seem to have influenced the results. Both are indicated with a continuous variable made up of 22 items in the former and 3 items in the latter case. The values are defined in such a way as to express the divergence from the average (e.g. attention above average =1). As the organisational forms of direct and indirect effects of religious practice appeared as sources of ambition at the individual level and channels for transmitting norms and information at the communal level, we introduced continuous variables to indicate personal religious practice (prays regularly =1), religious practice in a large community (goes to church regularly =1) and in a small one (member of a youth group =1), and we added another continuous variable to indicate the proportion of the above phenomena in the individual schools. The various orientations of relationship networks were also illustrated with a continuous variable based on the index calculated earlier. Regional inequalities were illustrated with dummy variables indicating places of permanent residence (city =1, village =1) and temporary residence during the school year (student hostel =1). The choice of programmes offered by the school and the types of religious motivation were represented by continuous variables calculated during factor analysis, and participation in extracurricular school activities was represented by a dummy variable (more active than average =1).

68

Table 2: Standardised regression coefficients of the model explaining students' academic achievement in Hungary, significance levels of respective explanatory variables and R² values of models

Church-run school	0,089 **	0,077 ***	0,078 **	0,067 *	0,052	0,021	-,129 **	-,156 **	-,177 **
High occupational status -Father		0.107 **	0.107 **	0.120 **	0.109 **	0.106 **	0.088 **	0.086 **	0.078 *
-Mother		0.132 **	0.130 **	0.110 **	0.107 **	0.118 **	0.112 **	0.114 **	0.101 **
Wealth			0.022	0.015	0.018	0.020	0.025	0.030	0.004
Parental attention				0.124 ***	0.069 *	0.057	0.062	0.060	0.057
Teacher attention					0.235 ***	0.224 ***	0.216 ***	0.216 ***	0.210 ***
Student's personal religious practice						0.101 **	0.095 **	0.089 **	0.081 **
Proportion of religious group members at school							0.194 ***	0.205 ***	0.220 ***
Lives in a student hostel								0.067 *	0.072 *
Academically oriented network									0.152 ***
R²=	0.009	0.049	0.05	0.065	0.117	0.125	0.139	0.143	0.164

Source: Secondary school students' plans for higher education (2006) N=868. A cell is marked with asterisks where the correlation is significant.
Levels of significance: *** =.000, ** < 0.03, * < 0.05.

On the whole, denominational schools in Hungary have a positive effect on students' achievement. Parents' high occupational status plays a minor role in achievement and their financial status plays none. Parental attention as the manifestation of the family's social capital contributes significantly to success at school, but the first really important component of the beneficial effects of denominational schools is teacher attention (conversations about private life and plans for the future, teacher's personal interest in the student). Another essential component is the student's personal religious practice. This seems to justify the argument for the direct effect of religiosity in the debate on direct vs. indirect effects. The further components result from the social context outside school. Among those we have detected are a high rate of youth group membership at school, student hostel environment and an academically oriented relationship network.

On the basis of our results, we think there are three main components of school achievement in both sectors. One of the two predominant components is teachers' attention to their individual students, which is a time and energy-consuming voluntary or, if you like, charitable activity. If a school invests in it, high student achievement is the profit it will yield. We have no information whether there is a correlation between teachers' attentive behaviour and their religiosity. We could not have relied on the students in this issue; it is only their impressions we could have inquired about. A future survey among teachers might suggest an answer.

The other predominant component is the proportion of youth group members at school, the benefits of which we have already noted before. This is a form of social capital that we consider as an indirect effect of religiosity, because the norms promoting academic progress operate through the community, helping even those who do not belong to such groups. Interestingly enough, this component cannot be replaced by the high proportion of churchgoers, which has no significant effect in this model, which weighs all factors together. This also suggests that different types of communal religious practice have different effects on school careers. It is close ties that seem to play a more important role.

The third component is personal religious practice, and the detection of its positive effects on school achievement is a very important result. We have referred to the explanations of the phenomenon in our summary of the relevant literature. In our sample the sources of the qualities (future and achievement-oriented behaviour, hard work, ability to respect fellow students' dignity) condensed into a dependent variable are most probably norms and inner control developed by a regular examination of conscience.

Table 3: *Standardised regression coefficients of the model explaining Hungarian students' academic achievement in Ukraine, significance levels of respective explanatory variables and R² values of models*

	1	2	3	4	5	6	7
Church-run school	0.431***	0.415***	0.413***	0.438***	0.419***	0.376***	0.293***
High occupational status -Father		0.074	0.075	0.090	0.059	0.082	0.019
-Mother		0.150**	0.141*	0.131*	0.093	0.083	0.070
Wealth			0.199**	0.202**	0.200**	0.214**	0.160*
Parental attention				-0.175**	-0.192**	-0.189**	-0.167*
Teacher attention					0.134*	0.100	0.124
Student's personal religious practice						0.160**	0.120
Academically oriented network							0.250***
$R^2=$	0.186	0.219	0.259	0.288	0.302	0.324	0.370

Source: Secondary school students' plans for higher education (2006) N=193. A cell is marked with asterisks where the correlation is significant. Levels of significance: *** =.000, ** < 0.03, * < 0.05.

In the border regions of Ukraine the gross effect of denominational schools on achievement is very strong and positive. Results show that parents' (especially fathers') high occupational and financial status plays a role, even if a minor one, in that positive effect. But a major part of denominational students' advantage comes from other sources. The tasks of parents have been almost completely taken over by teachers, as a major source of achievement is the same teacher attention as in Hungary. The two other components of the effect of denominational schools are personal religious practice and an academically oriented relationship network.

Table 4: *Standardised regression coefficients of the model explaining Hungarian students' academic achievement in Romania, significance levels of respective explanatory variables and R^2 values of models*

	1	2	3	4	5	6	7	
Church-run school	-0.273 ***	-0.285 ***	-0.284 ***	-0.278 ***	-0.227 **	-0.203 **	-0.173 **	-0.175 **
High occupational status -Father		0.089	0.083	0.091	0.084	0.108	0.100	0.099
-Mother		0.087	0.086	0.084	0.078	0.074	0.096	0.071
Wealth			0.047	0.036	0.024	-0.017	-0.021	-0.015
Parental attention				0.023	0.056	0.060	0.008	0.000
Teacher attention				0.206 ***	0.194 **	0.212 ***	0.164 **	0.144 **
Rate of churchgoers at school					-0.113	-0.081	-0.175 **	- 0.17 **
Residence: city					0.093	0.087	0.054	0.045
Experience-oriented activities						0.213 ***	0.241 ***	0.232 ***
Cultural activities						0.151 **	0.142 **	0.139 **
Self-oriented religiosity							0.168 **	0.135 *
Inconsistent religiosity							-0.178 **	- 0.178 **
Extracurricular activities								0.158 **
$R^2=$	0.074	0.114	0.116	0.159	0.181	0.249	0.301	0.324

Source: Secondary school students' plans for higher education (2006) N=385. A cell is marked with asterisks where the correlation is significant. Levels of significance: *** =.000, ** < 0.03, * < 0.05.

Contrary to the other regions, the coefficient of denominational schools is negative. We attempted to establish the causes of this in our analysis. If we ignore the impact of high-status parents, denominational schools even have a slightly more negative effect. Personal teacher attention has a positive influence, so the problem is not its absence. The density of churchgoers does not bring about any significant change elsewhere, but in this region it definitely has a negative effect. That is to say, if the majority of students practice their religion, it is insufficient for high achievement. Other religiosity indices show similar tendencies or have no effect at all. As far as places of residence are concerned, the influence of big cities is neither negative nor significant. As we have mentioned, the vast majority of denominational students in Romania come from two milieus: from rural, traditionally religious families with very low education and from non-religious worker families in big cities. It is obvious that these schools are open to the less fortunate strata of society and it is very difficult to make them produce good results.

The hypothesis of regional differences may provide an explanation of the relatively weak achievement of denominational schools in Romania. In a region with a dense network of denominational schools they fulfil a special function: low-status parents always choose nearby schools for their children, whether denominational or not and whether they themselves are religious or not. Given this, low-status students are present in large numbers at school, and therefore the school must have a much more marked denominational character including the intergenerational closures around the school (i.e. relationship networks organised along the religious community), the functional unity of the system of norms, teacher attention and extracurricular or weekend programmes. According to our analysis, achievement can be improved remarkably, apart from the great care provided by the teacher, by experience-oriented and cultural programmes provided by the school. By experience-oriented programmes we mean trips, camps and celebrations, by cultural ones we mean visits to the cinema and the theatre, which low-status parents fail to provide. However, not all schools provide those opportunities for their students, and that is how it may occur that it is students in Romania who most often make friendships at places of entertainment, becoming members of information networks with different value preferences. The help those networks offer are not enough for them to make up for the cultural disadvantages they have inherited from their families. What would have a beneficial influence on achievement in those schools is self-oriented religious motivation, but the renewal of old communal religious habits has not yet taken place. The existing hidden and rite-oriented motivations are of little help, and inconsistent religiosity has an undoubtedly negative influence. We use the term inconsistent to denote the religiosity of an individual who questions any correlation between religious practice and its consequences in either direction, because they are convinced that religiosity does not influence one's decisions or the quality of one's lifestyle. Resigning oneself to the contradictions between religion and behaviour in one's everyday life is an anomic symptom. An inconsistently religious student lacks exactly what is traceable in the differently motivated students of the two other regions, namely religiosity as a source of the inner drive and control that are realised in academic work. Another important factor is the defective extracurricular opportunities offered by some denominational schools in the border regions of Romania. There are a large number of families – just like elsewhere – that are unable to supply their children with "background schooling" i.e. private teachers in the afternoons, but while other denominational schools offer their students plenty of extracurricular opportunities, the above mentioned schools do not.

Conclusion

In this chapter we have attempted to reveal sector-specific differences in school achievement among last-year secondary students in the border regions of three countries. Using the various dimensions of achievement we created a summarising index of achievement that included aspects such as taking on extra academic work (taking language exams, participating in competitions), planning one's future academic career (higher education) and a subjective element, namely the importance attached to academic activities. In each region we constructed our regression model by continuously checking our hypotheses during our search for the components of the gross effect of denominational schools. We presumed that sector-specific differences are not rooted in the social backgrounds of schools and that students' school careers, religiosity, value systems, relationship networks and academic achievements are very diverse. Diversity is present in the whole sample area and is very significant.

Models have revealed that there are three essential sources of the effect of denominational schools. The first one is the powerful presence of special attention from the teacher. This is not based on the curriculum and not part of the hidden curriculum, either, but rather extra time and work devoted purposefully and voluntarily to the students by the teachers, realised in face-to-face conversations and various programmes organised by the school. The second source is students' personal religious practice enabling them to work persistently and ambitiously, act purposefully under strong self-control and respect the work of others (teachers and classmates). The third source is students' relationship networks developing predominantly through religious communities and appearing as an indirect consequence of religiosity in the sense that cooperating students in the relationship network support one another's purposeful and disciplined academic work.

In search of indicators of a school context effect

Abstract

The aim of this study is to reveal the explanatory capacity of the concept of social capital theory in connection with the variations in students' academic achievements in relation to individual and context-level religious variables. Thus, we focus on the structures and nature of students' relationships as they are organized in school. We carried out analyses based on individual students and tried to represent contextual effects with the attributions of aggregate students groups. We compared three context variables (the school composition based on parental social status, teachers' care aggregated at the school level, and the school-average of students' religious networks) with each other to find out what impact they may have on students' academic careers. According to the analysis, there is a significant divergence shown among the sectors in terms of the characteristics of school context.

Introduction

Authors of the international specialist literature dealing with denominational schools generally concentrate on deviations among students attending institutions of schools maintained by different administrative bodies. A sector specific deviation of students' achievement was first recognized in the 1960s. Analysing school reports of American high-school students coming from families with similar backgrounds but attending schools maintained by different administrative bodies, Coleman found diverging results, and he and his colleagues stated that the denominational institutions helped students achieve more (Coleman et al. 1982, Coleman and Hoffer 1987). The findings of European researchers also showed sector specific differences of school achievement (Laarhoven et al. 1990, Dronkers 1995, Dronkers et al. 1999). In a recent international comparison analysing PISA data, Dronkers and Róbert concluded that a special effect mechanism of denominational schools exists, and manifests its role in social mobility (Dronkers and Róbert 2004). Many researchers claim that certain kinds of characteristics of children or their families can cause deviations; others have started to pay attention to the character of communities in or around the schools. In previous studies we revealed that Hungarian denominational schools favourably influence the school career of students with disadvantaged backgrounds. We pointed out that these schools reduce the inequality of cultural capital with the help of organic relationships and cohesion between parents and children in the school community (Pusztai 2005).

Previous Research

Because of the high university acceptance rate among students in denominational schools, it is widely believed that the majority of denominational schools are elite establishments mostly attended by students with favourable social backgrounds. However, most religious people (in the church-adhering sense of the word) have, until most recently, been less qualified and have worked in jobs of lower esteem and lived in villages. In our studies since the turn of the millennium, we have revealed that denominational schools accept a variety of students, in both social and religious respects. Regarding the religiosity of students in denominational school families, 39% of families are homogeneously religious, 46% of families do not practise their religion and 15% are heterogeneously religious. Apart from the capital, where the neglected children of non-religious well-educated parents are also accepted, denominational schools students have an average social status, similar to public secondary school students. However, there are some differences: there are fewer intellectuals in leading posts and fewer unskilled workers among students' parents in denominational schools. In spite of their higher qualifications, these parents do not work in jobs of the highest prestige but rather as subordinate intellectuals, which indicates that the effects of negative discrimination against religious people, typical in former times, are still detectable. There are a larger number of entrepreneurs among the parents, but the reason why these people were forced to set up their own businesses was to avoid unemployment. Many denominational schools are located in disadvantaged peripheral areas, and almost 70% of students in denominational schools come from villages or small towns. The number of children in the families (2.34) is well above the Hungarian average, and thus the per capita income is lower (Pusztai 2005).

The former study showed that students in denominational schools have more definite plans for higher education than students in non-denominational schools of similar social status. Above all, there is a striking difference among children of less educated parents. In denominational schools the high occurrence of intentions to go on to higher education among children of less educated parents is significant. We interpreted this phenomenon by arguing that the effects of social reproduction are reduced by some factor in the denominational sector. According to our explanation this effect is based on the organic relations within the school community, the connectedness of parents, and children forming a community and following similar lasting and reliable norms, all of which become a resource for students' development, and have an important influence on their school career. The density of children with a homogeneously religious circle of friends in a school has the most important influence on the student's achievement. This form of social capital can also be beneficial to those students who lack this kind of resource.

Other Hungarian research has shown the long range effect of denominational schools. A larger number of students in denominational schools are admitted to higher education than could be expected on the basis of their proportion in the region. What is more, they do not drop out; on the contrary, the proportion increases slightly until the end of their higher education. Besides, there is a much greater proportion of university students than college students in the first year of higher education among former students from denominational schools compared to other school sectors (Imre 2008). Moreover, it is the children of parents who have no degrees that decide the most often to go on to universities instead of colleges.

The ways in which former students in denominational schools enter and get along in the world of work show their characteristic attitudes. Most become ready to start working by the end of their university years, in terms of their knowledge, persistence, zeal or expectations regarding the tasks and challenges they will face. About two-third of former students in denominational schools would like to work in socially useful, responsible jobs where they can deal with people and work in a team. A sense of efficiency is also important for them. Students from other school sectors, however, consider career advancement, prospects for promotion and a high salary important.

However, our research also showed performance differences between the schools and the students within the sector, and students from similar social status perform differently in different contexts. We started to look for answers to the school context factors that positively influence students' results. According to Coleman's theory (1988), this factor is social capital, which, just like other forms of capital, can itself be transformed into other kinds of capital, for instance, into human or cultural capital. Social capital can take various forms: it can be based on exchanges of favours and information or on norms generally accepted in a community. We have long been familiar with the effects the exchange of information and favours have on one's career (Granovetter 1973, Putnam 1993), but it was Coleman who first pointed out the use of effective norms and closed structures of relations during one's career at school. The relationships creating social capital can, with respect to form, be structurally open or closed, intergenerational or intragenerational; and with respect to duration, stable or less stable. According to Coleman, as a result of both students' individual attributes, i.e. "student input" (Coleman et al. 1985), and the influence of the school community, i.e. "school effect" (Coleman et al. 1985), it is both dimensions of social capital, content and form, that account for the better achievement of denominational schools. The content element in these relationships is the clear set of norms resulting from religious faith; the formal element is the intergenerational closure of the school's community of students, teachers and parents, effective through preventing deviant behaviour and rewarding achievement. This is the empirical basis of Coleman's hypothesis that it is closed structures of relations based on effective norms that are most capable of creating social capital best convertible into human capital; moreover, he maintains that this kind of closure of relations is capable of creating a larger amount of capital than any other resource (Coleman 1988). According to Coleman, formal closure is a typical structural property of social relations based on common and effective norms (1988:105). Norms are only effective if the structure is sufficiently closed for the members to be able to combine forces for possible sanctions. The closed structure of an opposite nature may, of course, have an influence in another direction: the student may become embedded in a community of contemporaries that does not support his or her work at school and does not regard studying as hard as one can as a moral duty or as a useful investment (Portes-Landolf 1996).

Hypotheses

In a previous study we attempted to reveal sector-specific differences in school achievement among secondary school seniors in the border regions of three countries. We revealed that there are three essential sources of the effect of denominational schools. The first is the powerful presence of special attention provided by the teacher. This is not based on the curriculum, nor is it part of the hidden curriculum, but rather extra time and work devoted purposefully and voluntarily to the students by the teachers, realised in face-to-face conversations and various programmes organised by the school. The second source is students' personal religious practice, which enables them to work persistently and ambitiously, act purposefully under strong self-control and respect the work of others (teachers and classmates). The third source is students' relationship networks which develop predominantly through religious communities and appear as an indirect consequence of religiosity in that cooperating students in the relationship network support one another's purposeful and disciplined academic work.

In the present chapter we examine which characteristic of the school context is able to compensate the differences in school career caused by social status[6]. In other words, we are interested in how the social capital and the presence of confidential relationships in a school community alter the reproductive impact of parental status on school performance. The most

---

6   The "Secondary school students' plans for higher education" project was supported by OTKA T-048820. This chapter is an updated version of previously published analysis of the institutional level data.

commonly examined index of school status is the frequency of high-status parents (education, profession, SES) in a school community. It can often be demonstrated that the composition of a school environment based on social status is also able to modify expected performance based on individual background. However, this is not the only characteristic of school context that is worth observation. Since Coleman's study, another frequently investigated feature has been the influence of dominant relationship networks in the school community, and the impact of dominant norms within it. Coleman linked this type of social capital to the form of relative structure, and emphasized that positive norms can function in a community if the structure is closed enough to let control operate appropriately (Coleman 1988). The school community operating according to collectively accepted norms can help students' performance by applying information, control and sanctions more effectively. Taking this as a starting point, we observed the impacts of the frequency of religious networks in schools. These networks proved especially strong and attracted our attention. Besides this, considering Bryk and Schneider's study, we examined the personal care provided by teachers, since these authors showed that an increase in trust within the school organization contributes to an improvement in academic performance in the school community (Bryk and Schneider 2002). From their point of view, for the development of a confidential atmosphere, it is essential that the actors have a shared conviction that the consideration of each other's interests is important to everybody, and that role partners pay personal attention to each other; furthermore, that they are able to fill the role, and do their jobs conscientiously. The effect of this principle is manifested in the everyday life of the school in such a way that the parents, teachers and students constantly analyse each others' behaviour from these perspectives. Consequently, a deficit in any of these factors can undermine the confidential security of the whole relational system. We compared the context variables to each other to obtain information concerning which one of them is the most able to modify reproductive determinism.

We modelled our hypotheses in the figure below. We believe that school context has a great influence on commitment relating to studying and academic performance. On the one part, we assumed that the social status of parents is a strong influence on academic performance, and that the context levels of the parents' previous education are of even greater significance.

Nevertheless, we assume that people practising religion, or members of religious networks bring norms into the school context that help the pursuit of good performance, and make cooperation with the school more popular. These norms will bring about the appreciation of diligent and well-balanced work, and eventually cause better results even from students coming from disadvantaged social backgrounds.

However, we can also presume that the personal care provided by teachers presents a sort of absent social capital which is a missing feature in today's problematic families, and that a strong presence of this care in the school context will encourage students to perform better. Finally, we presume that there are various off-sector compensating effects that modify the impact of family social status on student performance. Our analysis is also based upon the database entitled "Secondary school students' plans for higher education".

Figure 1: The impact of various indexes of school context on school performance.

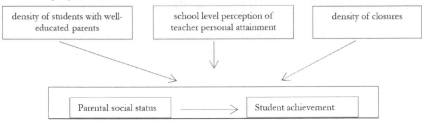

The proportion of the well-educated parents in the school context

According to both Hungarian and international research the social composition of individual schools has a marked influence on their students' academic careers (Coleman and Hoffer 1987). There is a debate in the specialist literature about the extent to which the existence of denominational schools brings about selectivity in the school system. Some experts claim that denominational schools, by gathering high-status children, cause selectivity and differences among schools, while others say that a school belonging to a religious or a national/ethnic community is, by its nature, inclusive (Dijkstra 2006). The social context of a school can be best characterized by an index showing the proportion of its students whose parents have a degree in higher education.

According to our findings, non-denominational schools turned out to be socially closed and segmented, compared to their denominational counterparts. Students in non-denominational schools go to schools which can be classified socially into five different groups according to the social composition of the schools. At one end of the scale, we find schools where the proportion of parents with degrees is only 10%, whereas at the other end this proportion is over 60%. There are no such cases in denominational schools. According to our experience, if a school is organized on a cultural (e.g. ethnic or religious) basis, identification with the given culture overwrites the vertical structure of social status in recruiting students. In this way, social segregation which negatively influences the capacity of the educational system is less characteristic.

Table 5: The distribution of students according to the percentage of parents with degrees in church-run schools and in the different sectors, percentages

	Church-run schools			State-run and other private schools			Altogether
	Hungary	Romania	Ukraine	Hungary	Romania	Ukraine	
Under 10%	0%	56.1%	0%	8.9%	19.6%	44.2%	15.7%
Under 20%	28.4%	43.9%	51.6%	30.4%	23.8%	31.2%	32.3%
Under 30%	47.1%	0%	48.4%	42.6%	56.6%	24.7%	39.2%
Under50%	24.5%	0%	0%	9.1%	0%	0%	9.7%
Above 60%	0%	0%	0%	9.1%	0%	0%	3.1%
N=	384	196	95	484	189	77	1425

Source: Secondary school students' plans for higher education (2006). The underlined figures indicate that the percentage in the given cell is higher than expected in a random distribution. Level of significance: ***= 0.000.

The rate of closures in the school context

It is our conviction that when researching school processes it is not sufficient to examine only the characteristics of individuals and families, since students connected via an organizational framework will acquire new and common characteristics. In this respect, we treated the religious practice of students as a characteristic of school communities. Despite the relatively high rate of students practising religion, one fourth of the students attend schools where those who practise are in a minority, and almost one third of the sample attend schools where three fourths of the students are believers by personal conviction. Therefore, we can see that while students in non-denominational schools can study in various environments in this respect, the students of the other groups are present in a predominantly religious environment, even in the case where the density of religious students is not the same in the different schools.

In terms of personal religious practice, the most homogeneous context is the Ukrainian ethnic Hungarian society. Two thirds of the Hungarian students attend denominational schools where religious students are in the bare majority, and one third go to schools where the religious students are in the great majority. These context figures can be seen as parallel to what we saw in the social backgrounds of schools. Thus the assumption gains support: the schools organized on religious foundations are similarly as little segregated in terms of religious practice as they are socially.

Table 6: *The distribution of students who practise religion personally, characterized by different proportions in church-run schools and in the different sectors, percentages*

	Church-run schools			State-run and other private schools			Altogether
	Hungary	Romania	Ukraine	Hungary	Romania	Ukraine	
Under 25%	–	–	–	17.4%	–	–	5.8%
25.1–50%	–	–	–	58.7%	–	–	19.6%
50.1–75%	65.1%	36.2%	–	24%	76.2%	56.1%	44%
75.1–100%	34.9%	63.8%	100%	–	23.8%	43.9%	30.6%
N=	384	196	95	484	189	98	1446

Source: Secondary school students' plans for higher education (2006). The underlined figures indicate that the percentage in the given cell is higher than expected in a random distribution. Level of significance: *** = 0.000.

The school-related density of students with a communal religious practice shows a different picture. The table clearly demonstrates the two extremes. Whereas the Hungarian students in non-denominational schools attend schools where less than one fourth of the students are churchgoers, the Ukrainian students in denominational schools attend schools where more than three fourths of the students go to church regularly. In three of the other four groups, it is clear what the most typical proportion is – i.e. the proportion which characterizes this feature of the school context. In the Romanian denominational schools, more than 40% of the students show a moderate but firm communal religious practice dominance, yet one third of them attend schools whose context resembles that of the non-denominational schools; there, churchgoer students are in a minority, despite the fact that in terms of personal religious practice, the Romanian denominational sector did not seem very divided.

Table 7: *The distribution of students who practise religion communally, characterized by different proportions in church-run schools and in the different sectors, percentages*

	Church-run schools			State-run and other private schools			Altogether
	Hungary	Romania	Ukraine	Hungary	Romania	Ukraine	
Under 25%	–	–	–	100%	23.3%	24.5%	31.7%
25.1–50%	7.8%	36.2%	–	–	31.7%	51%	16.1%
50.1–75%	66.7%	19.9%	–	–	45%	24.5%	30.9%
75.1–100%	25.5%	43.9%	100%	–	–	–	21.3%
N=	384	196	95	347	189	98	1309

Source: Secondary school students' plans for higher education (2006). The underlined figures indicate that the percentage in the given cell is higher than expected in a random distribution. Level of significance: *** = 0.000.

The symmetry of students doing communal religious practice is greater everywhere in the denominational sector than in the non-denominational one. On the other hand, the frequency of students from strongly religious families is greater among Romanian and Ukrainian students in denominational schools, than among Hungarians. This can be explained by the fact that during long years of oppression in a minority group, and having been repressed by the state, the only chance to preserve one's identity was religious and denominational affiliation. However, we noticed that while denominational secondary school-goers predominantly attend schools where personal and communal religious practice is in the majority, one third of the Romanian students in denominational schools, and less than one tenth of the students from north-eastern Hungary attend schools where religious students are in the minority. In other words, there are schools in the denominational sector where these resources are not chiefly available on the context level.

Networks in the school context

School context is also determined by what relation networks the students belong to, and, by being a member, what sort of outward or inward network norms and information they introduce into the school community. These networks can evolve from friendships and acquaintances. The literature names the former networks strong-, the latter weak bonds. As for friendships, based on the analysis of the range of personal relation networks, it seemed that the intimate, friendly relationships between Ukrainian and Hungarian students in denominational schools are particularly multiplex relation networks, i.e. these friendships serve various functions. In connection with building friendships, the school itself (especially the institution we visited during our research) represents the greatest source. Four-fifths of the secondary school students and more than two-thirds of the elementary school students made friends. Places of amusement and the local environment provided opportunities for building relationships for fewer than half of the students. Whilst in non-denominational schools students make friends at places of amusement and during extra-curricular and hobby activities, for denominational schools students, it is the dormitory and the religious communities that prove to be the most determining source for making friends.

The role of acquaintances in social mobility is much more appreciated by certain authors than that of strong bonds (Granovetter 1983), because they have a greater chance to bridge social class divides, and thus information inaccessible within a direct circle of friends can become a channel. Weak bonds can be examined in different ways as well. One can trace the range of relation networks, the number of networks, the central-, fringe- or intermediary situation in the networks, the build-up of the networks, and the homophile or heterophile characteristics found within the social classes. With the help of a questionnaire developed following our own conception and used on numerous occasions, we examined their relation to others with special social circumstances and subcultures, and tracked whether the students have any social actors in their circles of family, friends or acquaintances whose relation would (according to previous research) orient the student socially. The questionnaire listed twelve social actors. Among them there were people who progressed in the school system, people who made their way outside their studies, and others who abandoned the generally accepted legal way of life. Our starting point was that the people available in the social environment cannot only be treated as a confidential, supporting circle of friends, but also as a reference group. In this case we were not interested in recording statistics; it was particularly opportune to see the distorting effect of individual perceptions, since we considered it more important who it is they treat as significant than who really is significant.

Observing the frequency of the actors in family, friend and acquaintance circles examined in student groups, we detected that the potential reference individuals (who had been previously mentioned by the students) are related to those above them on the career ladder, and can be linked to religious relationships and professional positions. Hungarian students in denominational schools refer to more such actors within their families, and there was a major emphasis on people who have proceeded on to a higher academic level, or people important in the religious sense. For Romanians, the reference people of high significance seem to be family members who went to work or live abroad. This also refers to the fact that for an individual belonging to a minority, the homeland has a weaker retentive power. Among the sector-specific features it is obvious that in Romania the educated family members are important for students in non-denominational schools, and that apart from clergymen there is no outstanding reference person in the families of students in denominational schools. In the most economically underdeveloped parts of Ukraine, the common feature of the students' relation network is the unemployed family member, and in the students' families in denominational schools there is a figure reported more frequently than average: an individual making a living from illegal trade.

Table 8: Social actors found in the families of church-run schools and the different sectors, percentages

	Church-run schools			State-run and other private schools			Altogether
	Hungary	Romania	Ukraine	Hungary	Romania	Ukraine	
University student ***	45.6%	38.8%	25.3%	40.5%	49.2%	19.4%	40.3%
College student ***	40.6%	26%	16.8%	35.1%	18.5%	18.4%	30.8%
Graduate ***	68%	55.1%	64.2%	61%	68.3%	37.8%	61.6%
Working abroad1***	35.7%	45.9%	36.8%	27.5%	42.9%	43.9%	35.9%
Foreign citizen ***	27.3%	46.4%	45.3%	19.4%	51.6%	38.8%	32.4%
Religious ***	71.1%	64.8%	68.4%	41.9%	58.7%	36.7%	56.4%
Clergyman ***	15.6%	17.3%	18.9%	5.6%	15.3%	9.2%	12.2%
Successful businessman***	37%	28.1%	23.2%	39.9%	34.4%	19.4%	34.3%
Leader position***	45.6%	29.1%	29.5%	46.1%	33.9%	20.4%	39.2%
Unemployed***	26.6%	20.9%	45.3%	21.1%	12.7%	32.7%	23.8%
Illegal trader***	8.1%	7.1%	13.7%	7.9%	3.7%	9.2%	7.7%
Member of Parliament ***	9.1%	2.6%	9.5%	9.7%	2.6%	6.1%	7.4%
N=	384	196	95	484	189	98	1446

Source: Secondary school students' plans for higher education (2006). The underlined figures indicate that the percentage in the given cell is higher than expected in a random distribution. A cell is marked with asterisks where the correlation is significant. Levels of significance: *** =.000, **< 0.03, *< 0.05.

89

Considering acquaintances, there are no significant inter-sector differences, except for the fact that among Hungarian denominational school students, academically advanced individuals receive greater emphasis. Educated acquaintances are of great importance to the Ukrainian denominational school students, as well, although among Romanians this is more characteristic of the non-denominational group. However, the inter-sector difference is not straightforward in this respect. The acquaintances of Ukrainian students in denominational schools include people of both high and low professional status, although not always as positively referenced individuals. Among friends, it is more apparent that the students in the denominational sector are attracted to educated people, but the frequencies do not show any outstanding divergence.

The social actors are not interesting to us in themselves. Rather, they are worthy of notice because their frequencies in the students' relation network show relation orientations. We observed the social actors in terms of what orientations can emerge based on their frequencies. Considering the relationships with the specific actors, and detecting the closeness of these relationships, there are typical network types that can be traced around[7] the students. These network types are sure to influence their decisions in connection with their studies, as well. The five relation network types are the following: career orienting, study stimulating, religiously stimulating, showing an unsuccessful/illegal example, and attracting abroad.

In the following section we investigate the dominant network influence on individual students and groups.

---

7 Depending on how close a relation the actors had with the respondent, we assigned scores between one and three, and the scores of the representatives with the same orientations were added to each other. The value of the new variables became equal to the proportion of their presented scores, compared to the total maximum. The group average of these proportions were compared at the end.

Table 9: *The attraction of relation network orientations for groups of students in church-run schools and in the different sectors, averages*

	Church-run schools			State-run and other private schools			Altogether
	Hungary	Romania	Ukraine	Hungary	Romania	Ukraine	
Career orienting***	31.33	23.44	27.86	31.55	24.93	19.69	28.48
Study stimulating***	43.43	38.63	37.02	40.38	39.39	25.62	39.6
Religiously stimulating***	38.76	35.8	39.65	26.38	33.29	22.62	32.46
Showing an unsuccessful/ illegal example***	21.42	20.75	31.75	20.54	16.98	21.77	21.16
Moving abroad***	31.99	38.82	36.93	26.98	36.68	30.19	32.05

Source: Secondary school students' plans for higher education (2006). Level of significance: ***= 0.000.

The career orienting network is the most prevalent for Hungarians, but the biggest inter-sector divergence can be detected in Ukraine with the students in denominational schools. The study orienting network supports the activities of Hungarian denominational school students, but the non-denominational school students do not lag behind either. The most decisive divergence occurred among the students of the Subcarpathia (Ukraine) sectors in the study orienting network expansion. The power of the religious oriented network evidently influences denominational school students more, but the inter-sector divergence is traceable in Ukraine and in the north-eastern counties of Hungary. The relationships providing an unsuccessful, illegal example influence Ukrainian denominational school students most, but the same orientation can be seen in Romania as well. We notice that the Ukrainian ethnic Hungarian denominational school students spend their days in dormitories, as these schools are almost predominantly boarding schools. Thus, these relationships represent a much reduced risk than for the Romanian ethnic Hungarian students in denominational schools who come from a disadvantaged background, and many of whom are not in residence. We found it interesting that the denominational school students are in the majority almost everywhere with regards to the "moving abroad" orienting relationships. It is likely that a network arranged along religious organizations does not only counteract social class borders, but also networks closed within country borders.

Assessing special teacher attention and care in the school context

The interviews proved that teachers' behaviour has a decisive influence on students from disadvantaged backgrounds. We had come to the same conclusion in our survey of Romanian students' school careers (Kozma et al. 2006). We are convinced that, based on Coleman's theory, it would be possible to extend the law of symmetrical influence from the influence of schoolmates to that of all partners involved in school life. We wanted to know to what extent denominational schools are more efficient in their contribution to the inclusion of students with disadvantaged backgrounds. The fact that in this region these schools have a relatively low number of students increases efficiency in itself, as a higher teacher-student ratio increases the chances of giving personal attention. The present database provides us with more than meaningless statistical data and we can fill the structural framework of this relationship with meaning. Students told us whether they are able to discuss private matters and plans with their teachers, and even whether teachers pay personal attention to the course of their lives. There are students in denominational schools from north-eastern Hungary and Ukraine who turned out to be exceptionally successful in discussing private problems and plans. Students in denominational schools are more likely to share private problems with a teacher everywhere, but ethnic Hungarian students in denominational schools in Romania are less likely to discuss their plans for the future than their non-denominational peers do. Attention to students' personal lives is above average in every denominational school, but students in north-eastern Hungary experience it more intensely than the others do.

Given the influence this issue has on the atmosphere of schools, we created an index of teacher attention, involving the number of teachers (one or more) and the various forms of attention (with values from 1 to 6). The average result of the sample was 1.94 with students in denominational schools from north-eastern Hungary (2.24) and Ukraine (2.37) having results above the average, and students in non-denominational schools from north-eastern Hungary (1.92), Romania (1.66) and Ukraine (1.62) and students in denominational schools from Romania (1.62) having results below the average. Overall, according to students' general impressions, teacher attention is the most intensive in the denominational schools of north-eastern Hungary and Ukraine. We examined how much the atmosphere of individual schools can be characterized by a general feeling of a high level of teacher attention. One third of students in denominational schools in north-eastern Hungary and a quarter of students in denominational schools in the Ukraine attend schools where students generally experience more attention than average from their teachers. Altogether, students who experience a lot of teacher attention are in a minority in non-denominational schools, whereas they are in the majority in the denominational sector. We examined how the general perception of special teacher care pervades the atmosphere of different schools.

Table 10: *The distribution of students according to the proportion of students sensing special care from teachers in church-run schools and in the different sectors, percentages*

	Church-run schools			State-run and other private schools			Altogether
	Hungary	Romania	Ukraine	Hungary	Romania	Ukraine	
25.1–50%	37.8%	43.9%	–	50.6%	76.7%	65.3%	47.4%
50.1–75%	28.9%	56.1%	75.8%	49.4%	23.3%	34.7%	42.2%
75.1–100%	33.3%	–	24.2%	–	–	–	10.4%
N=	384	196	95	484	189	98	1446

Source: Secondary school students' plans for higher education (2006). The underlined figures indicate that the percentage in the given cell is higher than expected in a random distribution. Level of significance: *** =0.000.

There were no schools in the region where fewer than one-fourth of the children experienced special teacher care and attention; however, the relative ranking of the schools is typical in this respect as well. One-third of Hungarian denominational school students and one-fourth of Ukrainian denominational school students attend schools where the general experience is of special teacher attention above the average. One-third of Hungarian denominational school students and two-fifths of Romanian denominational school students study in an atmosphere where students who sense great teacher attention are in a minority. In the non-denominational sector half of the Hungarian non-denominational school students, two-thirds of the Ukrainians and three-fourth of the Romanians students attend schools with this kind of atmosphere:

A comparison of context effects

After having examined the school composition in terms of differing parental status, religious practice with its link to religious relation networks, and the perception of special teacher attention – in the interests of searching for a pattern in the regions and sectors under examination, we attempt to do something else. We intend to compare these context influences with each other to find out what impact they may have on the students' academic careers.

Examining the different context variables, it was the school composition in terms of parental social status, the school context of teachers' care, and the school rate of students having a religious network, which represented strong influences on school performance within our research. While comparing the different context variables, we attempted to understand whether these phenomena operate in exactly the same way in the different school sectors, or if there is any divergence to be detected.

As we intended to describe secondary students' school careers, we needed indices of achievement to help us assess students' progress at school. We introduced several variables to measure dimensions of success. We did not measure academic achievement by test scores; instead, we tried to find indices that matched our questionnaire. Using the various dimensions of achievement we created a summarising index of achievement that included aspects such as taking on extra academic work (taking language exams, participating in competitions), planning one's future academic career (higher education) and a subjective element, namely the importance attached to academic activities by the particular student. The numerical value of the index ranged from 1 to 5. The index is capable of giving a comprehensive picture as it unites past achievements, hard work, ambitions for the future, conscious preparations and favourable attitudes.

Among the explanatory variables the only index on the individual level is the education of parents, representing the social status of the students' parents. The other explanatory variables are on the context level: the school composition of the parental social status (the rate of graduate parents), the school context of teachers' care (the school rate of students sensing a greater level of care than the sample average), and the school rate of those having predominately religious networks.

We introduced the variables into the analysis step by step – sector by sector, and also across the whole sample so as to be able to sense the impact the variables had on each other.

Table 11: *The modifying effect of context variables on the correlation between parental social status and school performance by school sectors, standardized regression coefficients*

School-maintainer	Church-run schools				State-run and other private				Altogether
	1	2	3	4	1	2	3	4	
Parental social status	0.139 **	0.068	0.070	0.067	0.216 **	0.110 **	0.111 **	0.110 ***	0.091 **
Composition of Parental social status		0.183 ***	0.139 **	0.092 **		0.286 **	0.223 ***	0.218 ***	0.185 ***
School context of teachers' care			0.223 ***	0.150 ***			0.161 ***	0.164 ***	0.166 ***
School rate of students with religious networks				0.273 ***				0.143 ***	0.110 ***
R²				0.16				0.16	0.13

Source: Secondary school students' plans for higher education (2006). A cell is marked with asterisks where the correlation is significant. The level of significance: *** =.000, ** < 0.03, * < 0.05.

According to the analysis, it can be stated that there is significant divergence shown among the sectors in the mechanism of the context effects, as different variables proved to be strongest in the different sectors as regards the modification of the effect of parental social status.

The stepwise analysis showed that parents' higher education influences school performance effectively, although this effect was modified by the school proportion of graduate parents. This modifying effect is not the same in the two sectors; in the more selective denominational system it is not sufficient to overwrite the effect of the parents' education, since the children study in a markedly homogenic atmosphere. In the denominational schools with more inclusive school composition, the context of parental education is able to reduce the effect of parental education. The third point to include in the analysis was the school level perception of teachers' care. This did not modify the effect of parental educational status on an individual level in any of the two sectors, but reduced the influence of parental educational composition in the school. In the case of the two sectors, different orders developed when we included teachers' care on the school level. While with the denominational schools the effect of the latter turned out to be the strongest, i.e. the general perception of teachers' care was able to weaken the (individual and communal level) selective strength of social status, in the non-denominational sector, the major composition divergences which evolved along the parental social status of schools were impossible to reduce to any meaningful degree, even with special teachers' care.

The last step was to test the strength of the density of religious networks in schools among students. Its strength is weaker in the non-denominational sector, which naturally slightly moderates the strength of the previous variables. In the denominational sector there is a significant rearrangement of the model, as it further weakens the effects of the individual and communal level status differences. We also find that it moderates the formerly major influence of teacher care. It is likely, therefore, that the school density of the students' religious relation networks is a resource that, in itself, has dominant influence on academic progress, through the student's inner and outer communal control and norms prevailing in the community. Nevertheless, we can presume that religious networks of students and teacher care are in a peculiar co-action with each other, as it emerged that some of the context level strength of teacher care comes from the impact of religious networks. This may be the very co-action discussed by Bryk and Schneider, and named "trust in schools."

In a different analysis we intended to test the influences of the context based on the multilevel modelling technique (Hatos et al. 2010). We we were able to confirm that contextual effects have a determined impact on student achievement in some dimensions. Beside the strong impact of the school composition according to parental status, the strength of the effect of the density of religious networks in schools was remarkable in our HLM model. It is therefore likely that the school density of the students' religious relation networks has a dominant influence on academic progress, and this can be accelerated by the students' inner and outer communal control and the norms prevailing in the community. The compensatory effect of social capital based on the density of religious friend-circles in the school-community is also confirmed on the contextual level. This means that students in a school-community without their own religious friends can also use the resources available from classmates' religious networks. Consequently, the collective effectiveness originates from the intergenerational consensus on norms, which can be beneficial even to those students who lack this kind of resource. The school level perception of teachers' care proved to have different effects on achievement in the two sectors. This can be interpreted by the strongly relative perceptions of teacher's care depending on students' special expectations (Hatos et al. 2010). All in all, the results presented were also confirmed by the multilevel analyses.

Summary

This study aimed to discuss our previous results in connection with the effect of social capital on school performance. The key perspective of this further study was finding what elements of the school context are able to moderate the reproductive effects of the school. According to our findings, school context strongly influences school performance. The individual level influence of parental social status can be reduced by the school context rates of parental education mostly in the sector where the school system was less divided into castes. The personal care and attention of teachers and the perception of this phenomenon moderates the individual and communal effects of social status in both sectors, but not to the same degree. The school density of those linked to religious networks modifies the individual and context level determinism of social status, but in a very discrepant manner: whilst in the non-denominational sector it has barely any effect, in the denominational sector it becomes the dominant compensating factor. It is likely that members of religious based networks need to be present in the school context in a considerable density to be able to influence their peers from disadvantaged backgrounds to achieve cooperation with the school and teachers, decent performance, and balanced work. Therefore, the context level explanatory variables did not behave as sector-free compensating factors.

Student success in tertiary education

Who gets a degree in Hungarian higher education?

Abstract

Despite the increasing access to higher education there are some factors which negatively affect students' careers. It is a well documented fact that parental education and family social status are extremely influential factors, but we extend our explanation to take in spatial and network inequalities. The proportion of students and graduates is lower in underprivileged areas where the losers of the recent economic and social transformation are over-represented. We supposed that differences in students' achievement in higher education can also be explained by the social networks theory, and more isolated young people have limited aspirations and opportunities. The theoretical background of our analysis is also based on the Colemanian social capital hypothesis, according to which social capital from relational resources can compensate for the reproductive impact of social status on school career. The first steps were also taken to move towards an understanding of the impact of higher education on the future plans and prospects of Hungarian youth.

Introduction

Higher education attendance and students' success in obtaining a degree are continually at the centre of Hungarian and international educational policy. In Hungary, the number of students has multiplied fourfold in the decades following the change of the political system. Since 2005, however, the number of students has diminished in both the full-time and correspondence courses. The number of graduates is therefore also diminishing, after a long period of expansion (Pusztai 2011, Szemerszki 2012). At present, Hungary is lagging behind most other European countries in terms of the number of students –and the number of college/university graduates– in proportion to the entire population (Harsányi-Vincze 2012). It is possible to identify the reasons why the dynamic growth has stopped (introduction of the two-stage course, the economic crisis which has limited the resources of the government budget and of families, demographic contractions, increasing international mobility, the attraction of foreign institutions, the lack of the language proficiency required for a degree) (Szemerszki 2012, Veroszta 2012, Kwiek 2013). On the other hand, there has not been sufficient research into the factors influencing the career of the individual. Its significance is that in this way it would be possible to replace theoretical hypotheses with specific research findings, in order to conceptualize one of the most important dimensions of the transforming social role of higher education institutions (Pusztai et al. 2012).

Students' Success: a Moving Target?

It is possible to analyse students' success from the perspective of the return of the investment made by the community in the educational system, and also from the perspective of the individual's social mobility, and their movement towards a higher status, or a safer and better job. Research findings indicate that the individual's decision to obtain a higher qualification, to step up from one level to the next, is crucial (Róbert 2000, Varga 2013, Polónyi-Kun 2013). Determining what proportion of the applicants will be admitted is merely an issue of educational policy. The appearance of an intention to start studies, to overcome various psychological factors and the difficulties of the system itself, and then carry out the long-term and successful studies as planned, are different at an individual level, no matter whether meritocratic or reproduction principles dominate the system. It is important to know what factors influence this process.

In the international literature there is a debate as to whether the effect of social status and family background remains the same under the circumstances of the expansion of higher educational enrolments or the effect diminishes when one enters higher education (Treiman 1970, Goldthorpe-Erikson 2002). Domestic research findings have so far appeared to reinforce the assumption that students coming from different social-cultural backgrounds appear in Hungarian higher education in different numbers, and that they are distributed among institutions of different prestige in different ways. Furthermore, certain institutions are apparently inaccessible for the children of parents with low social prestige (Róbert 2000, Kiss L 2013, Szemerszki 2012, Veroszta 2012).

It is difficult to identify the students who can be regarded as successful among those who have entered a higher education institution (Szczepanski 1969). This is not only because there are so many different course types, but also because the definition of success varies from institution to institution, faculty to faculty, and often even within the same faculty (Pusztai 2011, Hrubos et al. 2012). It is noteworthy that the concept of students' success often includes highly subjective elements (Pascarella-Terentini 2005, Pusztai 2014). Our comparative and objective data are gathered at graduation, as that is when it can be clearly seen who has successfully overcome the greater and lesser trials and tribulations of the years spent in higher education. A number of phenomena formerly regarded as objective indicators (the number of repeated exams/courses, courses completed uninterruptedly or without changing institutions) are no longer reliable, as students often complete their studies despite these difficulties. At around 40%, the Hungarian drop-out rate is higher than the international average, but the usual time structure of the drop-out process has changed. We have no reliable data as to whether –to use Tinto's terminology– voluntary or forced drop-outs dominate, and where former students leave to when they depart from their institutions (Varga 2010, Tinto 1993). Let us not forget students who find a job without a degree, as success in a new job does not necessarily correlate with a degree and/or its grade (Kun 2013). Whether a student pursues interrupted or completed studies, the planning of further education always involves an evaluation of previous studies, and a confidence in learning. The purpose is self-improvement through education, and expanding one's chances in the labour market.

If we assess students' success not only within the scope of higher education, but also take into account external factors, our observations will not stop at graduation (Pusztai 2014). As a consequence of the expansion of higher education, and the far-reaching restructuring of the labour market, not even a very consciously and carefully constructed career plan finishing with a college or university degree can guarantee a good and well-paid job and a position of high prestige. The amount of time devoted to finding a job, the prestige of the job finally taken, the relationship with the individual's previous studies, professional mobility, plans for a future career and a range of other objective and subjective factors may all serve as indicators of success (Veroszta 2010). As opposed to previously generally used criteria which consisted mainly of employment and income, and were insensitive to regional economic circumstances, the success of an educational career can be better measured by considering employability (Kiss 20014). Although in the international literature the interrelation between the education and employability of an individual is emphasized, we believe that many of the employability skills and attitudes are not the direct results of the declared curriculum of the training institution. Instead, these skills emerge spontaneously as a result of social contexts (Yorke 2008, Kiss 2014). At the present time of the rapid obsolescence of professional knowledge and constant change in the labour market, certain inherent, personal skills may predict long-term success (Knox et al. 1993, Knight-Yorke 2006, Hirschi-Fischer 2013, Bocsi-Szabó 2013).

International comparative analyses suggest that social background, gender and the chosen training course largely influence the chances of obtaining the desired job (Kivinen et al. 2000, Teichler 2007). In addition to the hard social indicators, however, there are also some other influencing factors lying in the background. Very often the cultural/social capital, as defined by Bourdieu, is mentioned as the source of an ability to find rare and valuable jobs, and to acquire the manners and behaviour necessary for a good career (Bourdieu 1977). An important factor in a student's success as an employee is, as widely discussed in the international literature, the capital manifested in the system of family relations. With the help of that network it is easier to find a suitable job (Granovetter 1983), but chances are also improved by the number of satisfied school leavers finding a job in the context concerned (Veroszta 2010). A person's willingness to undertake a particular job is influenced by the working culture found in that person's formal and informal environment (McQuaid-Lindsay 2005, Kiss 2014). It appears that certain student competences can be ascribed to the curriculum of the higher education institution (Knight-Yorke 2006, Siklós 2006), whereas other competences are rooted in the respective communities of the students, and the information that is available to the individuals in those communities (Pusztai 2013).

As far as the communities of students are concerned, there is a lively debate in the international literature about what the most useful and helpful forms of connections are in terms of the students' careers in higher education. Coleman (1988) believes that the most useful environment is a close and tight structure of connections, but Granovetter (1983) argues that the best system is a that of loose bonds and an open network. Lin asserts that the highest degree of safety is afforded by close and homogeneous networks that support stability. An extensive network of loose bonds, on the other hand, helps the individuals in recognizing and utilizing the chances of mobility (Lin 2005). It remains an open question, however, what types of connections are needed in order to be effective and successful in the phases of entrance to higher education, earning a degree, continuing education or purposefully looking for a job.

Questions and Data for Analysis

In our essay we examined what social groups are reached by higher education, and who, among young people living in Hungary, will have a chance to become a student and earn a degree in order to find a job. We also examined what resources there are for young people to rely on in a successful career, and which of these resources are able to counterbalance the disadvantages caused by the low social status of their families.

For our analysis, we used the results of the most recent wave of a series of research studies dealing with Hungarian youth (2000, 2004, 2008 and 2012). The research, entitled "Hungarian Youth 2012", conducted by Kutatópont, involved young people between 15 and 29 broken down according to region, settlement, age and gender. The research project was conducted in the autumn of 2012. Only 43% of the entire sample of 8,000, and half of the students (52.5%) are still at secondary school. Although 83% of the sample was above the age necessary to enter higher education in the autumn of 2012 (they were born between 1983 and 1994), only a narrow one third of them (30.5%, 1,053 individuals) were students at a college or university[8]. In this study we deal with the so-called student-age group (N=6,632).

An answer was sought to the question of what factors have an influence towards a more successful educational career. We made attempts to define a successful educational career through various indicators. Some of the major indicators include admittance to (and staying in) higher education, and graduation. A mere 9.6% of the student-age group has a degree, and 15.8% of them are still studying. Somewhat more than one hundred people had already graduated, but were still in higher education. So almost one quarter of the sample (23.9%) have spent some time in higher education[9].

Another indicator of success is openness to further studies. Naturally, there are several ways of planning further education, and a young person may have different motivations. Positive previous experience may be one, dissatisfaction with the results of previous studies or qualifications may be another. As the marketability of the first degree depends on a number of things (social status, place of residence, the current state of the labour market, personal expectations), in terms of the student's attitude to studies we must interpret it as a success if a student intends to improve their career through study. A positive attitude to continuing education characterized more then one quarter of the individuals in the student age group (27.1%).

As a third indicator we aimed to find interrelations between learning and various interpretations of work. A powerful intrinsic motivation is, in our opinion, an optimistic and self-confident preparation for an educational career. This feature characterized slightly more than one fifth of the young people in the sample (22.4%). Another 7.3% of the respondents reported that they had already found their desired job. In this satisfied group, individuals with high qualifications were over-represented; the higher qualifications they had, the more satisfied they seemed to be. One of the objectives of our project has been to identify the previously well researched and the not so well researched factors which influence the commitment of young people to enter, and stay in, higher education, and their positive attitude to work.

---

8   NB: due to the delayed school start, 17.7% of them came of age in the year of sampling, and only 6.3% of them entered higher education.

9   This is a low proportion, as approximately 20% of the adult population has a degree. It may be caused by the peculiarities of sampling.

Social Stratification and Students' Success

Getting into higher education within a school system the elements of which are based upon the principles of consecutivity and interchangeability is certainly something which expresses success in one's educational career. The age group concerned completed secondary school in the period of the expansion of higher education and the demographic decline in the number of the age group, so they had considerably better chances in admission to colleges and universities than the previous generations had had. In the statistical data for 2011, the proportion of college and university graduates in the 25–34 age group is 28%, and the "Hungarian Youth 2012" data suggest that nearly one quarter of young people aged 18–29 were able to make use of the expanding possibilities in higher education and to begin their studies. Selection in higher education affected the members of the age group differently. Because of the high number of applicants, admission was relatively difficult in 2002. In 2008, however, admission to day courses was, relatively speaking, the easiest (Veroszta 2012). As the data base contains a heterogeneous population as far as age is concerned, and the career path of young people is strongly individualized, it would be difficult to predict how many of them are actually going to graduate (Gábor-Jancsák 2006).

We first wished to find out how an individual's position in the vertical hierarchy of society influences them in terms of entering higher education and obtaining a degree. Our findings correlate with our preliminary assumptions, and the children of educated parents are shown to be more successful. One difficulty, however, was that several of the respondents did not disclose the highest level of education achieved by their parents. Almost 10% of the young people in the age group concerned did not answer the question related to the qualifications of their parents. In the sample, the children of parents with basic qualifications are widely represented, as nearly every second respondent said their mother, and nearly two thirds of them said their father had an elementary school qualification. At the same time, the proportion of parents with advanced qualifications is low (10.6% and 9.8%). These figures are lower than what is suggested by census statistics, even if we take into account the fact that many highly qualified people do not have children.

A more detailed analysis revealed that children from different family backgrounds were able to make use of the expansion of higher education which has taken place in the past two decades to very different degrees. Only 5% of the children of parents with low qualifications were able to obtain a degree. The respective figure for parents with a secondary education is slightly above 10%, whereas 25% of the children of parents with an advanced education graduated from a college or university. Among students who are still at college or university, the statistics are similar: more than one third of the children of highly qualified parents are at college, less than a quarter of parents with secondary qualification pursue undergraduate studies, and a mere 5% of the children of parents with elementary education do the same. It is clear that there is a powerful interrelationship between the level of parents' education and the children's attitude to entering into higher education and obtaining a degree.

Table 12: *Interrelation between parents' level of education and their children's entry into higher education and obtaining a degree*

The young person's educational career	Mother's highest qualification			Father's highest qualification		
	Primary	Secondary	Higher	Primary	Secondary	Higher
At present in higher education * * *	6.4%	21.6%	37.1%	8.5%	22.3%	39.4%
At present not a student	93.6%	78.4%	62.9%	91.5%	77.7%	60.6%
Graduated from higher education * * *	4.3%	12.2%	25.8%	5.2%	14.3%	27.3%
Not graduated	95.7%	87.8%	74.2%	94.8%	85.7%	72.7%
Studies at present or has graduated * * *	10.0%	31.8%	59.6%	13.1%	34.3%	62.0%
Not a student, not graduated	90.0%	68.2%	40.4%	86.9%	65.7%	38.0%
N=	3.127	2.327	488	3.634	1.715	363

Source: Hungarian Youth 2012. The underlined figures indicate that the percentage in the given cell is higher than expected in a random distribution. A cell is marked with asterisks where the correlation is significant. Level of significance: * * * =.000.

The table above shows that a higher proportion of the children of highly educated parents go on to higher education and graduate. Furthermore, among the children of educated parents there are many who have already graduated and want to go on studying. This means that the effects of social inequalities are present among those who intend to pursue postgraduate studies. Among the first entrants, as described by Green, the number of those coming from a higher social background is higher, whereas the adverse effects of missed education multiply among those who come from families with lower social prestige (Green 1980).

In the course of our search for indicators of student success among young people, we found that almost one third of the entire age group intends to continue their studies. It is noteworthy that the individuals in the 18–29 age group with experience of higher education wish to go on learning in higher numbers than those without such experience. An average proportion of the children of parents with elementary and secondary qualifications entertain the idea of further studies. Only the children of highly qualified parents are over-represented among those are committed to continuing education.

*Table 13: Interrelation between the level of parents' education and their chil-
dren's plans for continuing (higher) education*

	Mother's highest qualification ***			Father's highest qualification ***		
	Primary	Secondary	Higher	Primary	Secondary	Higher
Plans further studies	25.4%	28.4%	**37.5%**	25.9%	28.8%	**34.2%**
Does not plan further studies	**74.6%**	71.6%	62.5%	**74.1%**	71.2%	65.8%
N=	3.127	2.327	488	3.634	1.715	363

Source: Hungarian Youth 2012. The underlined figures indicate that the percentage in the given cell is higher than expected in a random distribution. A cell is marked with asterisks where the correlation is significant. Level of significance: *** =.000.

The reserves of cultural capital in the families of young people not planning further studies are characteristically weaker. Those not planning further studies are over-represented among students coming from vocational
secondary education, either from schools providing GCSEs or from schools
that do not offer this qualification[10]. The parents of vocational students usually have low qualifications, so the disadvantage of vocational students does
not diminish as a result of the expansion of higher education (Fehérvári
2014). The largely divergent educational careers of students with different
preliminary studies seem to reinforce our observation that learning at an
adult age benefits groups of higher social prestige, and further increasing
educational differences.

The indicators of students' success are not restricted to a young person's
educational career and plans. In our earlier work we also emphasized that
the image a person has of their future job and career is also a typical indicator (Pusztai 2009, Pusztai 2014). We find it an interesting fact that no more
than 22% of the members of the age group believe that they will have a job
which is close to their expectations. The overwhelming majority of these
young people, almost four fifths of them, are sceptical in this respect. This
is not only a concern for the future of a region or even a whole country; the
personal, and individual dimensions also raise the interest of the researcher.
There is no doubt that the pessimistic attitude of young people in connection
with their future job is not the best incentive for them to carry on learning.
It undermines their chances in the labour market, and makes the work of the

---

10 In an optimistic interpretation it could even be suggested that no very high qualifications are needed for finding a job, which is why vocational school leavers do
not plan advanced studies in the long run.

educational institutions more difficult. Discussions with recent graduates in Hungary confirmed the importance of subjective factors in connection with job satisfaction, and drew our attention to the fact that these elements have a special relationship with the individual's general well-being and satisfaction with life (Kiss P 2013). Earlier research findings explained the generally low levels of satisfaction with job and career in Central and Eastern Europe in terms of high investment with a low return, and there are also macro- and micro-level factors that influence people's attitude to work. All these, however, only partially explain young people's general lack of enthusiasm about their future career.

Table 14: Interrelation between the parents' level of education and their children's views on work

	Mother's highest qualification ***			Father's highest qualification ***		
	Primary	Secondary	Higher	Primary	Secondary	Higher
Reached their objective	5.5%	7.6%	7.2%	5.9%	7.2%	9.1%
Optimistic	17.7%	26.3%	34.2%	18.5%	28.2%	28.9%
Pessimistic	76.8%	66.1%	58.6%	75.5%	64.7%	62.0%
N=	3127	2327	488	3634	1715	363

Source: Hungarian Youth 2012. The underlined figures indicate that the percentage in the given cell is higher than expected in a random distribution. A cell is marked with asterisks where the correlation is significant. Level of significance: *** =.000.

Those few who have already found their ideal jobs are, not surprisingly, among the oldest respondents within the age group. The low proportion of those who have achieved their desired goal may be explained by the fact that following the vertical expansion of secondary education –often by 2–3 years– the time students spend in higher education is also extended. It is therefore perfectly possible to spend as many as eight years in higher education, and the completed studies can still be regarded as successful and effective. But what influences somebody to be optimistic about finding their desired job?

Those who were engaged in shorter or longer higher education studies and graduated tend to report that they have already found their ideal job in much higher numbers than those who have never been in higher education at all. Optimism in connection with finding the ideal job in the future is rare, as only every fifth young person possesses that kind of inner certainty. The hope of finding an ideal job is, just as with the results already achieved, unevenly distributed among young people. Optimism increases as we proceed upwards on the social ladder. It is also evident that the high qualifications of the mother appear to be more important than similar qualifications of the father, since the children of mothers with an advanced degree are considerably more optimistic in terms of finding a good job than the others.

After surveying the first questions of our research we can conclude that there is a strong interrelationship between the three success indicators and the educational level of the parents which determines the social status of the families.

Regionality and Students' Success

In our earlier research projects we found that regional location is one of the outstanding factors determining the success of young people at school. It was emphasized that in Hungary geographical location strongly reinforces students' access to higher education and graduation (Kozma Pusztai 2005, Pusztai 2006, Rechnitzer 2009, Kozma et al. 2012). Disadvantages rooted in social status and the difficulties caused by geographical distances usually mount up. In this analysis, we do not only examine regionally uneven socio-economic levels of development, but also the geographical location of higher education institutions. It is obvious that people living in large national or regional higher education centres will easily enter a college or university, while those living in regions where there is no university, or where there are no long-established traditions of higher education, are at a distinct disadvantage. It seems that young people living in the north-eastern and northern counties (Nógrád, Szabolcs-Szatmár-Bereg and Jász-Nagykun-Szolnok) find it the most difficult to start college or university studies. In these regions the number of people living in underprivileged circumstances is higher. Young people have a much higher chance of getting a degree in the counties with the three large universities. From the data one may conclude that the proportion of the age group concerned within the entire population of a region further complicates the map of chances. The chances are the highest for young people living in the vicinity of the University of Szeged, followed by Pécs and Baranya county, then Hajdu-Bihar county and the University of Debrecen. Obtaining a degree is the most difficult in northern and north-eastern Hungary (Nógrád, Borsod-Abaúj-Zemplén and Szabolcs-Szatmár-Bereg counties), where the proportion of young people in the entire population is high, but where many young people come from underprivileged families. In addition to this, the chance for a young person to obtain a degree in the northern plains (Jász-Nagykun-Szolnok) and in western Hungary (Somogy county) is relatively low. It emerges from the data that in some regions there is a shortage of institutions which can detect and prepare gifted young people for a college or university career. Young people in these areas are not attracted powerfully enough by the large regional universities, which are, in turn, unable to integrate these youngsters.

Map 1: Young people (18–29 years) who currently pursue their studies in higher education or have already earned a degree (broken down according to counties).

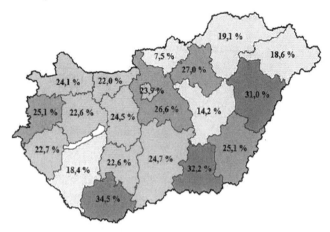

Source: Hungarian Youth 2012

The influence of the region or county on people's educational career is further boosted by the effects of the settlement. As has been by previous research projects, the type of settlement where the individual lives greatly influences their attitude to obtaining a degree. Almost one third of those who live in a city acquire experience in higher education, whereas only one quarter of the inhabitants of smaller towns do the same, and the respective figure for villages is less than 20%. We emphasize that disadvantages rooted in the region and those rooted in the settlement reinforce each other, and are further worsened by the low qualifications of the parents.

Table 15: Interrelation between the type of settlement where a young person lives and their chances of entering into higher education and earning a degree

	Type of settlement		
Educational career of the young person	City	Town	Village
Studying in higher education at present * * *	19.0%	15.8%	12.6%
Not a student at present	81.0%	84.2%	87.4%
Graduated * * *	13.4%	8.3%	7.3%
Not graduated	86.6%	91.7%	92.7%
Studying at present or already graduated * * *	30.0%	22.8%	18.9%
Not a student at present and not graduated	70.0%	77.2%	81.1%
N=	2.135	2.341	2.156

Source: Hungarian Youth 2012. The underlined figures indicate that the percentage in the given cell is higher than expected in a random distribution. A cell is marked with asterisks where the correlation is significant. Level of significance: * * * =.000.

The type of settlement apparently has less influence on an individual's plans regarding further education than on the actual implementation of those plans. Regional differences are, on the other hand, more important, especially the differences between counties. It is likely that the specific combination of higher education supply and an attractive job market is the reason why young people living near the capital city and in the neighbourhood of the western border are the least active in planning further studies. The case is similar with those living in northeastern part of Hungary. Though young people in northern Hungary live in a disadvantageous situation in terms of access to higher education, they are still the most committed to continue their studies at a higher level. All this indicates that researchers should also pay attention to the attitudes of potential students who are interested in further study but who are impeded in reaching their goals. Studying the attraction and spill-over effect of higher education institutions in itself is not sufficient.

Regional differences rooted in social and economic characteristics are confirmed by our research findings as well, since we experience considerable regional differences when we focus on the hopes and expectations of young people regarding their future careers. The proportion of those who have found their dream jobs is the greatest in the area of the capital city and in the relatively developed western counties. The results are in accordance with the levels of economic development of the regions. Still, the regional differences we found in the numbers of those who expect to find their dream jobs were smaller than we had originally anticipated. The results indicate that young people are basically pessimistic in every region. There are, however, minor differences among the regions. In dynamically developing areas one quarter of the young people interviewed were confident they could find the job they longed for. In the north-eastern region, on the other hand, young people are much more pessimistic in this respect.

Table 16: Interrelation of the home region and job expectations of young people

In connection with a job	Central Hungary	North-Western	South-Eastern	North-Eastern	South-Western	Northern	Middle-Western
Achieved their goal	**8.8%**	7.6%	6.9%	4.8%	4.7%	4.6%	4.5%
Optimistic	21.3%	22.7%	**25.1%**	21.5%	23.5%	18.4%	**26.6%**
Pessimistic	69.9%	69.6%	68.0%	**73.7%**	71.8%	**77.0%**	68.9%
N=	1.805	642	894	1.079	621	835	756

Source: Hungarian Youth 2012. The underlined figures indicate that the percentage in the given cell is higher than expected in a random distribution. A cell is marked with asterisks where the correlation is significant. Level of significance: *** =0.000.

Although the number of young people who have achieved their goals is higher in cities, it is noteworthy that those who come from villages have almost as many optimistic expectations as city dwellers. There are, furthermore, large regional differences in the employment statistics of people from settlements of similar status. The relatively high level of optimism of people living in villages is only partly explained by their willingness to harmonize their desires with reality by moving from one place to another, since the distances between their homes and jobs are largely different.

As we have seen, the explanations for success (entering into higher education, earning a degree, planning further studies and the perception of employability) as reflected by social status indicators and regional differences are largely confirmed by the results of the research entitled "Hungarian Youth 2012." In Hungary today the social status of the family, the region and the direct environment of the home (settlement) determine who will become a student, or a professional, ambitious postgraduate student and a young person optimistic about their employment. Since we had also been looking for factors able to counterbalance this social determinism in our previous research projects, we intended to find out whether such factors were present in the 2012 data. Previously, we pointed out the interrelation between students' success and the structure of the individual's social connections; now we also wished to find out whether the network of personal connections are able to refine the well-known mechanisms of social differences.

The Network of Social Connections and Students' Success

Researches seeking the explanation for students' success find it important to examine the personal social connections of an individual, in addition to examining their general social background (Pascarella-Terenzini 2005). Researchers analysing the effects of peer connections, however, tend to focus on the informal (friends, membership in voluntary organizations) and formal (school, place of work) contexts (Tinto 1993, Tierney 2000). The "Hungarian Youth" project was based upon an individual analytical approach, and while it tells us little about an individual's institution (school, higher education), it does provide us some information about informal connections. The cross-sectional survey does not make it clear whether the interpersonal relations of the respondents existed at the time they entered higher education, or only emerged later during their years as students. So the data should be treated and used with special care. It is still worth considering the data, because interpersonal connection patterns and inclinations tend to be stable over a person's career (Fonyó 1970, Pusztai 2011). The young people involved in the research spend most of their time at school or at work, and we learn little about these environments from the research; however, the data base contains much information about the relationships of young people in their free-time and their membership of voluntary organizations.

Three quarters of the age group had friends and social groups they spent their free time with on a regular basis. More than half of those aged between 18 and 29 mentioned that they spent their free time with friends at the weekends, and 30–40% do the same during weekdays. Permanent friends proved to be an extremely sensitive dividing line in terms of success[11]. Some of the findings of the research into people's social networks suggest that the connection resources of individuals are unevenly distributed along the vertical hierarchy, similarly to social status differences. Our present data also confirm this observation, as a much higher number of students and graduates claim that they have friends and a social group. Although the designers of the inventory were not concerned about the composition of the group of friends, or the borderlines of that group, it seems to be a part of students' way of life to spend their time in the company of friends, both during weekdays and weekends, more often than for young people who are not students. The difference between the two groups in this respect is 10%. Although graduates are at a distinct advantage in having a permanent group of friends compared to those without a degree (82% and 74% respectively), they are at a disadvantage in terms of the amount of time they are able to spend with their friends. Social networks appear to play a much more important role in the life of students than in the life of the other respondents. At weekends almost two thirds, and on weekdays half of the students spend their free time with friends, whereas the respective figures with young people who do not attend higher education institutions are a half and two fifths. For a large number of students the most frequent free time activity at weekends and on weekdays is being with friends (60%, 40%); others do not spend their free time with friends so often (47%, 30%). In our earlier research we proved that the orientation of students to their studies, working norms, extracurricular activities, and their trust in the actors of higher education is not determined by their social status, but to a much larger extent by the community of peers.

If the company of friends is interpreted as a resource, in accordance with the concept of social capital it is worth examining the data in terms of the young people's opinions about further training and future career. We experienced that the group of friends is extremely valuable; those who plan further studies and have an optimistic attitude to work tend to have a stable group of friends, while the amount of time spent with friends as reported by the respondents is hardly significant.

---

11 A stable circle of friends was surveyed by an open inventory related to free time activities.

Table 17: The interrelation between the stability of the social network and the plans for further education/views on the future in groups with parents with different qualifications

	No stable company of friends			Stable company of friends		
	qualification of parents			qualification of parents		
	Primary	Secondary	Higher	Primary	Secondary	Higher
Planning further studies	19.0%	20.7%	35.0%**	27.3%	32.0%***	34.5%***
Not planning further studies	81.0%	79.3%	65.0%	72.7%	68.0%	65.5%
Optimistic or successful	20.4%	28.2%***	50.0%***	25.6%	35.7%***	38.1%***
Pessimistic	79.6%	71.8%	50.0%	74.4%	64.3%	61.9%
N=	1.046	560	60	2.498	1.984	386

Source: Hungarian Youth 2012. The underlined figures indicate that the percentage in the given cell is higher than expected in a random distribution. A cell is marked with asterisks where the correlation is significant. Level of significance: *** =0.000, ** < 0.03.

In the case of students the group of friends is interpreted as a part of the students' way of life, but the interrelationships between the existence of a stable group of friends, plans for further studies and the desire to find a good job is not only characteristic of students; it is relevant to all the respondents in the age group concerned. The data indicate that the children of parents with secondary qualifications plan further studies in much higher numbers if they have a stable group of friends. It seems that ambitions for further studies evaporate more easily, if such desires appear at all, if the young person does not enjoy the support of their peers. Interestingly, this factor is not that significant in the case of children of parents with advanced qualifications, since the influence of parents and other members of the family are able to sufficiently motivate the individual to make plans for further studies.

It is also possible to conclude from the data that young people with a stable group of friends are more optimistic than the average in terms of finding the desired occupation. A glance at parental background further refines the image. The share of optimistic students is higher among those who have a stable group of friends and who come from families where the parents have secondary qualifications. The students whose parents have advanced qualifications are influenced by their group of friends to a much smaller extent; what is more, they are sometimes even hampered by their friends. Perhaps it is because friends may relay mixed news and opinions about further studies and careers. The effect of peers is therefore basically positive, but it seems to be rather a compensating factor, acting against the control for parental education and qualifications, than a purely supporting one.

We examined how varied the support of peers for students and graduates is, and we found that the effect of a stable network of peers is positive. It supports an individual's plans for further studies among those students who come from families of lower social status, and increases their optimism regarding their future career plans. The analysis took into account the social background and the respondents' own status, and the findings suggest that status group differences are not as sharp among those who have a stable network of friends as are the differences among young people who do not have such a network.

Contrary to expectations, those who have a stable network of friends do not only have a chance to talk with their friends, but they also read more, use the internet and do sports more than people without friends. Only one third of students with friends go regularly to the same place; the others seem to visit each other instead. The significance of this fact is that in this way they do not only meet each other, but they also meet each others' parents, and the network surrounding the individual is extended to an intergenerational level, and the young people may find role models in other families.

It is possible to identify bonds of different strengths in terms of young people's belonging to various voluntary organizations. 9% of young adults reported they were members of at least one organization (hardly more than 3% of them belonged to more than one organization). Besides formal members, one fifth of the young people in our panel are connected more or less closely to civil organizations. Membership of voluntary organizations or groups characterizes only a small fragment of the young people involved in our research but it shows a close correlation with the indicators of study success. Among individuals linked to the activities of various organizations those who are successful and efficient in their studies are over-represented. In connection with the professional debates regarding the students' success in terms of their weaker or stronger bonds we may conclude that membership of a civilian organization is the most effective when the individual is only loosely connected to the activities of an organization. This appears to underpin the importance of loose links.

When the effects of belonging to a voluntary organization are subjected to the control of the most important family status indicator, that is, the education of the parents, we find that the children of parents with low qualifications make up for much of their disadvantage by belonging to some sort of a civil organization. The children of parents with secondary and advanced qualifications also largely benefit from the support of these networks, which relay norms and values to them. The positive effects are measurable when entering into higher education, planning further studies and in an optimistic attitude to work. In terms of earning a degree, the children of parents with secondary and advanced qualifications do not seem to be at any advantage. What is more, the effects are adverse, as these factors relativise the objectives set by the parents. We may therefore conclude that a loose connection to a voluntary community has a generally positive effect in terms of three of the success indicators, regardless of the social status of the family of the individual concerned. The effect is different when we consider acquiring a degree, where the children of parents with low qualifications benefit most.

Table 18: *The connection between belonging to a voluntary group and learning efficiency in groups with various social and parental backgrounds*

	Not connected to any voluntary group			Connected to a voluntary group		
	Primary	Secondary	Higher	Primary	Secondary	Higher
	qualification of parents			qualification of parents		
HE students	7.0%	15.2%	34.2%: ***	24.3%	35.2%	51.1%: ***
Not HE students	93.0%	84.8%	65.8%	75.7%	64.8%	48.9%
Graduate	5.0%	12.4%	26.9%: ***	8.5%	12.7%	22.6%: ***
Not graduate	95.0%	87.6%	73.1%	91.5%	87.3%	77.4%
Planning further studies	21.4%	25.0%	29.7%: ***	41.0%	42.8%	43.8% NS
Not plan study further	78.6%	75.0%	70.3%	59.0%	57.2%	56.2%
Optimistic or successful	21.4%	31.4%	35.4%: ***	36.4%	41.7%	47.4%: **
Pessimistic	78.6%	68.6%	64.6%	63.6%	58.3%	52.6%
N=	3.031	1.935	316	585	628	137

Source: Hungarian Youth 2012. The underlined figures indicate that the percentage in the given cell is higher than expected in a random distribution. A cell is marked with asterisks where the correlation is significant. Level of significance: *** =0.000, ** < 0.03.

The "Hungarian Youth 2012" survey does not provide any further details about the composition of the groups of friends, and if we wish to study the character of the social networks, we are able to learn a lot relatively easily about those who belong to some religious community. The reason why this dimension deserves attention is that communities organized on a religious basis very often serve as social capital that is highly useful from the perspective of progress in education, as would be expected when dealing with status indicators. In the following we attempt to find evidence verifying this assumption.

Before attempting to analyse the interrelationship between belonging to a religious community and educational career, it is necessary to survey what proportion of the age group is characterized by a dense or loose network of religious connections. None of the original variables included that information, but we possess data about religious upbringing, the respondents' self-description regarding their own world-view, and religious practices within the community. In this way we are able to outline the basic types[12]. 30% of the respondents reported that they had been brought up in a religious environment, allowing us an insight into the parents' orientation and educational value preferences[13]. In the self-description session, only 7% of the young people said that they followed the teachings of the church, and a further 32% said that they were religious in their own way. Active religious practice in the community served as a better tool for identifying the individuals belonging to a religious community, as no more than 10% of the sample attend church services with a regularity of at least once a month, and there is an even lower percentage of those who regularly attend smaller religious communities or services. Of the members of the 18–29 age group who were brought up in a religious way, only one quarter are regular churchgoers, one third of them go to church irregularly, and more than 60% of them say that they are believers in their own private way. We used cluster analysis

---

12 It is important to know that 10% of those entering adulthood were unable or unwilling to answer the questions related to religion. Rosta (2013) pointed out that the reason may be methodological, since those who left the questions related to religion did not reach 3% of the panel in 2008. The drastic increase may be explained by the self-completed inventory, which differed from the other elements of the research. In our earlier research we noted that willingness to answer largely depended on the regional location and social background of the individuals. The lowest number of answers were received in Budapest and Pest County. Usually children of parents with secondary and advanced qualifications were the most reluctant to answer (Pusztai 2014).

13 In 2012, one third of young people in Hungary said that they had been brought up in a religious spirit. Since that time, the proportion changed, and the number of non-responding interviewees has increased.

in order to survey the differences, and the three groups were sharply differentiated from each other. The most populous group (72%) was those who did not have any religious education whatsoever, and who were not connected to any religious community (it should be noted, however, that one third of this group consider themselves religious), and we referred to them as the group isolated from religion. Members in the second group (20%) were brought up in a predominantly religious environment, are open in a spiritual way, and two thirds of them declare themselves as religious, but visit religious communities very rarely. They are regarded as the group with open networks from a religious perspective. For them, a practising religious community may primarily serve as a reference group. The young people in the third group actively practise their religion in the community (8%). They were all brought up in a religious atmosphere, and they all firmly believe in God. Half of them say that they are members of their respective churches, and half of them say that they are religious in their own way[14]. They are all organically integrated into the network of religious people.

An approach based on the educational level of the parents revealed that among the young people with a close religious network the proportion of children of highly qualified parents is slightly higher (1–2%), and young people belonging to the open network tend to come come from a families with lower qualifications; the difference here being 5–6%.

When we intended to chart the interrelations between groups of various profiles and the indicators of success, we found considerable differences among the young people. In terms of entering higher education and obtaining a degree, the group with an open network did not differ much from the group isolated from religion, but the close, practising religious group performed significantly better.

---

14 In the course of our survey among students of denominational secondary schools we observed that the students described their own parents as less religious than had been expected in terms of the religious life and practices of the parents. It is likely that the more religious education and training one has, the more easily one discovers the differences between individual interpretations and official norms (Pusztai 2004).

Table 19: Entering higher education and earning a degree in the groups with different religious networks

Educational career of the young people	Non-religious network	Heterogenous open network	Member of religious network
HE student at present * * *	14.9%	15.4%	**24.8%**
Not a student at present	**85.1%**	84.6%	75.2%
Graduated from HE * * *	8.8%	10.2%	**16.0%**
Not graduated from HE	**91.2%**	89.8%	84.0%
Has HE experience * * *	22.4%	23.8%	**37.3%**
No HE experience	**77.6%**	76.2%	62.7%
N=	4.757	1.355	520

Source: Hungarian Youth 2012. The underlined figures indicate that the percentage in the given cell is higher than expected in a random distribution. A cell is marked with asterisks where the correlation is significant. Level of significance: * * * =0.000.

The difference between the success of the members of the various networks is obvious: those who have a network of religions connections have a definite edge over those who do not have such relations, and the members of the group open to religious connections also have better orientation in terms of continuing their studies than those isolated from religion. The fault line is therefore between those having religious connections and those not having such connections in terms of their plans for continuing education. For study success in education, the best situation is to have a close network of religions connections.

Table 20: Planning continuing education in the groups arranged according to the characters of the social networks

	Non-religious network	Heterogenous open network	Member of religious network
Not planning further studies	**74.7%**	68.7%	67.7%
Planning further studies	25.3%	**31.3%**	**32.3%**
N=	4.757	1.355	520

Source: Hungarian Youth 2012. The underlined figures indicate that the percentage in the given cell is higher than expected in a random distribution. A cell is marked with asterisks where the correlation is significant. Level of significance: * * * =0.000.

When we talk about the expectations related to finding the ideal job, those who have already found the desired occupation and those who are optimistic about it are more numerous in the network of those who practise their religion than in the other two groups. The number of pessimists is, on the other hand, higher in the group isolated from religion. The network open to religion did not save young people from feeling pessimistic in connection with their prospective jobs. The proportion of individuals who are very optimistic about finding the right job is outstandingly high among the group closely related to religious communities.

Table 21:Views in connection with the prospective job in the different groups

	Non-religious network	Heterogenous open network	Member of religious network
Achieved their goal	6.3%	6.1%	7.7%
Optimist	21.3%	23.4%	<u>30.6%</u>
Pessimist	<u>72.4%</u>	70.5%	61.7%
N=	4757	1355	520

Source: Hungarian Youth 2012. The underlined figures indicate that the percentage in the given cell is higher than expected in a random distribution. Level of significance: ***=.000.

The analyses did not only reveal the considerable differences in success between the groups with different attitudes to religion; two other phenomena were also observed. One is that the differences caused by the different levels of education of the parents generate almost unbridgeable difficulties in the group isolated from religion. The differences are only detectable in three indicators in the group open to religion. The indicators sensitive to social status reduce to two in the group with a close network of religious connections. It is also clear that the success indicators of the children of parents with elementary and secondary education are much better in the group open to religion and also in the one with a close network of religious connections than in the group isolated from religion. Although the intensity of the positive effects may be different, its direction is the same, and it is not reversed in the case of the children of parents with high qualifications.

126

Table 22: Interrelations between students' success and the characteristics of the social networks in the groups arranged according to the parental background of the students

Network of connections	Non-religious network qualification of parents			Heterogenous open network qualification of parents			Member of religious network qualification of parents		
	Primary	Secondary	Higher	Primary	Secondary	Higher	Primary	Secondary	Higher
HE student	9.4%	18.7%	37.5% ***	8.3%	21.7%	42.3% ***	17.4%	29.6%	46.8% ***
Not student	90.6%	81.3%	62.5%	91.7%	78.3%	57.7%	82.6%	70.4%	53.2%
With a degree	5.1%	11.2%	24.1% ***	5.4%	14.5%	28.2% ***	10.7%	19.2%	31.9% ***
Without a degree	94.9%	88.8%	75.9%	94.6%	85.5%	71.8%	89.3%	80.8%	68.1%
Would continue	22.4%	27.9%	33.5% ***	29.8%	32.8%	35.9%	30.7%	34.0%	34.0%
Not planning continued education	77.6%	72.1%	66.5%	70.2%	67.2%	64.1%	69.3%	66.0%	66.0%
Optimist	22.7%	32.4%	38.4% ***	25.1%	34.5%	39.7% ***	31.1%	46.8%	42.6% **
Pessimist	77.3%	67.6%	61.6%	74.9%	65.5%	60.3%	68.9%	53.2%	57.4%
*N=	2.585	1.844	328	761	516	78	270	203	47

Source: Hungarian Youth 2012. The underlined figures indicate that the percentage in the given cell is higher than expected in a random distribution. A cell is marked with asterisks where the correlation is significant. Level of significance: *** =.000, ** < 0.03.

Force Fields in Interaction

As the last step of our analysis we undertook to compare the factors derived from the social networks surrounding the young people with those stratificational and regional status indicators traditionally acknowledged as important. Success was analysed by examining the different variables combined, and the estimates formulated for the expected values. The variables were arranged into three major categories, and their effects were examined in single- and multi-step models. In this study, however, we are not concerned with the effects the variables exert on each other, but with the combined effects of the same variables on different performance dimensions.

Table 23: The chances of efficiency of student-age young people controlled for social, regional and social factors and their networks of social connections

	obtaining experience in HE		intention to continue education		optimism in connection with work	
	Sig.	Exp(B)	Sig.	Exp(B)	Sig.	Exp(B)
Gender: female	.000	1.698	.000	1.558	.190	1.084
Mother with degree	.000	4.592	.001	1.469	.000	1.649
Father with degree	.000	3.863	NS	1.128	NS	.980
Mother with secondary qualification	.000	1.899	NS	1.067	.003	1.242
Father with secondary qualification	.000	1.677	NS	.996	.005	1.241
Regional force field						
Permanent address in small town	–	1.025	NS	1.103	NS	.910
Permanent address in big city	.000	1.534	.000	1.454	NS	1.072
Vicinity of regional university	.000	1.393	.001	1.311	NS	.979
Force field of connections						
Stable company of friend	.000	1.685	.000	1.628	.000	1.302
Civilian participation	.000	2.226	.000	2.333	.000	1.498
Member of religious network	.000	1.769	NS	1.089	.003	1.366
Institutional effects			.000	.735	.000	1.895
Constant	.000	.032	.000	.091	.000	.141
Reduction of 2LL		12		3.7		3.5

Source: Hungarian Youth 2012.

From a gender point of view, it seems that young women in Hungary have a higher chance in getting into a college or university and they also complete their studies in higher numbers than men do. They are also more motivated in continuing their studies at postgraduate level. Their optimism about finding a good job does not, however, really differ from that of young men. Parental qualifications higher than elementary level is a serious advantage for young people in their efforts to get into higher education. It is particularly clear with parents with a college or university degree. The children of mothers with a degree appear to have a significantly higher inclination to develop a need for continuing their studies and confidence they will find the right job. Parents with secondary qualifications afford a tangible advantage to their children as they seek to become professionals. It is to be noted, however, that the positive effect of the parents' qualification level is considerably reduced by the effect of the young person's social network. This fact draws our attention to the importance of the force field of connections surrounding young people. As educational institutions provide the major framework for social networks, it is necessary to pay special attention to this dimension of institutional effects.

The regional force field surrounding a young person plays a major role in shaping their career. When it comes to entering HE, and obtaining a degree, living in a big city has a definite advantage for the person concerned, as we anticipated beforehand. However, regional advantages do not show a linearly increasing pattern according to the hierarchy of settlements. Those who live in small towns are not at any advantage over those who live in villages. Similarly to what we found at the two-variable analysis, the advantage of the vicinity of a large regional university in terms of entering into higher education and developing an intention to continued education remain the same under the control. But the hope of finding the right job is not extended to those who live in a big city or near a large university.

We included several elements of the force field of connections as the third element of our analysis. A stable company of friends, and belonging to a voluntary organization are significantly positive, even when controlled for all factors. The positive effects are the most obvious when entering HE, planning further studies and earning a degree. The advantageous effects are not so spectacular in terms of making the individual optimistic about finding a good job. Controlled for the other variables the fact of belonging to a religious organization definitely increases the chances for the person concerned in terms of starting studies in higher education and earning a degree. It moderately increases the person's optimism in the hope of finding the right job, and appears to make no difference to an individual's desire to continue their studies. With two success indicators we intended to survey the effects of student life, i.e. the fact that the respondent is already a student at a college or university. Given the available data, it was the only way of observing the effects of learning in a higher education institution. Several analyses provided the same result: living as a student does not encourage the person to make efforts to continue their studies at a higher level, but clearly increases their optimism in finding the right job. The latter is a positive development, but the two results together appear to suggest that student life does not make young people realize that learning and making a career in the labour market are both moving targets. Instead, they are lulled into the false illusion that a degree is, without any further effort, an entry ticket to their desired job.

Conclusion

In our study we have analysed data relating to young people between the ages of 18 and 29 with the help of indicators of their expected social mobility. When analysing their position in the vertical –social hierarchy– and the regional –geographical location– dimensions of their existence, we were able to detect considerably uneven situations. This unevenness predicts that the original social and family status of the young people concerned will be reproduced, despite the fact that unprecedented possibilities have opened up in Hungarian higher education. Upon observing these uneven chances, we analysed the alleged compensating force of individuals' social networks by using two- and multivariable procedures. The of elements of the network resources we examined proved to be genuine compensating factors, alleviating the disadvantages of family status. We are encouraged to conclude that the force field of connections is in itself an important factor in shaping the career of young people and deserves the attention of researches in its own right, in addition to family status. A further important factor is belonging loosely to a voluntary organization or group. Loose connections are especially useful in relaying inspiring information to young people. The advantage of these connections is that they do not require any major effort, so 20% of the young people make use of them. Although Hungarian youth – similarly to the rest of the society– are not very active in communities, a relatively large number of people benefit from various communities, although, naturally, this number could and should be greater. The loose bonds are a generally inspiring force for young people's educational career, in raising their motivation to continue their studies and find the right job. A closer network of connections, manifested in its formal permanence and stability, is a more modest, but still palpable resource. The community of a campus, where students spend their daily life, offers us a special area for observations. There we can study the students' expectations, and their optimistic or pessimistic views on their future careers; however, it seems the energy inspiring students to continue their studies at a higher level is missing there. All these points appear to confirm the results of earlier research projects that have found the dominant attitudes of students at a campus not particularly favourable from the perspective of students' further education (Pusztai 2011).

Should I stay *(on campus)* or should I go *(to work)*?

Abstract

Educational researchers have highlighted that schools can have various insti-tutional characteristics in compulsory education (stable relationships in the school community, mutual trust between actors and expanded faculty role models) that can serve as resources of social capital. Recent changes in high-er education and increasing diversity in student populations have turned sci-entific interest towards students and communities. Tinto and colleagues have argued for the statement that students' institutional integration and institu-tional social context attributes have a strong effect on student achievement in higher education as well. Our question was whether students' integration into higher education institutional and external communities and associa-tions during the university years can also contribute to the improvement of higher education outcomes in an East Central European region where the proportion of graduates is lower than the EU average and the majority of students' parents have had no experience with HE. We analysed the The Role of Tertiary Education in Social and Economic Transformation data for full time bachelor (2008) and master (2010) students, who were the first cohorts to enter the two-cycle higher education system. When comparing ex-planatory variables we found it noteworthy that it was the informal aspect of intergenerational relationships that proved to be highly efficient, whereas the most prominent areas of intragenerational relationships were those based on the expansion of knowledge and attachment to a voluntary community.

Introduction

In its so-called elite phase before its large-scale expansion, higher education was characterised by input selectivity (Trow, 1974). Also in Hungary, the structure of secondary education which prepared for the entrance exam, the process of making a decision to apply for admission, the highly competitive entrance exam and later the distribution of students among different types of institutions and training took place in a socially selective way (Kozma, 2008), although after entrance the drop-out rate was not high. After the transition to democracy in Hungary, regardless of alternating periods of full speed ahead and halt in the expansion process the strictness of entrance se-lection has gradually decreased owing to the joint influence of the funding system and demographic changes (Kozma, 2008, Polónyi, 2013). Nowa-days European higher education policy no longer has strict selection on its agenda; instead, recent general aims include widening participation and raising the proportion of disadvantaged students and supporting their academic careers (Reay et al., 2009, Thomas, 2002, Greenbank, 2009, Teichler, 2008, Pasternack and Bloch, 2008). This certainly raises the question of how competitive mass higher education really is across particular regions, institutions and faculties, since in most higher education institutions of the surveyed region non-traditional students are in such a majority that one can actually speak of non-traditional campuses.

As regards the diversity of the student community, some of the literature discusses the heterogeneity of students in terms of sex, social origin, ethnicity and religion (Harper and Quaye, 2009). Studies in educational sociology and the pedagogy of higher education are consistent in describing certain groups as non-traditional if they show new features in the above senses or are under-represented compared to their social significance. The concept of non-traditional student does not have a stable semantic field; its meaning is continually broadening. The following risk groups have also been identified in Hungary: students from low-status families (Fónai et al., 2011), women, family providers and those who work while studying (Engler, 2013), those who belong to an ethnic or religious minority (Pusztai, 2007, Forray-Kozma, 2013), and those who come from secondary technical schools or start their studies at a somewhat later age (Györgyi, 2008). Risk groups usually include students who entered higher education as new target groups in the second wave of expansion. A possible lack of integration threatens mainly first-generation students, whose former social and intellectual background differs sharply from the culture of the institution. Low achieving middle-class students had also appeared in higher education by the 1990s, introducing "middle-class drop-outs" in massive numbers as a new crisis group (Tinto, 1993, De Witte and Cabus 2013).

The Implementation of Multicycle Higher Education

Higher education in the region under investigation followed the Soviet pattern after World War II., which was characterized by centralized direction, a low rate of participation, and the binary structure of the system. This can be linked to the fact that a binary structure of universities and colleges evolved in Hungary with relatively small sized institutions. The changes in Hungarian higher education did not start with the Bologna process. Higher education went through so many changes that the period after 1990 is known as the quarter of a century long reform of Hungarian higher education. After the political transformation of 1989–90 the number of higher education students has risen fourfold and the student/teacher ratio is more than two and a half times higher. Inconsistency – manifest in growing needs and fewer resources – is the common denominator in the restructuring of Central and Eastern European higher education, while the same processes were spread over a longer period in the western countries. During this time many significant questions of higher educational policy remained unresolved. During the alternating cycles of restrictive and expansive educational policies the processes currently in course attempt to deal with the effects of this rapid restructuring. The changes are termed 'reform' in Hungarian, an expression which carries a positive secondary meaning in the Hungarian historical mind (Pusztai-Szabó 2008, Szolár 2010, 2012).

The first higher education act (Higher Education Act) was passed in 1993; previously all levels of education had been regulated by the Unified Educational Act (1985). The importance of the Act of 1993 was in its decentralization of higher education, in the establishment of the autonomy of higher education institutions, and in the replacement of the Soviet type of higher education with a modern type. A major element in making Hungarian higher education 'euro-compatible' is the application of the European Credit Transfer System (ECTS), which is the result of a long process. Since 1990 there have been institutional attempts to restructure the old student assessment system and to introduce an assessment system based on credit accumulation. The introduction of the European Credit Transfer System (ECTS) as a legal requirement dates from the modification of the Higher Education Act of 1996 and became compulsory for all institutions from 2002. The question of diploma supplements is also linked to the subject of internationalisation. Their introduction was included in the modification of the Higher Education Act in 2003.

In 1999 Hungary was among the countries signing the Bologna Declaration, which meant that Hungary undertook to establish a multicycle higher education system. The whole system has four levels in practice. Firstly doctoral studies (PhD programmes) were introduced from 1994 (ISCED 6 level), based on the previously mentioned 1993 Act. As for post-secondary studies, advanced vocational programs (ISCED level 5B advanced vocational programs) were introduced from 1997. The launch of three-year-long bachelor studies became possible from 2004 with the modification of the Higher Education Act of 2003. However, at this time only a few programs were started in the field of ICT. The launch of the multi-cycle system took place in 2006, and was the result of the new Higher Education Act of 2005. BA and BSC programs started at this time in all study fields. Master graduate programs were launched in 2008. In some fields –medicine, veterinary studies, pharmacology, dentistry, law, architecture, and from 2013 also teacher education– the system retained the long single-cycle studium.

It became apparent that Hungarian higher education –just like other Central and Eastern European systems– has had to face different problems since the introduction of the Bologna process (Szolár 2011, Kozma et al 2013). After the turn of the millennium increasing student enrolment and institutional diversification challenged the quality of higher education. Some bachelor programmes have set very low threshold scores for admission, which favours low-status students, but several of them have proved to be of little value as entry points for the labour market or further studies. As a result of the expansion of the institutional system, Hungary, with 3.1 institutions of higher education per million inhabitants, has been approaching the levels of other Central European countries. However, the introduction of multi-cycle higher education coincided with diminishing state subsidies owing to the economic crisis, a demographic slump and increasing international mobility, so –just as in Poland– the number of students entering higher education started to drop precisely in that period, which has led to competition for students among the institutions (Pusztai et al. 2012, Kwiek 2014). At the time of the introduction of the new system the hottest issue of debate was the marketability of the new type of qualifications. Compared to the framework of the old binary institutional system there was a sudden increase in bachelor programmes and the holders of certain degrees could only find employment in positions that had earlier required no more than secondary education. In the 2010s the government has been making efforts to regulate admission to programmes with poor labour market relevance by imposing strict controls on threshold scores and admission quotas, which makes institutions re-evaluate the quality and relevance of their programmes and keep better track of their graduates' careers.

The internationalisation of the Hungarian system of higher education manifests itself not only in the increasing mobility of both students and faculty, but also in the launch of German and English-language degree programmes as well as the support given to Hungarian-language programmes and institutions that have been launched on the initiative of ethnic Hungarian communities in Romania, Ukraine and Serbia.

Research Questions and Data

We view the society of an institution as a network of personal relationship structures. We make a distinction between students' intergenerational and intragenerational contacts and compare their importance. Several studies point out that in higher education there is a widening generation gap because of the diverging interests of students and faculty. In all segments of formal education there is a tendency for faculty to lose some of their authority and public activity and to have less confidence placed in them. We examined to what extent and with what consequences these phenomena appear in higher education. There are further questions on organisational social impacts. We do not have clear-cut answers to the questions of whether it is formal or informal, intergenerational or intragenerational, close value-based homophilic or loose heterogeneous relationships that provide students with really supportive resources during their studies. It is difficult to mark out one's organisational reference group in a large organisation, but the circle influencing one's career is supposed to be wider than one's personal relationship network. Beyond that network, which presupposes reciprocal relationships, we have to take into account people in the same organisational position, e.g. students of the same faculty, functioning as a reference group. Both the sources and content of the information regarding them are unclear, and the exchange of information is not reciprocal, yet it seems to influence how students make sense of their experiences of HE, and they also adjust their decisions to this constructed picture.

This research is based on the serial quantitative research conducted by the Center for Higher Education Research and Development among Hungarian-speaking higher education students in seven institutions of a cross-border region, which is situated on the eastern edge of the European Higher Education Area. Data were gathered in the border regions of three Central Eastern European countries, namely Hungary, Romania and Ukraine. In the project entitled The Role of Tertiary Education in Social and Economic Transformation[15] full time students on Bachelor courses preparing for their finals (2008, N=1211) and students on the first year of a Master's course (2010, N=600) were surveyed. The samples are representative in terms of the faculties. We have carried out cluster sampling; we asked all the students at the chosen seminar groups, which were selected at random.

Indicators of Student Success

In the world of mass higher education the concept of student success is even less clearly defined than in compulsory education. One interpretation, on which researchers reached a consensus long ago, takes a negative approach. Studies published around the turn of the millennium showed a growing tendency to search for the reasons for students' failures, attrition, and disappointment with their academic goals or institutions. The primary question was why different student groups were unable to take advantage of expanded higher education.

In overseas higher education research, which was launched in the 1960s, the first outcome comparisons among institutions sought to establish criteria

---

15 The Impact of Tertiary Education on Regional Development survey was supported by OTKA T-69160. In the present essay we rely on our paper published previously on the same subject (Pusztai 2014). This chapter is an updated version of previously published analysis of the TERD data.

for the excellence of universities and colleges. A remarkable -and still influential- contribution to the project was the creation of the expanded notion of student outcome (Astin, 1993), which cast new light on the achievements of both students and institutions. Another essential step forward was a new concept of institutional outcome that took into account the make-up of the incoming student population and their attributes at entrance. Realising the importance of student (self-) selection and the institutions' individual impact mechanisms, Astin created the IEO (Input-Environment-Output) model of the impact of higher education institutions, which gives a comprehensive model of students' characteristics at entrance, the impacts of the environment and student outcomes (Astin, 1993). With this, he has made a remarkable contribution to the research into added value in higher education. The concept and methodology of this research are becoming subtler all the time and the notion is well on the way to becoming the key concept of the quality of higher education. On our part, we see the necessity for a broader interpretation of student outcome in tertiary education, which is undergoing a transformation and adjusting itself to the school system. Factors to be considered are the changes in students' knowledge, skills, value preferences and attitudes to higher education and work. We look for the so called inner indicators of student outcome within the world of higher education. Indicators of success are successful entrance to various stages of higher education in accordance with one's career plans, persistence, (fulfilled) aspiration to move one stage forward, exam result averages (taken individually or in comparison to others), advancement (presupposing input and output measurement), and even commitment to one's studies and doing one's work in compliance with academic norms (Tinto, 2006, Klein et al., 2005, Banta and Pike, 2007).

Planning One's Master Studies

As our research focused on the very first students entering two-cycle higher education courses, it is no surprise we are looking forward to data on the proportion of students who have identified with the message implicit in the structural change, namely that it is not necessary to spend more than three years at university to obtain a degree. We had expected the majority of students to be determined to spend a longer period of time in higher education for some reason or other. However, only slightly less than half of the students approaching the end of their bachelor years expressed their intentions to continue their studies. Their intentions were significantly but not exclusively correlated with their fields of study.

Our earlier research led us to the assumption that strong integration into institutional relationships helps students not to lose sight of what, according to the inner logic of the educational system, is the primary goal, namely the acquisition of the highest qualification (Green, 1980). We do not claim with certainty there is a direct and conscious correlation, but rather an influence exerted by the context that supports students' persistence in their goals through the stability provided by everyday interactions. As academic aspirations are powerfully influenced by parents' social status and qualifications, we wanted to know how indicators of embeddedness influence plans to continue one's studies when controlled for parents' education and various other strong determining factors.

Having examined the indicators one by one we found that, with similarly qualified parents, the following had an unambiguously significant positive impact: trust in faculty and university management, the impression of being taken care of by the institution, e.g. by career counselling, involvement in research and other academic activities, participation in the institution's adult education programmes, membership of the institution's academic and interest organisations and students' enlarged relationship networks (compared to their parents' and their own previous ones) now including persons attracted to academic mobility.

Table 24: Predictor coefficients of the formation of students' aspirations to continue their studies (Exp (B) values)

	1	2	3
Student attributes			
Father with degree in higher education	0.748	0.716	0.689
Mother with degree in higher education	1.815**	1.783**	1.755**
Father with secondary education	0.948	0.944	0.904
Mother with secondary education	1.846***	1.865***	1.872***
Sex.	538***	0.508***	500***
Minority student	0.518	0.429**	0.372**
Secondary school providing general education	1.390**	1.393**	1.402**
Intergenerational integration			
Trust in faculty		1.270**	1.299**
Perception of mentor attention		1.583**	1.525**
Intragenerational integration			
Participation in adult education within the institution			1.322*
Intragenerational public activity within the institution			1.446*

	1	2	3
Intragenerational integration			
Harmony with fellow students' world views			1.332*
Constant	0.665**	0.508***	0.381***
Reduction of -2LL	3.4%	7%	9%

Source: The Role of Tertiary Education in Social and Economic Transformation: Bachelor Students (2008). The significance of Wald statistics: ***: p<0.000, **: p<0.01, *: p<0.05. The fit of models is indicated by the decrease of -2* loglikelihood value in percentage terms.

When we examined the impact of the above factors in a single model, the first thing to take into account was the impact of students' attributes at the time of their entrance into higher education. As regards the qualifications of the two parents, the education of mothers, (who are more highly qualified anyway), has a strong influence on graduating bachelor students' intentions to continue their studies. The impact of this factor is long-lasting, and it is only close contact with faculty that is slightly able to diminish its distinguishing influence. Thus bachelor students gain a definite advantage from the fact that their parents, especially their mothers, are highly qualified. As far as sex differences are concerned, our earlier regional research had already revealed the weakness of males' academic commitment. Only those males whose families have more cultural capital than their female peers' families take the risk of entering higher-level university training. This is due to their aspirations to obtain economic status in the surveyed region, where unemployment is very high.

Our findings have also revealed minority students' more uncertain future planning. Although the most important outcome that the two decades of the new political system has produced for them is the establishment and academic legitimisation of minority higher education institutions, the restructuring of higher education has posed further serious obstacles for them because in a minority position it is even more difficult to meet the accreditation requirements of higher levels of training (Kozma, 2008). Although some institutions have coped with the task successfully, the insertion of another point of divergence in minority higher education institutions might bring with it the risk of students emigrating. This follows from minority status rather than the structure of training, as our research findings have failed to confirm the assumption that students from faculties where no master programme has been launched are automatically less motivated to continue their studies.

Since in the region's higher education there is an increased number of students coming from secondary technical schools as opposed to secondary schools providing general education, this inevitably raises the question of what chances non-traditional students have of continuing their studies.

We have come to the conclusion that in spite of their growing numbers, students from secondary technical schools are in an obviously disadvantaged position in higher education. The phenomenon is still present after the exclusion of the impact of parents' education, which implies that the years spent in a secondary technical school orientate students towards other goals. We attribute this to the social impacts of the school rather than the different nature of the curriculum.

That leads us to the question of student embeddedness, which is represented by two sets of variables in our model. The first refers to the dimension we call intergenerational integration. The impact of other variables having been excluded, the unambiguous and significant variables have drawn attention to the informal side of student-faculty relationships and made it possible to ignore the impact of research and academic activity. Although the correlation systems of the trust in faculty and the creditability of other public and university figures were already detectable with simple descriptive statistics, what we have found noteworthy now is that trust in faculty has such a marked and independent influence on planning one's further studies.

The analysis of explanatory variables (which control one another) reveals that a lecturer's efficiency best manifests itself in what we call the influence of mentoring. That is to say, the most powerful component of the student-faculty relationship is that students perceive that their lecturers follow their personal careers with attention. Our survey uses the concept of intergenerational relationships in a broader sense, including extracurricular cooperation and informal interactions as well as lecturers' classroom efficiency. Our findings confirm that student success is essentially influenced by the form of lecturers' employment, availability, professional identity and attitudes towards students. In the future, these factors are likely to carry even more weight on campuses with an increasing number of disadvantaged students.

In search of a correlation between students' intragenerational embeddedness and academic persistence we have taken into consideration all kinds of activities that relate students to one another. Our results show that commitment to continue one's studies is definitely promoted by frequent participation in adult education courses offered by one's own institution, active community work within the institution and harmony between one's own and one's fellow students' free-time activities.

We should keep in mind that the impact of intragenerational embeddedness is less significant than that of lecturers' personal attention. Besides, intragenerational interaction among students does not become a stimulating force in itself but only in a meaningful context alongside certain values and norms. When students take adult education courses together within the institution, which undoubtedly demands some extra effort from them, they mutually reaffirm one another's conviction that it is worth studying. Also, voluntary community work on campus -just like all investment in a public good- is a stimulating force both at individual and public levels (Coleman, 1988). As for harmony with fellow students, this encourages students to persist in their goals by creating the impression of congruence.

As we did not intend to find a holistic answer to why bachelor students arrive at the decision to continue their studies and how the idea becomes a serious resolution, we did not aim to increase the fit indices of our model. Instead, we examined the functioning of those potential explanatory variables that could indicate students' embeddedness in higher education and were able to act as independent factors after other influences had been taken into account.

Intention to Find a Job

As regards the correlation between embeddedness in the higher education institution and job search, on the basis of Astin and Tinto's hypotheses and the theory of student integration we assumed that institutional integration would result in decreased willingness to look for a job, because strong attachment to campus society obviously makes separation more painful. Our data has shown that there is a strong, significant correlation between embeddedness and job search, but, contrary to our expectations, it operates in an opposite direction. Our two-variable analyses show that among inter- and intragenerationally embedded students those who are prepared for employment are strongly over-represented. In contrast, less embedded, isolated students do not look for jobs, although their admittance into the master programme cannot be taken for granted. Moreover, they do not want either to start working or to continue their studies, which suggests that students who have fallen out of relationship networks even have difficulty coping with the need to plan their future. All things considered, it seems that embeddedness in the society of the institution does not only support the individual in planning their further studies but also in their preparation for employment.

The formation of an image of work that gives high priority to social usefulness and public good (Pusztai, 2007) is promoted by different relationship aspects in differently qualified parent groups. Students whose parents have primary education tend to adopt this image if their free-time activities are centred around the campus community or if they practise their religion. For students whose parents have secondary education the factors contributing to the development of an altruistic image of work are participation in extracurricular and free-time activities within the institution, belonging to permanent groups formed on the basis of religion or some cultural activity, as well as trust in faculty, intellectual partnership with lecturers and professional support from them. As for students with highly qualified parents, the formation of an altruistic image of work is stimulated by religious relationship networks, whereas out-of-campus free-time activities have the opposite impact. As we can see, student's social embeddedness is a complex factor but one that cannot be overlooked.

Therefore, we made an attempt to compare the factors influencing one's image of work. Although there is low explanatory value in models that assess the chance of the formation of an image that looks upon work as socially useful, performance centered and requiring responsibility and teamwork, the student relationship variables tend to have coefficients of similar direction and strength in the different models. Among social background variables, the majority of which can be ignored, residence in big cities plays a negative, while minority status plays a positive role in the formation of a socially useful image of work. Among students' relationships within the institution the most powerful positive impact is exerted by their varied personal interaction with lecturers. The all-around attention from mentors even overshadows the influence of unidirectional trust in faculty, so its significance cannot be overemphasised. In order to enter into such relationships based on extensive communication lecturers need an extended role image, which may have an impact on students as a direct role model of someone doing altruistic, socially useful work. Two of the indices of intragenerational embeddedness (multiplex friendships and participation in free-time religious or cultural community activities) have proved to be able to bridge the dividing line between society within and outside the institution. They are characterised by value and interest orientation that connects the individual to smaller or larger, but relatively stable communities. Harmony with fellow students has a positive influence in this respect as well, but it is not a significant condition of aspiration for socially useful work.

Table 25: Predictor coefficients of the formation of an altruistic image of work among students approaching the end of their bachelor studies (Exp (B) values)

	1	2	3
Student attributes			
Father's qualification	.971	.952	.964
Mother's qualification	.942	.952	.947
Secondary grammar school	.937	.933	.960
Residence in a city	.720**.	694**	.709**
Financial status above average	1.011	1.016	1.003
Minority student	3.134**	2.758**	2.171

	1	2	3
Intergenerational integration			
Perception of mentor attention		3.568***	3.237***
Trust in faculty		1.001	1.017
Intragenerational integration			
Multiplex friendships			1.074**
Religious – cultural community activity			1.430**
Harmony with fellow students			1.020
Constant	1.344	1.261	.797
Reduction of -2LL	1.69	3.47	4.35

Source: The Role of Tertiary Education in Social and Economic Transformation: Bachelor Students (2008). The significance of Wald statistics: ***: $p<0.000$, **: $p<0.01$, *: $p<0.05$. The fit of models is indicated by the decrease of -2* loglikelihood value in percentage terms.

Conclusion

We assumed bachelor students' embeddedness in the society of the institution helps them persist in their aspirations towards their goals in higher education, so it acts as a special campus-related source of social capital. Our findings have led us to the conclusion that during their series of interactions with various institutional co-actors, students gradually identify with the norms and values of their immediate institutional environment and adapt to the formal and informal expectations of the community. Meanwhile they receive confirmation that -even if for different reasons- it is important for them to obtain a high qualification and develop a valuable vision of work. In campus communities intergenerational embeddedness had a more powerful and marked impact, whereas intragenerational embeddedness had a relatively weaker influence. When comparing explanatory variables we found it noteworthy that it was the informal side of intergenerational relationships (involving lecturers and based on reciprocity) that proved to be highly efficient, whereas the most prominent areas of intragenerational relationships were those based on the expansion of knowledge and attachment to a voluntary community or activity.

Our conclusion is that beyond students' original demographic, social, cultural and regional attributes there is a set of resources evolving from social experiences and contact with the main socialising agents within the institution during one's higher education. They seem to be able to have an independent and measurable impact on students' careers. Although the structure of these social experiences needs further analysis, it is clear that the institutional influences we have been trying to outline in this paper may receive considerable weight among recently more and more heterogeneous student groups, especially those with rather disadvantaged backgrounds. By exploring some essential indices of inter- and intragenerational institutional social context and surveying their impact on students' plans to continue their studies and on their visions of starting work our analysis took a major step towards putting students in the focus of attention again, as in recent times higher education research has ungenerously treated them as one-dimensional beings, either as consumers to be tempted or as labour market commodities. Our findings also encourage further research in order to identify independent subcultures in the world of higher education. Subsequently, the elements that influence students' academic careers need to be analysed further.

Testing a complex indicator of student success

Abstract

Until recently, the validity of the ranking lists of higher education institutions based on quality indicators were not questioned, but some new international research programmes have found that the quality lists of colleges and universities, and even the students' concepts of success are constructions that do not rest on unquestionable and objective foundations. While conducting research into the origins of and alternatives to these constructions, we had to come to terms with the idea that researchers' concepts regarding success in higher education are rooted in individual or social (e. g. disciplinary or regional) value preferences, previous theoretical assumptions, epistemological orientations, and beliefs in various measurement methods and schools of thinking. The "university map" research projects, showing the wide variety of institutions with different missions encouraged us to deal with the idea of students' outcomes. A number of concepts, ideas and expressions are used very frequently, although they do not rest on any scholarly or scientific consensus. We therefore intended to identify some of the factors that help students in achieving outstanding results in the course of their studies.

Competing Quality Concepts in Higher Education

In the multi-cycle course system which was created as a response to the expansion of higher education, a comprehensive model appears to have emerged at the lower levels (Szemerszki 2013, Veroszta 2013). In this way, there is a growing sense of responsibility in higher education in terms of the social integration of students (Hrubos 2009, Veroszta 2010). At the same time, Astin and Antonio (2011) point out that there is apparently slow progress with a number of students, in fact in terms of social integration half of them seem to spend their time in higher education in vain (Arum-Roska 2011). It is difficult to confront and analyse this fact, since in higher educational outcomes there is no consensus; different academic, pedagogical and economic value systems compete with each other. Astin (1973, 1993) argues that some of the dominant excellence concepts emphasize the wealth of resources (high scoring entrants, quality infrastructure), whereas others focus on the academic excellence of the faculty (qualifications of, and selection of replacement researchers). A possible third concept should perhaps address the care offered to talented students, and development potential, i.e., how a higher education institution is able to shape the knowledge, skills, value system and attitude of its new students. The potential for skills development has not become a prominent research issue, for several reasons: the traditional approaches to higher education, and different interpretations of input and output indicators. The increasing integration of post-secondary education into the system of higher education, however, necessitates more detailed research on the topic (Kiss 2011, Hrubos 2014). A condition of learning more about an institution is specifying the level of outcome measurable at an individual level. Estimating the achievement and progress of students is difficult for a number of reasons. To that end, some sort of data regarding the personal/individual performance of the student is necessary. The objective of this essay is to contribute to the creation of more reliable indicators of student success for the education-sociological research projects of the future.

In Search of Student Success Indicators

When we attempt to conceptualize the higher education outcomes of students, we encounter a number of dilemmas. Is there really a need for a standardized measuring system, or should the institutions themselves, or even the students, decide what is success for them? Should we rely on objective data, self-classification, or the perception of classification by the environment? It is important to decide what is a suitable time to register success; whether it is at the moment of graduation, or should it be done much –perhaps years– later? A further dilemma is whether we should approach the issue of outcomes from the positive or the negative side. From the negative side, drop-out, failure, disillusionment with the institution or the original learning objectives may serve as indicators. We find positive indicators among the enrolment and output requirements, but these are not defined, and we do not collect such data. It is also disputed whether student success should be evaluated within the system of higher education, or external factors are also to be included?

The external factors include a good job, and the ability to offer the working attitudes sought by the employers. Education research, however, tends to accept the approved international indicators of success in the labour market indiscriminately (Hrubos 2010, Varga 2013, Pusztai 2013). In the various models the success of an employee is usually indicated by extrinsic factors such as salary, employment, and finding a job matching one's qualifications. Intrinsic factors, such as whether the individual's original expectations are fulfilled, or whether they like their job or not, are less common (Garcia-Aracil-Van der Velden 2008, Beck 2001, Derényi 2010, Kiss 2012). A basic principle of the theory of human capital is that education and success in the labour market are closely interrelated (Schultz 1971), but the predictors that can indicate the future success of professionals who are at present still at college or university have not yet been researched. A degree or its grade does not correlate with the performance of the individual at their job. Some economists believe that a degree in itself may lead to an increase in productivity, but the sheepskin effect only explains a part of this (Kun 2013). Those who attempt to measure working productivity identify value orientation, dispositions and attitudes as predictors. Similarly, researchers often list the ability to work independently, commitment, responsibility for the closer and broader social environment, self-control, willingness and ability to cooperate and to plan and the ability to work as a leader (Knox et al. 1993, Bunderson–Thompson 2009, Hirschi–Fischer 2013). Higher education learning outcomes measuring projects in Europe usually rest upon a set of key competences, as indicated by research into the social consensus on the issue (Rychen–Salgarik 2003). The concepts of learning outcomes are based upon these competences, although the emphasis is on interactive skills, cooperation within a varied environment and conflict management. The third set of competences, i.e. the skills of autonomous action, receives less attention, although these are the ones that include most of the predictors that may forecast the future success of the students mentioned previously.

Other models approach student success from a social cohesion perspective or analyse the complex indicators of the quality of life, rather than from the perspective of an individual's success in a job. These models include social and ethical factors, in addition to economic ones (Camara–Kimmel 2005, Heuser 2007). It is possible to derive the elements of education indicators of the success of students as used in higher education from these models. These models also emphasize the social success of a graduate as well. A successful student finds studying a sensible activity, so they are willing to do extra work voluntarily, and they find it natural to identify with the system of norms of the institution (Heuser 2007). These models operate with the obligations of a citizen, social responsibility, and services rendered to the community, since these factors play a major role in measuring the learning outcomes of students (Pascarella–Terenzini 2005, Koltói–Kiss 2011). Several research projects have clearly shown the interrelationship among these factors and the competences of individuals as leaders (Smart et al. 2000).

Researchers appear to concentrate on the indicators of teaching and learning, instead of the not easily accessible, unreliable and disputed external factors. The dimensions to be examined, however, have extended significantly. A range of other predictors have been identified, in addition to teaching and learning. These are able to forecast the future success of an individual. Such predictors include long-term skills, including social and citizen's competences or performance (by the latter we understand the state in which routine activities, attitudes and opinions are amalgamated into a comprehensive system).

Some of the indicators are arranged into the affective-psychological, others into the affective-behavioural dimension (Astin 1993, Pascarella–Terenzini

2005). To survey the practices of cooperation, social problem solving methods and the attitudes of students, we used a statistical analysis based upon a voluntary inventory. When students' intrinsic system of conditions, and the knowledge and abilities required to execute these activities are compared to each other or to a pre-set system of criteria, a psychometric method is used. When the data thus obtained are analysed, a certain level of competence, or any difference from the values measured at an earlier survey are regarded as a result. The social and intercultural competence of students, made up of their cognitive and affective characteristics, brings with it the promise of effective cooperation with others (Berardo 2005, Deardorff 2006, Spitzberg–Changnon 2009, Polyák et al. 2012), but the question is how these potentials are realized in real life. The results of the psychometric measurements are therefore not sufficient in themselves; a multi-dimensional approach is needed (Buhrmester et al. 1988).

In Europe, the outcomes of students' higher education studies are usually measured in terms of their success in their jobs. In America, on the other hand, most of the concepts of the achievement of students are competence-based. There is no consensus as to whether performances measured under laboratory circumstances can be recreated in real-life. The most sophisticated education-based achievement concepts measure the increase in students' knowledge by comparing the specialized or general knowledge of entrants and graduates. In that respect student success is what the standardized means are able to detect and measure. In order to be successful in one's job, a wide range of skills and competences are required. Higher education institutions promise to create and develop all those competences, but little information is available as to how the skills are realized later on. Collegiate Learning Assessment is similar to the methods used to measure competences at secondary level in terms of assessing critical thinking, analytical arguments and problem solving skills. The system known as Assessment of Higher Education Learning Outcomes (AHELO) attempts to measure specific skills and competences at the faculties of economics and engineering. There are experts who argue, however, that the Collegiate Learning Assessment entries used in the general element of the AHELO also primarily serve to measure general business planning skills (Shavelson 2012). As has been shown, those who formulate objections to standardization argue that course-specific features, and regional and social differences make it difficult to achieve a consensus. A competence to be measured is always distorted towards this or that training course; regional and social distortions are present even within the same country, as there are different training requirements and social missions in various regions. The different attitudes of different social groups also considerably influence the interpretation of social integration. Another reason why measuring schemes of learning outcomes is not fully reliable is that they all use a lengthy data gathering procedure, and often require an IT infrastructure that is not always available everywhere. At evaluation, the subjectivity and costs of measurement are increased by various methods, for instance when selection tests are complemented or replaced by textual sections. In order to reduce the workload of an individual student, several students work on various parts of the inventory, so it is not possible to carry out data analysis at the individual level (Klein et al. 2007). These tests are therefore not suitable for analyses conducted separately for individual and institutional levels.

In Astin's taxonomy, several elements of the answers in the research inventory related to learning are listed with the cognitive-behavioural dimension. When educational progress is the focus of a student's career, i.e. the emphasis is on entering new levels of higher education, achieving these goals in the system may well be considered as success. Similarly, above average results, commitment to one's studies, and meeting the norms of one's respective institution are also indicators of success (Klein et al. 2005, Pascarella–Terenzini 2005, Tinto 2006, Banta–Pike 2007).

A characteristic of the educational system is that it measures performance in grades, marks and points. It seems to be logical to take the points or grades earned by the student as input data, and those earned at graduation as output data. Several research projects use the grade of the degree or the grades earned by the student. The grades are included in the research as objective indicators, in order to eliminate differences, and are used as a basis for comparison between the student concerned and the others studying at the faculty or institution (Pusztai 2011, Veroszta 2013, Nyüsti–Ceglédi 2013, Gáti–Róbert 2013). By using these data, it should be possible to calculate the expected performance, but this is usually not done in domestic research projects. In international research projects it is also heavily criticised, as performance is influenced by so many different factors (Rodgers 2007).

An approved student success indicator is progress to a higher level of education, although this is not independent of the possibilities available in the institution or region, the branch and form of training. What is more, there are often differences between the student's plans and actual progress to a new training course (Mullen et al. 2003, Pusztai–Fináncz 2003, Schomburg–Teichler 2011, Pusztai 2011, Veroszta 2013).

Less objective achievement indicators include the individual's commitment to studies which, in its narrow sense, means a determined and value-centered participation in studies. In a broader sense it is active involvement in the learning environment. Researchers usually differentiate between the inner (cognitive, ideological) and external (daily routine, activities, behaviour) dimensions. Commitment to studies also includes learning efforts (Pace 1984), and involvement (Astin 1993). Researchers emphasize various aspects of the model[16], and several inventories used for measuring it have become widely used[17]. Further subjective success indicators are the student's attitude to factors such as choosing an educational career, personal competences, integration into the life of an institution, the goal of obtaining a degree, and loyalty to the chosen institute (Bean–Bradley 1986, Tinto 1993, Thomas 2000, Rautopuro–Väisänen 2002).

Questions and Data

We have seen that a number of indicators are able to represent students' achievement in various research projects, and a wide variety of concurrent, more or less relevant factors vie to become an independent and decisive variable in these examinations. Since in the course of our previous examinations we always paid attention to using only internationally approved indicators of students' achievement, so in our new research project we also worked with a multilateral, empirical approach. In this study an attempt is made to introduce our ideas concerning a complex achievement indicator that, in Astin's typology, belongs to the cognitive behavioural dimension. We first wish to highlight our interpretation of success and its dimensions, as well as the most important modes of its operationalization. Subsequently, we summarize the major interrelations between the components and the appearance of the complex indicator in the data obtained from the students. There, however, we do not focus on a description of a model, but the behaviour of the achievement indicator. For the analysis we used the international data set entitled "Higher Education for Social Cohesion Cooperative Research and Development in a Cross-border Area" (2012) (N=2728)[18].

---

16 In certain interpretations, this is one of the dimensions of the professional competence of a student, and it is measured by the time the student devotes to learning. Others consider it as an attitude, through which the individual's capacity for constant further development increases. (Astin 1993, Klein et al. 2005, Carini et al. 2006, Pusztai 2011).

17 One of its components is meeting the academic requirements, e. g. comparing, using and analysing learned theories, or arguing with those, and meeting the expectations of the teacher. Other indicators concentrate on cooperative learning and the individual's attitude to the campus environment (Kuh et al. 2005, Pusztai 2011).

18 The "Higher Education for Social Cohesion – Cooperative Research and Development in a Cross-border area" project was supported by the Hungary-Romania Cross-Border Co-operation Programme (HURO/0901/2.2.2).

The Dimensions of the Concept of Success

As has been shown, student success is not an objectively existing goal in educational policy. It is, instead, a construction created by researchers. Since our concept of achievement operates with intra-institutional, multi-dimensional and long-term predictors, we believe that a minimum of five components is necessary to build it up. The first dimension contains the unbroken educational career, and the importance of continual progress, even though the age of fully linear educational careers is apparently over. The indicator of an unbroken career means that the student smoothly passes the selection points of the system, and has a lower number of interruptions, or started but unfinished semesters, than the average at their respective field of training. We basically interpret an unbroken educational career as an indicator of the future of the student; an unbroken career means persistence in their chosen subject major, and loyalty to the institution. We examined the inclination of the students to give up their original goal with questions in the inventory related to the interruption and suspension of studies, and the number of unfinished semesters. We did not ascribe too much significance to the intention to change institutions, since in our experience this may indicate a course correction on the side of a committed and conscious student. We weighed the positive vectors of an unbroken educational career, and not only the negative ones. Persistence in one's studies is an important element of the success dimension which also includes the recognized value of the studies for the student, and the confidence to be able to complete those studies[19].

In the second dimension we identified the intention and capability of the student to exploit the learning opportunities offered by the higher education institution as an important factor. Here we included the credit courses and the non-credit ones, i.e., voluntary activities and their results. The first component of this dimension reminds us of the traditional, narrow success indicators, which is somewhat similar to the ideal student in the Humboldt

---

19 Agreement with statements like "My studies are going to be useful to me in my professional career," or "I do my best to attend lectures, seminars and practical classes" may appear as explanatory variables in certain models examining the reasons for the efficiency and success of students. They are powerfully bound to the dimension of the student's persistence in their studies, as they show rational commitment to the individual's studies. Confidence in connection with various challenges ("I can") also represents rationality and consciousness.

University model[20], and partly to the successful specialized professional[21]. The advantage of discussing them together is that in this way they are not faculty- or course-specific. The second component of this dimension addresses the routine of activities inside and outside the classroom. Naturally, certain elements are not present in various fields of training, so the success of individual students was examined in terms of the average achieved at the faculty concerned. Those above that average were regarded as successful students. The learning characteristics examined here included learning intensity[22], class attendance and exam efficiency.

The third dimension of success contains the acceptance of the declared educational and professional norms and goals of the institution. In our interpretation this independent dimension is a predictor of the behaviour patterns of a professional able to contribute to the cohesion of the smaller and larger communities in society. As usual in international practice, we also separated the moral judgments of students and their daily practice, and did not ask questions regarding their actual actions and the moral classifications of those actions. In this dimension, students were divided into successful and less successful ones according to their moral judgments about situations that pose various moral challenges during the daily work of a college or university student. In our earlier projects we detected a considerable uncertainty among students regarding norms to be followed, and under these circumstances a decision to follow certain norms is a significant achievement (Barta 2010, Pusztai 2011).

Our fourth success dimension is that of the willingness to start a job during the time when the individual is still studying. If we accept the presupposition that the basic attitude of an individual to work and to social responsibility are important from the perspective of future performance, then the decision to start a job is a predictor of success after graduation. The emergence of that attitude, and its gradual shaping during the years of study, is an important aspect of success even if specific economic and social circumstances are not always favourable in terms of finding the desired job. In this analysis, we have combined the affinity to work into one unit from the various elements of plans and experience, when students identified any

---

20 The possible success indicators of a student at a research university may include the following: a research topic of their own, writing special theses, attending competitions and conferences, receiving appointments from the department, publishing essays, earning special scholarships within and/or outside their respective institution.

21 Here we refer to competences in management, advanced language exams, acting as a private tutor to students in lower years.

22 Here study efforts, involvement and commitment appear, measured with the adapted inventory of NSSE.

kind of work as part of their life experience[23] and from plans to start a job in the near future. When students find a job during the time they are at college or university which matches their studies and qualification, it is often regarded as a predictor of future success, but in our region this issue must be treated with care. Earlier analyses revealed that it largely depends on the social status of the student (Gáti-Róbert 2013), and it is to be noted that the chances of finding a part-time job for a student vary greatly in the centre and on the periphery within the same country.

The fifth dimension of success is the willingness of the student to continue their studies and to educate themselves, since this factor is simply unavoidable in our dynamically changing world. Here we do not only refer to entering a higher level of training; the openness to any kind of additional studies has been interpreted as a condition and predictor for adaptability in the future.

In order to draw up a detailed and complex set of success indicators, we used 151 items in our inventory, and 16 variables derived from those items. Since there is complex content in every component, we first prepared the indices for every component, and then the contents of the components were summarized in a complex index. A continual and normally distributed variable was the result, with 0 as the minimum, 14 as the maximum value, and 6.2 as the average. 47% of the students were better than the average, and 16.5% fell into the top third. In order to detect success in a sensitive way, a variable was created for students better than the average and one for those in the top third.

The Operation of Student Success Indicators

In accordance with related international practice, we approached the issue of the progress of students from the perspective of the factors that may impede that progress. We noted that while less than 10% of all the students had had an interruption during their career, more than twice as many students had this experience in Hungary (12%), as their colleagues in Romania. A vacant year after finishing the secondary school is not included here[24]. It is noteworthy that the reasons were not primarily financial, or bound to the institution. Suspended or interrupted studies were not primarily characteristic of male students and those coming from lower social status backgrounds. Very often

---

23 Work experience includes the activities done in the family farm or family business, performed in addition to a paid main job, as well as any voluntary work undertaken by the student.

24 The proportion of students who do not begin their advanced studies right after secondary school is much higher in Hungary than in the other two countries concerned. In 2012, 16% of the students reported that they had interrupted their studies before going on to college or university.

the children of highly qualified parents interrupted and then resumed their studies. The proportion of such students is almost two times higher among the children of mothers with advanced qualifications. One of the reasons may be that the secondary schools are not always able to prepare students for the increasingly difficult entry requirements, whereas in Romania the institutions of higher education shape their admission requirements in a more flexible way, to meet the training output of the secondary schools. It is necessary to consider whether interrupted or suspended education means the same in Hungarian higher education as it does in the neighbouring countries or, as a matter of fact, in the other European or overseas countries. If there are considerable differences, not all the components of that dimension can be used as a reliable, international indicator of success in higher education.

More than two thirds of the students in the international sample share the belief that their studies are sensible and useful in the long run, but the proportions are not the same: while in Hungary 60% of students believe this, in Romania the respective figure is 70%. Here we need to know that the difference is not influenced by the ethnic minority or majority status of the students in Romania. The form of the course does not seem to influence the statistics either, but the faculty and the form of financing apparently do. A higher number of fee paying students trust in the usefulness of their studies than those who attend free courses. This confirms our earlier observations that some free training courses in state-owned colleges and universities, usually with lower admittance requirements, are considered by students as a temporary solution. The situation may easily become even worse if the college or university is unable to convince the student during their years of training that their studies are useful. This may lead to the appearance of large numbers of disillusioned students.

Significant differences have been observed in terms of the confidence of students in connection with the completion of their studies. There were differences in the international comparison: 63% of the Hungarian students had a positive image of themselves, and 71% of the Romanian students had the same. There were also differences at the different training levels, as three quarters of the students at postgraduate level believe that they are competent, while at undergraduate level the respective proportion was a mere one third. We can conclude that there are differences between the training systems of the different countries and naturally, between the various institutions, too, in terms of bridging the gap between the secondary school and the college. In this analysis, the qualifications of the parents did not have a great influence on the confidence of the students regarding the success of their students. Women tend to be a lot more confident in this respect.

The two-variable analysis of the first component of the educational activities, aimed at the quantitative group differences in extra-curricular activities, revealed that only one third of the students are involved in non-compulsory study or research work. Out of the eighteen activities offered, students do three on average. Differences between the countries appear in this respect, too. At institutions in Hungary, individual differences among students are low, and the general level is lower than what we find in Romania, where more students reported taking part in a great number of extracurricular activities. The higher performance of correspondence and postgraduate students in this respect is partly explained by the longer course time. It is obvious that in this respect we cannot use the same standards for fee-paying students. Of the individual characteristics, parents' high qualifications play an important –supportive– role in this respect. One quarter of children of parents with basic qualifications, and more than 40% of children with advanced qualifications perform above the average in this dimension. The same differences are observed in the productivity of students coming from rural and urban environments. The advantages enjoyed by students from big cities are considerable in both systems, although the dividing line in terms of parents with differing qualifications is more conspicuous among students in Romania. In Hungary, the disadvantage of students with parents whose qualifications are low is greater[25].

When we discussed the activities inside and outside the classroom, we first examined the active participation of the students in their own courses, and then we addressed the product of the specific academic year. The differences between the two countries, observed earlier, were present here as well. In Romania students, according to the answers they themselves provided, participate more intensively in activities related to their studies, and the level of their end product is also higher. Postgraduate and correspondence students often make more effort in Romania than their Hungarian counterparts, and here the parents' qualifications was not found to be a significant influencing factor.

In an analysis of the norms related to work in higher education we compared the judgments of the students to the average of the sample, and not to the regulations themselves. In this way, we found that almost 60% of the students behaved in compliance with the norms. The national border made a difference in this respect, too. More than one third of Hungarian students, and more than 50% of Romanians were found to be in breach of the norms, to an extent exceeding the average. Postgraduate students and those studying in integrated master courses, as well as women are closer to the declared norms of their institutions and, contrary to our original expectations, the effects of the qualifications of the parents were found to be negligible.

---

25 There is a difference between the countries in terms of the parents' qualifications. In Romania the numbers of fathers and mothers with elementary qualifications is approximately the same, but in Hungary the number of fathers with elementary qualifications is remarkably high.

Hardly more than one third of the interviewed students had an above average affinity to work. The respective figure in Romania was over 40%. Postgraduate students, fee paying students, men, and children of parents with lower qualifications had more work experience than others, but their home settlement was not an influencing factor. After the first futile efforts at finding a job, 17% of them found it a logical option to apply for unemployment benefit. Every tenth student would like to avoid taking a long-term job, but two thirds are more determined than the average to become an employee. The data suggest that the structural characteristics of the training influence the attitude of students to work, while the social status of the family does not. Territorial differences are tangible in this respect, too: in Hungary almost three quarters of the students plan to find a job, while in Romania the proportion is hardly more than half of them. At this point we have probably encountered feedback from some external factor.

Almost two thirds of the students have some idea about the course of their future studies, i.e. whether to continue or correct their career paths. In this respect there is no difference between the two countries. It is primarily undergraduate students who intend to continue their studies (almost 60%), and hardly more than one third of those studying in integrated master courses. Surprisingly, there was no difference in terms of the different forms of course in terms of intention to start future doctoral studies, with every fourth student intending to enter doctoral courses. Students in the integrated master courses plan to pursue postgraduate studies, but not in a doctoral school. In Romania the number of students planning doctoral studies is considerably higher, and it is more common among students whose parents have higher qualifications (the difference in this respect is 10%).

Complex Indicators of Student Success

In the following we intended to find out how our two variables (created as a result of the dichotomization of our multi-dimensional index (which separates the excellent and above the average students from the others) behaves in connection with various common background variables. We attribute importance to this because it is necessary to know whether there are outstanding differences in the success of social groups which are different in a nominal and not in a gradual way. These include the differences between the genders and belonging to different educational systems.

The methods used to measure the success indicators tend to distort to some degree, these methods being biased to either of the two genders, emphasizing the feminine or masculine features. We therefore asked the question of how our success indicator behaves among female and male students separately, and we found that both genders are represented in the top group. Among those who are better than the average, girls are slightly over-represented, which is a result of the advantage enjoyed by female students in the system (Fényes-Pusztai 2006, Fényes 2014), but the difference barely reaches the level of significance. We believe that the multi-dimensional model of success is also a good choice because it helps to eliminate distortions by genders.

Table 26: Proportion of successful students among male and female students

	Women	Men
In the top third	17.3%	15.3%
Outside the top third	82.7%	84.7%
Above the average performance	48.6%*	45.1%
Below the average performance	51.4%	54.9%
N=	1,672	887

Source: Higher Education for Social C\ohesion – Cooperative Research and Development in a Cross-border area 2012. The underlined figures indicate that the percentage in the given cell is higher than expected in a random distribution. Level of significance: *< 0.05.

It is expected that a higher education success indicator should be applicable in international terms, and that it should emphasize individual performance and not merely the common features of aggregate samples. As a result of our observations described above, we found that the components of our success indicator were applicable to the students of institutions both in Hungary and Romania. It was also noted that some features were characteristic of Hungarian, whereas others of Romanian students. The differences found in the components also appear when using the complex indicator, though we were unable to detect any difference between the two countries with above average students. The number of students in the top third is somewhat higher in the Romanian institutions.

Table 27: The proportion of successful students at the Hungarian and Romanian institutions

	Romanian institutions	Hungarian institutions
In the top third	18.5% **	14.5%
Outside the top third	81.5%	85.5%**
Above average performance	48.1%	46.0%
Below average performance	51.9%	54.0%
N=	1,323	1,295

Source: Higher Education for Social Cohesion – Cooperative Research and Development in a Cross-border area 2012. The underlined figures indicate that the percentage in the given cell is higher than expected in a random distribution. A cell is marked with asterisks where the correlation is significant. Level of significance: **=0.002.

The success indicator must pass the test of being able to work reliably when analysing the location in the educational structure. It behaves neutrally in terms of financing the course, but when it comes to the form of the course, postgraduate courses are at an immense advantage. Even a carefully compiled, multi-dimensional student success indicator may contain components that make it impossible for undergraduate students to be included in the successful student category. It is natural, since the very fact that over a longer period spent in higher education students are able to accumulate and show more results demonstrates the efficiency of higher education. Nevertheless, we still face the dilemma of how to develop a student success indicator specifically tailored to undergraduate students, i.e. in what ways should such an indicator differ from those used for postgraduate students and those studying in an two stage system. We may be led to the conclusion that when it comes to measuring success, institutions doing different types and levels of training cannot be compared without reservations.

Table 28: *The proportion of successful students in various types of training*

	Undergraduate	Postgraduate	Integrated
In the top third	15.1%	23.7%***	17.2%
Outside the top third	84.9%***	76.3%	82.8%
Above the average performance	44.5%	60.8%***	47.3%
Below the average performance	55.5%***	39.2%	52.7%
N=	2,062	380	169

Source: Higher Education for Social Cohesion – Cooperative Research and Development in a Cross-border area 2012. The underlined figures indicate that the percentage in the given cell is higher than expected in a random distribution. A cell is marked with asterisks where the correlation is significant. Level of significance: ***= 0.000.

We then continued by examining gradual differences among students, and found that the gradual differences generate really powerful effects on our student success indicators. We concentrated on three types of gradual differences: those caused by differences in social-family status, those rooted in the social capital manifested in the student's civil environment, friends and family, and the differences caused by the social capital afforded by the institution.

We have experienced that inequalities observed at the lower levels of the educational system are repeated in higher education, since students' social status is in close correlation with their success. This is true despite the fact that the indicators of the various dimensions of success do not reflect the advantage enjoyed by students coming from higher social status backgrounds. Parents' qualifications, their financial situation, and the home settlement of the student in the hierarchy of settlement types all play a major role in shaping students' success. 14% of students from a financially modest family and living in a village find their way into the excellent students group, while 20% of those coming from wealthy families achieve excellence. 45–47% of the former and 51% of the latter groups will perform better than the average. As far as the education level of the parents is concerned, the fathers' high qualification is closely linked to excellence. The effect of the mothers' qualification, however, appears to be much less powerful. When seeking explanatory factors for student success, it is essential to compare the individual performance of students coming from similar social backgrounds, and it is not enough to compare the summarized institutional data of students, as it leaves the differences caused by the input of students hidden. Let us point out here that the social status of students' families is not only important at an individual level, but appears as an independent factor in the composition of the institution (Pusztai 2011).

Table 29: *The proportion of successful students broken down according to their parents' qualifications*

	Mother's highest qualification			Father's highest qualification		
	Primary	Secondary	Higher education	Primary	Secondary	Higher education
In the top third	14.4%	16.7%	19.7%**	12.8%	17.7%	22.1%***
Outside the top third	85.6%**	83.3%	80.3%	87.2%***	82.3%	77.9%
Above the average performance	44.9%	48.8%	50.1%	44.0%	49.6%	51.9%**
Below the average performance	55.1%	51.2%	49.9%	56.0%**	50.4%	48.1%
N=	617	1,125	758	802	1,070	603

Source: Higher Education for Social Cohesion – Cooperative Research and Development in a Cross-border area 2012. The underlined figures indicate that the percentage in the given cell is higher than expected in a random distribution. A cell is marked with asterisks where the correlation is significant. Level of significance: *** = 0.000, ** <0.03, * <0.05.

The network resources of students are recognized as an important factor in helping students to achieve excellence. We examined three dimensions of this student resource: that of the social capital coming from the family[26], that of multiplex relations with friends[27], and that of membership of voluntary organizations[28]. The connection among these was one-way and positive, but not particularly strong. Since these resources are important for students in reaching excellence, and we supposed their role is cumulative and not alternative, we included them as a compound index in our analysis. In this way we believe that we are able to point out an important gradual difference that may be instrumental in moving students towards excellence. An examination of the students' social capital within the institution revealed that this factor, similarly to the social status of the family, powerfully influences our student success indicators.

---

26 Coleman (1988) defines family social capital as the time, attention and energy devoted by parents to children. We produced an index from the variables used for measuring this, in order to summarize parental care (conversations about culture, public issues, books, movies, how the student spends their free time, involving them in household chores, showing interest in their studies and friends, financial support, joint cultural programmes, keeping touch with teachers).

27 Multiplex, multi-functional relations with friends was analysed by an index derived from the data of a group of variables, and we intended to find out whether the student has a friend outside the institution to talk about their educational, cultural, private problems and plans for the future, or to help them in their studies and other issues.

28 Membership of voluntary organizations outside the institution was examined by an index, derived from the data of a group of variables, and we intended to find out whether the student is a member of a cultural club, circle, art group, dance ensemble, orchestra, choir, conservationist group, professional organization, church, small religious community, environmental protection group, charity- or hobby club, political organization, party, interest negotiating organization or any other association or movement.

Table 30: *The proportion of successful students according to their social capital within the institution*

	Social capital below average	Social capital above the average
In the top third	12.6%	<u>21.3%</u>***
Below the top third	87.4%	78.7%
Above the average performance	42.8%	<u>52.7%</u>***
Below	57.2%	47.3%
N=	1,129	1,176

Source: Higher Education for Social Cohesion – Cooperative Research and Development in a Cross-border area 2012. The underlined figures indicate that the percentage in the given cell is higher than expected in a random distribution. A cell is marked with asterisks where the correlation is significant. Level of significance: ***=0.000.

A definite and recurrent statement in the course of our research is that the institutional social capital should also be taken into account, in addition to a number of often examined characteristic features of institutions. Institutional social capital is the summary of formal and content features of the inter-relations of the institution, and these features add up to a cohesive force. The reason why we find it important is that it is part of the educational system, and is different from and independent of other factors that greatly influence the career paths of students. Institutional social capital for a student is what is available to them on campus, provided that the capital is strong enough to support the students in their progress.

The third gradual factor examined in this analysis is therefore social capital obtained from institutions. We identified two of its dimensions, multiplex intergenerational[29] and intragenerational[30] relations. We built an index out of these, and dichotomized this according to the average of the sample. The connection between the two indices was one-way, positive, and weak to moderately strong. We assumed that the factors needed for achieving success

---

29 The social capital manifested in the intra-institutional multiplex, and the inter-generational relations index, was derived from the data of a group of variables, and we intended to find out whether the student is able to discuss study matters with their faculty, as well as other topics, such as science, art, public affairs, and their plans for the future and whether the teachers offer assistance to their students, if they are in e-mail connection with them, or monitor their career path.
30 The strength of the intra-institutional, multiplex, intragenerational relations was analysed by an index, derived from the data of a group of variables, and we intended to find out whether the student has a friend to spend their free time with, and discuss problems and plans for the future with, and whom they can rely on when in need of help.

in studying function as cumulative resources, so we included them in our research as a compound index. Since in our earlier research we had demonstrated that intra-institutional social capital can be more than simply weak or strong and there are groups with a varied level of social embeddedness, we attached three attributes to the variable. Contacts in groups with no or hardly any inter- and intragenerational relations are defined as weak, ties in groups with multi-funcional inter- and intra-generational connections within the campus are considered strong, and those the institutional environment was completely unable to integrate into multi-functional relations we treated separately.

Table 31: *The proportion of successful students according to their social capital within the institution*

	Weak	Medium	Strong
In the top third	9.1%	16.0%	26.8%***
Below the top third	90.9%	84.0%	73.2%
Above the average performance	31.9%	50.5%	60.1%***
Below the average performance	68.1%	49.5%	39.9%
N=	667	1,074	672

Source: Higher Education for Social Cohesion – Cooperative Research and Development in a Cross-border area 2012. The underlined figures indicate that the percentage in the given cell is higher than expected in a random distribution. A cell is marked with asterisks where the correlation is significant. Level of significance: ***=0.000.

When we examined the effects of the students' intra-institutional social capital, we found that that this factor has, similarly to the social status of the students' families, a powerful influence on our success indicator. Although our objective here was not a comparison of the factors assisting students in achieving excellence, it was noteworthy in the two-variable analyses that strong institutional social capital is a very powerful factor, and its absence generates a serious shortage of resources, impeding students more than anything else in becoming successful. Analysing this phenomenon and its possible consequences is a task for the future, but our multi-variable analyses aptly demonstrated that the gradual factors influencing success are certainly not a uni-dimensional world, and education researchers must discuss inequalities influencing the educational career of students in much greater detail. It is not sufficient to focus on the inequalities caused by the different family backgrounds, as there is a wide range of factors to be taken into account within the institutions as well.

Table 32: The chances of achieving excellence, controlled for families' social status, and intra- and extra-institutional social capital

Gender (male)	,799	,767	,832	,808
Country (Romania)	1.366**	1.349**	1.321**	1.321**
Father's qualification (at least secondary)		1.552**	1.504**	1.410**
Mother's qualification (at least secondary)		1.040	1.009	1.000
Permanent address in a city		1.338**	1.365**	1.330**
Extra-institutional social capital			1.889***	1.627***
Level of training (other than undergraduate)				1.669***
Institutional social capital				1.797***
Constant	.141***	.084***	.061***	.033***
Reduction of -2LL		0.5	1.5	3

Source: Higher Education for Social Cohesion – Cooperative Research and Development in a Cross-border area 2012. A cell is marked with asterisks where the correlation is significant. Level of significance: *** =0.000, **< 0.03.

Our complex student success indicator worked well, reflecting the nominal differences of the society of students to a much lesser degree than any of the unidimensional success indicators. It was, on the other hand, highly sensitive to the gradual inequalities that really exist in the system of institution and that require different investments. We pointed out that the differences in the levels of success achieved by students were not only caused by the unequal investments, but are also the results of causes rooted within institutions.

Summary

The objective of our study is to contribute to the development of individual student success indicators for future education-sociological research projects. Most researchers use unidimensional student success models, but it is necessary to recognize the multitude of concepts related to students success, and the increasing demand for distortion-free indicators. After presenting an overview of concepts related to student success, we introduced a complex indicator that opens up possibilities for creating new dimensions of success in diagnosing the possibilities, dispositions, experience and customs in students within institutions. All these may be interpreted as predictors. After comparing the individual components and the complex indicator to institutional, demographic and social background variables it seems that it is possible to create a tool based upon multidimensional student success concepts, and, furthermore, that this tool may be suitable for international analyses, operating without distorting nominal differences. With the dimensions of inequality where gradual differences dominate due to the level of control over the available resources, our indicators reflect the varying levels of return on the different investments. When dealing with the social (cultural, financial etc.) background of the family, and the intra- and extra-institutional social capital, our model behaves similarly to previous models. The conceptualization of student success at various levels of the institutional structure will probably pose a challenge, and it is likely that both identical and varying components might equally well constitute elements of the student success concept.

Institutional impact in higher education

Social capital in campus settings

Abstract

According to research into the institutional contribution to students' progress it is clear that it is not primarily the structural and infrastructural conditions of an institution of higher education that effectively support the success of a student. Among the theories that might function as interpretative frameworks for the campus impact research findings available on the subject the most influential are Astin's theory of student involvement (Astin 1993), Tinto's theory of student integration (Tinto 1993), Bourdieu's theory of reproduction and its improved version, the theory of institutional habitus (Tierney 2001), as well as Coleman's concept of social capital (Coleman 1988). As a result of our previous research findings, we give priority to the effects of informal ties (Pusztai 2009, 2011). While in Tinto's interaction model it is the network of interpersonal links that forge students into a community, in Coleman's functional community concept shared values accomplish the same and maintain integration.

The Many Faces of Diversity in the Student Body

As regards the diversity of the student community, some of the literature discusses the heterogeneity of students in terms of sex, social origin, ethnicity and religion (Hu–Kuh 2003, Harper–Quaye 2009). Studies in educational sociology and the pedagogy of higher education are consistent in terming certain groups non-traditional if they show new features in the above respects or are under-represented compared to their social significance. The concept of non-traditional student does not have a stable semantic field; its meaning keeps expanding. The following risk groups have been identified: students from low-status families, women, those who belong to an ethnic or religious minority, those who start their studies at a somewhat later age (over 21 in Europe), family providers and those who work while studying (Forray 2003, Thomas–Jones 2007, Harper–Quaye 2009). Risk groups usually include students who entered higher education as new target groups in the second wave of expansion. Lack of integration threatens mainly first-generation students, whose former social and intellectual background differs sharply from the culture of the institution. Badly achieving middle-class students had also appeared as a new crisis group in higher education by the 1990s, with the massive increase in middle-class drop-out rates (Tinto 1993, Koucky 2008).

We interpret the role of higher education in terms of its function in supporting social cohesion, and its contribution to establishing common social knowledge which is based on recognising and harmonising individual and collective interests and the ability to cooperate. Indeed, the concept of social cohesion is not limited to the inclusion of students and different diversity groups in the higher educated social strata and the job market, but extends across all student groups with the idea of embedding more holistic approaches to student learning and long-term development, and equipping students to be socially purposeful professionals and citizens. There is no doubt that the links between student achievement in higher education and equality and diversity factors (such as social status, ethnicity, gender or disability) are well documented, but less documented are the effects of societal context and integration into social networks in campus-society on minimising the impacts of social status differences. We elaborated a hypothesis about institutional social capital. The theoretical background of our hypothesis is based firstly on the Colemanian social capital hypothesis, according to which social capital from relational resources can compensate for the reproductive impact of social status on a school career. On the other hand, educational researchers have highlighted that schools can have some institutional characteristics in compulsory education (stable relationships in the school community, mutual trust between actors and expanded faculty role models) which can serve as resources of social capital. Recent changes in higher education and increasing diversity in student population have turned scientific interest towards higher education students and communities. Astin, Tinto, Pascarella and Terezini argued that students' institutional integration and institutional social context attributes have a strong effect on student achievement (for example their attendance and persistence) in higher education as well. Finally, the thesis of institutional habitus further modulates the picture. This feature of an individual campus seems to affect the career paths of non-traditional students more definitely than others. Our question is whether integration into institutional and external communities and associations of higher education, such as professional and research groups during the university years, can also contribute to the improvement of higher education outcomes in our multi-ethnic and multi-confessional region where the proportion of graduates in the general population is lower than the EU average and the majority of students' parents had no experience of HE.

Social Capital and Higher Education Students

The explanations for student advancement are grounded in the reproduction of the family's social status and the transmission of cultural capital, but these theories do not work among non-traditional students, for example

172

in a campus community which they dominate. As our earlier research had shown that social capital in the Colemanian sense was able to compensate for the determinism of reproduction to a certain extent, we wanted to know whether this positive effect of social capital could be detected in the context of lower-status higher education students and campuses. Accordingly, first we will give a review of how the literature on social capital and relationship networks in higher education takes this phenomenon into account and then we will present our own theoretical framework.

The majority of studies on higher education that use the concept of social capital set out from Coleman's concise definitions published in 1988 and 1990 (Arcidiacono–Nicholson 2005); elsewhere one finds Bordieu's three categories of capital (Berger 2000, Thomas 2002, Greenbank 2009), whereas the third group of researchers rely on both authors' interpretations without reflecting upon the fact that they are linked to essentially different paradigms of social theory (Martin–Spenner 2009, Thomas 2002). Most studies are empirical, and the most frequently discussed definitional problem is how difficult it is to distinguish social capital from its benefits. It is worth accepting Lin's (2005) distinction between the types of ties, the nature of capital and benefit(s). His concept not only draws a distinction between the source of capital, form of capital and benefit but also throws light on the differences between network types. He holds the view that the nature of the relationship network is no more than a source of capital. The capital itself -in the case of dense relationship networks- lies in homophily and the benefit appears in shared norms and common value preferences, while in case of loose networks the capital comes from diversity and the benefit is members' competitiveness.

In the discourse of higher education research the crucial matter for debate is which form of social relationship helps the development of that particular type of social capital which is the most supportive of the individual throughout their career. When Coleman claimed that social capital is rooted in the structure of social relationships and gives the individual stimulating support in achieving their academic goals (Coleman 1990: 302), he pointed out closed and tight relationship structures as the most efficient. Others argued for weak ties and open networks (Granovetter 1973), adding that the resources inherent in loose relationships are efficient if they mediate between cohesive social formations (Angelusz–Tardos 1991).

In this debate our train of thought is furthered by Burt's (2000) and later Lin's (2005) consensus-creating suggestions. Their models lead to the assumption that both tight, homogeneous relationship networks and looser ones are able to bring benefit to members, albeit in different ways. Lin holds that tight and therefore homogeneous, so-called closed relationships, although unable to channel information from outside, offer their members a safety of norms, thereby providing the individual with solidarity and cohesion. Extensive macro-level networks of weak ties promote the recognition and realisation of the individual's opportunities for mobility, mainly through their heterogeneity and ability to bridge wide social gaps. As a result, they are able to give the individual access to various cultural and economic resources and information, which gives them considerable advantage in competitive situations. (Lin 2005). In terms of the higher education system this means that at times of transition between the stages of the system it is the open relationship network with its loose ties that may come in useful, whereas within a given stage of one's education successful socialisation and good academic achievement are helped by closed and tight relationship structures (Pusztai 2011).

As long as different relationship networks bring their members different benefits, the question is which type of capital is the most necessary in higher education? Provided that higher education is a competitive field, it seems that a loose and -whether in terms of age, generation or social status- heterogeneous network is more useful; however, if young students still need reinforcing, redundant norms in order to be well prepared for later competition, a dense and homophilic relationship network is more expedient (Pusztai 2011).

In its so-called elite phase before its large-scale expansion, higher education was characterised by input selectivity (Trow 1974). In Hungary, too, the structure of secondary education that prepared for the entrance exam, the process of making a decision to apply for admission, the highly competitive entrance exam and later the distribution of students among different types of institutions and courses took place in a socially selective way (Ladányi 1994), but after entrance the drop-out rate was not high. After the transition to democracy, regardless of the expansion's alternating periods of full steam ahead and halt, the strictness of entrance selection has gradually decreased, owing to the joint influence of the funding system and demographic changes (Polónyi–Timár 2001, Kozma 2010). Nowadays European higher education policy no longer keeps strict selection on its agenda; instead, recent general aims include widening participation and raising the proportion and supporting the academic careers of disadvantaged students (Reay et al. 2009, Thomas 2002, Greenbank 2009, Teichler 2008, Pasternack–Bloch 2008). This certainly raises the question of how competitive mass higher education is as it is realised in particular regions, institutions and faculties, since in most higher education institutions of the surveyed region non-traditional students are in such a majority that one can actually speak of non-traditional campuses. The numbers of applicants and students admitted are not the same, so there is still some entrance selection; yet degree grades bear almost no significance in the labour market, which is to say that higher education can hardly be regarded as a competitive field. Attrition seems to be rather high by international standards (around 40%), but there are no data on whether students mainly drop out voluntarily or out of necessity (Varga 2010). Presumably it is due to a failure to meet graduation requirements.

Other authors look upon higher education as the last period of institutional education. At those levels of higher education which are gradually becoming united with compulsory education and therefore have an increasingly comprehensive function, objectives of training are shifting towards the acquisition of common social norms (Kozma 2010). Consequently, it would rather be the other benefit type, namely solidarity and the safety of norms that would lead to success (Pusztai 2011).

Some researchers claim that in adolescent groups dense and homogeneous networks are still more efficient (Burt 2000), whereas others think that the benefits obtainable in different network types are different in character because they offer different types of resources. When these considerations are applied to the world of HE, the first problem we face is age differentiation. Burt speaks of closed networks as dense networks where the flow of information is very secure and rapid and does not become distorted, and therefore this form of relationship is the most helpful in the development of young people searching for their identity. Redundancy, i.e. repeated information, is particularly supportive at this age as basic norms are better interiorised as a result of repetition (Pusztai 2011).

Having re-examined Coleman's findings, Burt stated that closed networks are really beneficial to adolescents as they promote good achievement at school. In contrast, in the competitive world of work adults are successful if they themselves influence their environment and advantage is gained primarily with the help of new information. The question is whether, in a social sense, higher education students can be regarded as adults or post-adolescents. It is beyond the scope of this study to examine the characteristics of this age group from the point of view of developmental psychology, and neither would it be expedient to do so, because youth as a phase in one's life cycle has been individualised and restructured to a great extent. From a sociological perspective, it is looked upon as being outside adulthood as students live in complete or partial economic dependence, their way of life is characterised by temporariness, open-endedness and a lack of full responsibility, so by the above logic closed networks and regular norms would suit them best (Pusztai 2011).

The features of a network do not only produce different effects by age but also by the individual's social status. However, there is no consensus on whether low-status individuals benefit more from homophily or relationships that bridge status differences. One opinion is that those who abound in some kind of resource benefit from a loose network where they play a bridge role, whereas closed networks are the sources of really efficient social capital which prevents them falling behind and helps them catch up (Burt 2000). Others argue that low-status individuals benefit from upwardly directed relationships that span a great social distance. This view, when one defines homophilic and heterophilic relationships, presupposes an exclusive one-to-one relation between the network type and the redundancy of the accessible information (Lin 2005). Burt says that good achievement requires a tightly closed group and a large number of non-redundant relationships outside the group and he dismisses all other combinations as less efficient (Burt 2000). Speaking of students' relationships, this would mean strong embeddedness in the community and, at the same time, the existence of outside ties (to teaching staff or outside the institution) that provide new information.

No consensus can be expected until the meaning of homophily is clarified since it can be interpreted in several dimensions. In an earlier study we concluded that with respect to the fulfilment of academic objectives it was more useful for a school community to be organised on the basis of value homophily (see Lazarsfeld and Merton's distinction), which crossed the borders of status homophily (McPherson et al. 2001), and thus low-status students were able to benefit from the community's resources (Pusztai 2004, 2009). Status homophily is based on the similarity of social and demographic features, whereas value homophily is rooted in shared values, attitudes and convictions. In other words, when an educational institution recruits its students on the basis of cultural (religious, ethnic) affinity, it is able to integrate a wider range of social strata and give a bigger boost to academic achievement (Pusztai 2009). Overseas social stratification research classifies ethnicity and religious-denominational affiliation as essential status factors, therefore our statement does not challenge the view that value homophily can be a consequence of status homophily (Blau-Duncan 1998, McPherson et al. 2001).

Of all the features of relationship networks, Coleman considers value homophily the most important source of social capital. It is based on the similarity of attitudes, convictions and aspirations on the one hand, and the similarity of behaviour on the other. We think students' relationships can be based on their academic orientation, attitudes to the institution's norms and participation in academic and social events. Opportunities inherent in relationships that are established within an organisation are of special relevance to our subject. Networks that are kept within social and organisational limits but are not based on value preferences are typical of the modern age. It is generally accepted that their low stability is due to one-dimensional, "functional" and "convenience" friendships limited to short periods at various stages of one's life cycle (Simmel 1949, Riesmann 1956, Pataki 2003, Albert–Dávid 2007).

176

Most friendships are based on educational homophily. The educational system is perhaps the most versatile channel of homophilic relationships. Hungary is a characteristic example of the rule that besides work, the majority of measurable friendships originate from school, mainly because the population of educational institutions are sociologically rather homogeneous owing to the free choice of schools[31] (McPherson et al. 2001, Albert–Dávid 2007, Utasi 2008).

Another tie among those who pursue the same discipline is shared interests and orientation (Huber 1991, Becher 1989). Before the demographic expansion of HE, the student population was not only characterised by demographic but also social homophily, and Tinto's theory, whether this is consciously expressed or not, is based on the supposition that if one aspect of a network's multidimensional homophily ceases to exist, it can be balanced by another dimension. That is to say, the increased cohesion of educational-organisational homophily compensates for social (and demographic, ethnic and religious) heterophily, and the result is value homophily, which supports academic success.

Theoretical Routes of Campus Social Capital

Prompted by his longitudinal comparative survey of higher education students, in 1984 Astin developed his influential theory of student involvement, which attributes students' advancement to their involvement in the higher education institution's academic and social life. A distinctive feature of the theory is that involvement and identification with the student role both refer to students' actual activities rather than their motivation. As the author puts it, it is not what students think or how they feel that is important, but what they do.

While looking for the reasons for dropping out, Astin noticed that students do better if they are in harmony with their institutional environment. He found that cultural attachment at a denominational college, for example, supports the achievement of the members of the particular denomination, because it is easier for them to identify with the institution and they take pleasure in participating in its events. He also observed that entrance to higher education influenced world views, religious orientation, ways of life and taste in several cases and concluded that the common changes must be

---

31 Moreover, relationships and friendships established in adulthood also attract people with similar schooling. This kind of homophily is the most common among people with the lowest and highest levels of education. Intellectuals and manual workers are much less likely to enter into a relationship across their social strata than within their respective groups (McPherson et al. 2001).

rooted in students' interaction with their institutional environment. This is the observation on which the theory of involvement grounds its explanation of student outcome (Astin 1993).

The theory considers students as purposeful actors who make good or bad use of the institutional environment for their advancement. Naturally, the extent and quality of student involvement reveal essential differences in institutional environments, which were classified by Astin according to how much they stimulate their students to invest more time and energy in their studies. The four dimensions of institutional environment consist of institutional characteristics (type, proportion of sexes, size, faculty-student ratio, proportion of students taking part in various types of training, expenses allocated to training and research, payment of faculty), curriculum indices (unity of curriculum, proportion of general subjects, written assessment, special requirements), faculty environment constructed from faculty's responses (research orientation, using student activity-based teaching methods, commitment to developing students, willingness to integrate non-traditional students and tailor the curriculum to their needs, political orientation, workload, perception of working conditions, perception of the institutional administration's sensitivity to problems) and peer environment (selectivity, economic and social status, proportion of different majors, political orientation, commitment to academic life, ethnic and religious composition, way of funding one's studies, cultural profile) (Astin 1993).

One of the outstanding theories of student integration is Tinto's theory (1987, 1993) based on his empirical research on student attrition. In the 1980s, to satisfy the urgent need for theories felt by the independent sociology of higher education, he interpreted the findings of his decade-long research on student attrition within the frameworks of rites of passage, a concept borrowed from ethnography, and Durham's theory of anomie. The choice of the interpretational framework suggests that the author intended to break with the almost exclusively psychological approach of student sociology. He emphasised that the difference between the attrition rates of selective and comprehensive institutions cannot be attributed to different personality types (Pusztai 2011).

The theory of student integration originated in the presupposition (formulated by Parsons) that the most fundamental basic function of action systems is the integrative one, which provides the unity of norms, cohesion and reciprocal loyalty in a societal community. Tinto's theory integrated the findings of Coleman's early research (1961), namely that students' behaviour is best explained by the social context of the school. Coleman did not only realise that the factors determining students' favourable sociometric status reveal what kind of achievement is appreciated in the student community but also that the more people value non-academic achievement highly in an institution, the worse the school's grade average is. A recurring question in educational research is how it is possible to make a constantly changing population interested in identifying with values and norms that help them achieve their goals. After the 1960s Coleman tried to find out how students in increasingly widespread secondary education environments can be given the chance of success at school, and he realised that the make-up of students in a school is of key importance mainly because it determines the school's subculture (Pusztai 2009). According to the theory of student integration, both individual success and the efficiency of the institution crucially depend on the stability of the higher education institution's societal community, the condition of which is a significant shift between ties outside and inside the institution: a change of community. This model, drawing from the theory of rites of passage, puts a strong emphasis on that dividing line and crossing it successfully, since the function of rites of passage is precisely to indicate clearly one's successful separation from one's earlier community and, simultaneously, its values and norms. The theory stresses incorporation into the new system of relationships through phases of transition and acceptance and identification with its values and norms. In Tinto's model the divide between relationship networks and communities within and outside a higher education institution is very clear-cut, and membership is mutually exclusive because his earlier empirical findings show that lack of commitment and embeddedness lower certain student groups' chances of obtaining a degree. He conducted his research mainly among disadvantaged students (Tinto 1993).

The above idea of community integration and the theory of functional community, described by Coleman and Hoffer in 1987, have similar roots. However, in Coleman's theory, achievement at school is supported by students and parents being integrated into the school community, whereas in Tinto's model it is separation from the community outside the institution and its replacement with a new one which are capable of preventing both the identity crisis experienced by students which stems from multiple identities, and the resulting threat of a loss of confidence or even attrition (Pusztai 2011). A common element of the two theories is the idea of connecting the organisation and the community; yet Tinto, considering the characteristics of student existence, the social strata which have recently appeared in higher education and generational rearrangement, draws a much closer and more marked borderline around the institutional community. During the three stages of student socialisation (separation, transition and incorporation), in order to achieve competent fulfilment of the student role it is indispensable to cut down on and transform interactions with the previous environment, to change the system of governing norms and to acquire new patterns of interaction. Students leaving their previous communities inevitably arrive in a cultural no man's land and a state of anomie. According to the theory the individual is helped to overcome this condition by rites of passage or the solidarity of the community currently undergoing transition (Tinto 1993). The theoretical (and not temporal) separation of the three stages calls attention to the fact that leaving one's previous communities (primarily family and place of residence) does not go hand in hand with the acquisition of the culture of the new higher education environment, but students inevitably go through periods of uncertainty, and if they are unable to cope with the stages of transition, they will never become real members of the academic community. This statement has never been questioned by later critics of the theory (Berger 2000). Moreover, British qualitative research has confirmed how dramatic the crisis is (Reay et al. 2009, Thomas–Jones 2007).

According to the theory of student integration, the success of a career in higher education is crucially dependent on the success of the third, incorporational phase. Modelled on Durkheim's (1997) concept, it is possible to make a distinction between the intellectual and social layers of students' integration, corresponding to academic (classroom) and social systems in higher education society (Tinto 1993). The former follows from the formal educational function of HE, the latter from informal everyday college or university life. The concept holds that inappropriate integration leads to academic-intellectual isolation on the one hand, and unsatisfying social embeddedness i.e. social isolation, on the other. Tinto draws a parallel between institutional attrition and Durkheim's categories of suicide (Durkheim 1997). Incorporation can be unsuccessful because the collapsing structure of the community is unable to integrate the individual (egoistic model), the individual cannot find a way out of the temporary crisis of the norm system (anomic model) or the environment is excessively regulated (fatalistic model) (Tinto 1993).

The question arises of whether the field of extra-institutional relationships really are a distant and unfamiliar world for students. Tinto's train of thought on separation and integration is supported by some findings from our region, which point out that the society of a campus is secluded from wider society (Kozma 2004) and even the academic world outside the institution might be dangerous for PhD students if they are not backed by their mentors from the campus (Pusztai 2009). Another theory, relying on the analysis of student constructions, sees the outside world as divided into a (mainly emotionally) supportive micro-world and the hostile and confusing macro-world of wider society (Kálmán 2012).

In Tinto's view, institutional experiences can be looked upon as a continuous series of interactions that influence the extent of integration and, as a result, students' commitment. Positive, i.e. integrative experiences confirm students in the purposeful completion of their studies. The institutional environment is surrounded by the social formations of the outside world with

180

norms and value systems different from those of the campus community, so students have to find a balance between forces attracting them both inside and outside the campus. Institutional experiences obtained through integration are made up of formal (academic achievement) and informal (interactions between faculty and students) experiences. Likewise, integration into the institution's social subsystem has the same division into formal (extracurricular activities) and informal (peer influence) elements (Tinto 1993). The interaction among experiences deriving from different layers of the relationship system makes individuals continually revise their views on their goals and institutional commitment. Stronger integration increases, whereas weaker integration decreases chances of achieving ultimate academic goals. Meanwhile, dispositions are also shaped by involvement in outside communities, not necessarily directly but rather to the extent that it diverts students from being integrated into the institution. A later interactionist interpretation of Tinto's model considers this very important because during students' interactions inside and outside the institution, there is a meaning-making process going on in their minds even when they do not discuss their studies in a direct way. Thus, insufficient academic achievement is primarily due to a lack of academic integration, while failure to continue one's studies stems from a lack of social integration (Tinto 1993, Brundsen et al. 2000).

Since higher education is becoming more heterogeneous with respect to the basic status indicators, Tinto thinks that status similarity originating from the student role can develop, influenced by integration, into value homophily. Status similarity refers to members of the student community as they have the same position in the structure of HE, and therefore they do not only enter into communication more easily but, being connected by similar challenges and experiences, they are also more likely to remain in touch. The opinion-shaping power of these relationships is very relevant, especially because the same higher education institution -or the same unit within it- can be seen extremely differently by different actors, and for students, the organisation comes to life through their words (Lawrence 2006, Pusztai 2011).

The homophily on which relationships are grounded can not only be based on shared student status but also on the similarity of position in the relationship network. Tinto's model also makes a distinction between central and peripheral student status with regard to whether students are attached to the dominant student culture or merely a subculture of the campus. This tells us a lot about the influences students are exposed to and about their distance from academic norms (Clark–Trow 1966, Tinto 1993, McPherson et al. 2001).

It is primarily incorporation into a student society made up of loose ties that Tinto regards as a valuable form of capital, while those who have empirically revised his concept opt for close friendships (Bean 2005). Others, relying on the ecological analysis of student relationships, hold the view that the closeness or distance of relationships cannot serve as a basis for distinction or contrast. Since interpersonal relations in the narrow sense (such as roommates, groups of friends, work teams, sports club, connections between faculty and students) interact as independent microsystems, they only serve students' development if they support one another (Renn–Arnold 2003). As the student society within an institution consists of networks of subcultures and one student can belong to several of them, it is not enough for a student to find support for their views on studying in only one microsystem – the entire perception of student culture should be stimulating.

Advocates of the reproduction theory criticise Tinto for devoting less attention to social status than they think is necessary. In their opinion, both the choice of institution and selection within an institution are kept in motion by the reproduction of cultural capital, therefore institutions admit and retain the kind of students who contribute to their cultural capital (Berger 2000). Academic and social integration are determined by students' cultural capital alone, as the range of social contacts is both a direct and, through communication skills, an indirect consequence of the family's cultural capital (DiMaggio–Mohr 1985).

Another distinctive formation at the medium level of organisational relationships in higher education is the organisational reference group, which can exercise a special influence between the levels of close friends and the entire student society of the institution (Lawrence 2006). This is the sum of relationships that are not necessarily based on actual communication but on unidirectional visibility. Its members are those who are perceived by the individual as their environment. There is no standard definition for its size and scope, because it always depends on the individual's standpoint. It includes peers who shape students' plans and behaviour, and although they are only in loose connection, students still internalise their viewpoints. The organisational reference group is only partly similar to Merton's reference group. It is not actual or desired group membership that unites members but a similar organisational position and social status, so students collect the kind of information about their reference individuals, i.e. those to whom they can compare themselves and adjust their own decisions (Lawrence 2006) in a mechanism of social comparison.

This particular and extensive gathering of information helps the individual orientate themselves in the organisation. Owing to the constructive nature of students' minds, the emerging picture of the organisational reference individual or group seems to be fairly coherent, although the information has been randomly picked up rather than systematically collected; it may not even be factual and it may come from everyday observations, non-verbal communication or fragments of indirect information spread by word of mouth. The missing fragments are then completed by the mind in a creative way. All this, of course, raises some doubts as to the possibility of an objective exploration of relationship networks, but it agrees with the statement that 21st century relationship networks have no local limits and what sociologists find important is not the networks' scope or the identification of members but the content they convey; not the network in its objective reality but its perception (Wellmann 1999).

Empirical analysis of the organisational reference group has shown that the individual, leaving behind the dilemma of homogeneity and heterogeneity, chooses similar individuals as regards sex, ethnic group, age and position in the organisation and different ones as regards rank and schooling. Therefore a student's organisational reference group is not very likely to include faculty, but it possibly includes someone from a student's original place of residence who is studying at a higher level, although female undergraduates or PhD students might well compare themselves to a female lecturer (Tornyi 2009, Harris–Lester 2009). They attribute value preferences and behaviour to reference group members and on the basis of this they construct the expectations and behavioural norms of the organisational environment (Lawrence 2006, Renn–Arnold 2003).

In conclusion, in the case of Coleman's functional community it is shared values that create and maintain integration, whereas in Tinto's interactional model connectedness is expected to integrate students and turn them into a community that shares the same values. Tinto's theory has been criticised mainly for assuming the realisation of organisational norm congruence, expected as a result of structural incorporation. Critics have pointed out that the process goes hand in hand with the acculturation of non-traditional students from culturally non-dominant groups, which is made difficult partly by the cultural gap and partly by the fact that mass institutions do not help the integration of a student society which shows the traits of a real community. Thus students, looking for homophilic relationships, integrate with those who are near them either culturally or in the organisational structure.

Towards a Theory of Campus Social Capital

Having analysed the large amount of literature on the subject, one is led to the unambiguous conclusion that institutions of higher education do not contribute to the development of their students through structural or infrastructural factors but by providing them with an interactional force field. Moreover, within the interactional force field there has been a shift of emphasis towards informal and intragenerational forces. Simultaneously, there has been an increase in the proportion of non-traditional students, who do not only lack any passed-down higher education experience, but are also attracted out of the higher education milieu by their social status and micro-environments.

Among the theories that lend themselves as interpretational frameworks to the more noteworthy research findings available on the subject the most influential are Astin's theory of student involvement, Tinto's theory of student integration, Bourdieu's theory of reproduction and its improved version, the theory of institutional habitus (Tierney 2001), as well as Coleman's concept of social capital. The most popular of these, Tinto's integrational paradigm, worked well, especially as an explanation of lower-status students' integration into HE, based on the observations made when the first wave of non-traditional students streamed into higher education in the 1980s. The theory relies on a concept of socialisation with a more traditional, passive and static student image and a somewhat simplified picture of organisational society. Revisions of the theory lead one to the conclusion that it does not apply equally to all student groups; e.g it works better with residential students than commuting ones and it works differently with the two sexes.

Since then, during recent waves of expansion, higher education has also been attracting students that do not (only) differ from traditional students in their hard indicators of social status, but (also) in other respects. These are students who have already entered institutions with strongly heterogeneous faculty and student societies. Perhaps now it is time to seek a more precise explanation for the achievement of various student groups in higher education by using a more sensitive, multidimensional approach to social status, taking into consideration subcultural lifestyles and value and identity categories that influence personal relationship networks and thereby detecting subtler social categories. Within the interpretational framework we are interested in paying special attention to the dimension of relationships because, beyond their help in creating a more sensitive status assessment, we assume that network resources as well as traditional forms of capital prove to be very useful in academic advancement. Accordingly, we have reviewed theories and research that count on the power of relationships among students.

Tinto analysed students' integration into the society of the institution as an explanation of success. In his comprehensive model he reflected on students' connectedness to formal and informal social systems and concluded that integration into these systems influences achievement in such a way that it cuts the ties that attract students out of the world of higher education and means that through frequent interactions they conform to forces attracting them inside. They are integrated to such an extent that they are able to share fellow students' norms and values and meet the long-term formal and informal requirements of the community of the institution or a closer student community. As long as integration strengthens, or remains strong, students'

184

commitment to both their personal goals and the institution increases, which has a beneficial effect on achievement. Lack of integration, on the other hand, leads to distancing, marginalisation and attrition. For a long time the theory of academic and social integration counted as the only dominant explanation of the issue, and although several of its details were debated, it was generally considered applicable. We also think there are limitations to the applicability of the theory because one cannot assume the existence of a tangible common culture in institutions, and neither is the student community the kind of entity that incorporates newcomers smoothly. When compared, the theory of student integration and Astin's (1993) theory of student involvement have a number of contact points. Whereas Astin does not give a coherent explanation as to what determines the differences in the extent of student input, differences in the success of student integration, as formulated by Tinto, give some guidance. Bean, Spady, Astin and Tinto all come to the same conclusion that the state of commitment necessary for success is a result of integration.

The other influential theoretical model which has contributed to research into the connection between relationships in higher education and success is the interpretation of Bourdieu and his followers, which claims the individual's relationships and achievement are related to the interplay between student habitus and organisational habitus. This theory fails to give a satisfactory explanation for the success differences within non-traditional student groups. Habitus is closely linked to hard indicators of social status, so it cannot be helpful in the interpretation of achievement differences within a class or class fraction. Whether they speak of the individualisation of young people or disciplinary socialisation, the authors remain close to the paradigm of the structural determinism of students.

The majority of the literature focuses attention on insufficient student resources when it comes to finding explanations for success or the lack of it. Less attention is paid to an important dimension of student socialisation, namely how, and in cooperation with whom, dispositions and goals are shaped and reinterpreted. What our model, based on international theories and research findings, considers relevant is students' personal relationship networks, which have a powerful influence on students living on heterogeneous campuses.

We find Coleman's theory appropriate for the examination of higher education students' resources because it gives high priority to individual decisions and considers one's class of origin important but not crucial to one's career, which makes it possible for us to explain the achievement differences among non-traditional students. In Coleman's theory differences are accounted for by the existence, composition and strength of personal relationship networks. It does not presuppose a unified or domineering and enforcing organisational community and norm system, but takes the relationship network approach, which is more sensitive to the diversity of subcultures. Therefore it is better applicable in the heterogeneous culture of higher education institutions. It is also sensitive to the fact that in a microenvironment formed by personal networks students' resources do not flow in one direction but are exchanged. Not only does this dynamic and mutual exchange of resources keep networks alive, it also explains how they are shaped by newly-entering members. Meanwhile, it is not only individual resources which receive emphasis but also the structural characteristics and the content of student relationship networks, which modify the achievement one would expect on the basis of individual resources. We think what really influences student achievement is values and norms shared and which speak to life in these microcommunities.

According to our concept, institutional social capital in education is based not only on formal (written, codified) norms, but mainly on informal norms and values, which are created by networks of students and teachers. We look upon the society of an institution as a network of personal relationship structures. We make a distinction between students' intergenerational and intragenerational contacts and compare their importance. Several studies point out that in higher education there is a widening generation gap because of students' and faculty's diverging interests. In all segments of formal education there is a tendency for faculty to lose some of their authority and public activity and have less confidence placed in them. We need to examine to what extent and with what consequences these phenomena appear in higher education.

Limitations of the Concept

There are further questions on campus social capital. We do not have clear-cut answers to the questions of whether it is formal or informal, intergenerational or intragenerational, close homophilic or loose heterogeneous relationships that provide students with really supportive resources during their studies. The impact of relationships as resources seems to be different for different age groups. We find it an important question whether among higher education students and at other levels of training there are the same impact mechanisms working as in compulsory education, and whether the individual is strengthened by surrounding relationships that reinforce formal contacts with informal ones and also perceive inter- and intragenerational cohesion at a context level. The exploration of public and higher education from this perspective may contribute to the definition of the pedagogical identity of higher education, an urgent need these days. In addition, we do not have unambiguous findings on the issue of whether certain student groups are more sensitive to any type of organisational social impact. The role of the wider student community still remains to be defined. It is difficult to mark out one's organisational reference group in a large organisation, but the circle influencing one's career is supposed to be larger than one's personal relationship network. Beyond that network, which presupposes reciprocal relationships, we have to take into account people in the same organisational position, e.g. students at the same faculty, functioning as an organisational reference group. The source and content of the information about them are certainly unclear, and exchange of information is not reciprocal; yet it seems to influence how students make sense of their experiences of HE, and they also adjust their decisions to this constructed picture.

Embeddedness in interpretive communities

Abstract

In our previous research we have pointed out that religious student groups contribute to the formation of distinctively novel patterns of socialisation within the institution, which is a good reason to pay attention to this aspect of student diversity as well. An important question for the education researcher is whether religion-based communities support or hinder young people's higher education careers. In this paper we examine in what ways membership in a religious student groups affects students' academic and social integration as well as their academic success. After reviewing the most important correlations between religiosity and social status, we analyse the connection between belonging to a religious community and relational and cultural embeddedness in campus society. Finally, we examine the willingness to do extra academic work among members of religion-based communities, controlled for variables of family status.

Introduction

Although educational studies on academic performance generally ignore the influence of religiosity, our research into the impact of religiosity on academic career over the past decade has convinced us that the phenomenon is worth taking into consideration. At first sight the subject may seem to bear little social relevance and raising it may even appear pointless as for a long time studies on the sociology of religion have tended to maintain that the higher the level of education, the lower the level of religious affiliation in European society. However, recent analyses have pointed out that in our region this correlation was due to socialist modernisation and state-supported secularisation (Tomka 2011, Gautier and Singelmann 1997). Moreover, nowadays there is a definite boom in religious practice among highly qualified young people (Doctór 2007, Gereben 2009, Tomka 2010, Rosta 2010). The subject becomes all the more interesting when we examine a student population in which the majority come from families with a lower-than-average level of education in a region that is struggling with economic difficulties and a range of related and unrelated social problems (Pusztai 2011). We have examined minority students (Kozma-Pusztai 2006, Pusztai-Nagy 2005) and students belonging to religious communities (Pusztai 2009, Pusztai 2011) in a number of studies. We have pointed out that not only is religiosity an essential personal trait influencing individual career and prospects but religious student groups contribute to the formation of distinctively novel patterns of socialisation within the institution, which is a good reason to pay attention to this aspect of student diversity as well. A further question for the education researcher is whether religion-based communities support or hinder young people's higher education careers. Relying on the findings of our quantitative research among students finishing their BA and starting their MA studies (Pusztai 2011) and our qualitative research on student microcommunities and organisations (Pusztai et al. 2012) we will examine in what ways membership of a religious student group affects students' academic and social integration as well as their academic success. After providing a review of the most important correlations between religiosity and social status (along with academic career, which forms the basis of the latter), we will analyse the connection between belonging to a religious community and relational and cultural embeddedness in campus society. Finally, we examine the willingness to do extra academic work among members of religion-based communities, controlled for variables of family status.

Religiosity and School Career, and Social Status

The study of the correlations between religiosity and social status and between religiosity and academic advancement receives high priority in the sociology of religion. It is widely debated whether decreasing religiosity is a clear and inevitable consequence of modernisation, rationality and the growing proportion of highly qualified people and whether the power of religion-based communities irreversibly diminishes in an open society (Tomka 2011). However, research results in our region have drawn attention to the fact that the process of modernisation here has been different from that in Western Europe, and, in addition, the education system played a central role for decades not only in achieving one's status but also in the interpretation of religious views, so the correlation between religiosity and the level of one's education cannot be simply attributed to the influence of modernisation. It is probably due to the ideology-based educational systems in our region that essential indicators of social status correlate so forcibly and negatively with religiosity. The facts disclosed in the first decade of the political transition confirmed the view that there is a cause and effect relationship between religiosity and social status, but in this context religiosity rather acts as an explanatory variable, i.e. the low social status of religious people is mostly the result of the ideological discrimination against religious people as well as their self-selection (Hegedűs 2000, Görgőy 2001, Bögre 2004, Pusztai 2004).

The above inverse relationship between social status and religiosity seems to have been losing significance in recent decades: with respect to the frequency of churchgoing, for example, people with the lowest qualifications are followed by the population with university degrees. Besides, at both ends of the religiosity scale young people with highly qualified parents are over-represented, and the background of young people who are practising church members is also characterised by somewhat higher economic status as well as a higher level of education, especially in big cities (Tomka 2010, Rosta 2010).

Our research findings show that the issue of religiosity and education level should be examined separately from the issue of religiosity and attitude to academic work and achievement. There is a large amount of research attempting to find an explanation as to how the attainment of the highest qualification is distributed across society; and it comes to the conclusion with great certainty that –although the educational level of the previous generation is a powerful impact factor in this question– there are certain factors that have been left unconsidered so far. Of those, we have already drawn attention to the structural and cultural characteristics of the context of religion (Pusztai 2009). It is a classic idea that religiosity in itself can be beneficial to social mobility (Riesman 1983, Weber 2001), but empirical evidence has been sought ever since by a whole range of analyses, some of which claim that academic success is promoted by religious practice, while others hold the view that it undermines high achievement (c.f. Pusztai 2009).

The majority of researchers can detect the impact of individual and communal religious practice on academic work, aspirations towards further studies and the individual's subsequent social status, and several of them claim that it serves to compensate for the lack of cultural capital in the family (Darnell and Sherkat 1997, Lehrer 1999, Regnerus 2000, Loury 2004). There are various interpretations as to the working mechanism of the impact of religious practice on one's academic career. The question is whether the correlation is direct or indirect. To put it more precisely, religiosity results in an attitude that helps achievement, and what we want to know is whether this attitude embodies a central and organic component of religiosity, for example, conscientiousness, or simply a particular side-effect of a religious upbringing, for example, respect for authority (Iannaccone 1998). Some think that religiosity and academic success have a common root, which has to do with obedience or, in other words, the ability to cooperate, a typical feature of religious communities. As for descriptions of the working mechanism, we have found the following alternatives the most interesting: firstly, the impact of religious practice may manifest itself, owing to personal contemporary relationship networks, as contemporary group pressure (Sewell et al. 1969, Darnell and Sherkat 1997), serving as a condition of cooperation with religious friends. Secondly, through the cognitive dimension of religion, value preferences and norms exert a direct influence on the individual's everyday decisions, as well as crucial decisions concerning school (Lehrer 2006).

Thirdly, religion can influence one's decisions on education through one's attitude to work, family and the like, as a consequence of decisions taken in these areas (Lehrer 2006). It can also provide security for disadvantaged pupils, easing the acculturation shock caused by the school and the stress caused by a lack of success (Clark and Lelkes 2005).

Religiosity in Higher Education

Since Newcomb's Bennington College study, we have suspected that the years spent in higher education are the formative ones with respect to the shaping of an individual's way of thinking, and political and religious views. Recent research has proved that these are the years which –depending on the institutional environment– bring about more or less decisive spiritual changes (Feldman–Newcomb, 1969, Schreiner 2000, Morris et al. 2003, Astin et al. 2011). Lately, higher education research has devoted special attention to religious students from another point of view. They have been identified as a special risk group, along with other minority student groups, family providers or students from low-status families. What these so called non-traditional students have in common is that their integration into the social milieu of higher education is only partial (Spady 1970 Tinto 1993). A fact noteworthy not in itself but in terms of the range of studies which confirm the assumption that poorly integrated students lack ambition in terms of continuing their studies, are less attached to the institution, more uncertain in interpreting academic objectives and more likely to change institutions, drop out or become unsuccessful (Bean -Metzner 1985, Tinto 1993, Pascarella-Terenzini 2005, Reay et al. 2009).

Still, the question arises of whether the concept of student integration is absolutely valid in the culturally heterogeneous student society of the post-millennium years, where integration into the dominant student culture does not necessarily represent real support for everyone. In our most recent studies we have argued that external relationships can also produce the kind of commitments that support learning-related decisions, achieving academic objectives or even identification with the institution (Hurtado 2007, Pusztai 2011). When we look at non-traditional students' higher education careers, it is crucial to understand with whom students formulate their views on academic objectives and obligations.

Previously, we analysed the influence of religiosity on one's school career and confirmed the importance of religion-based relationship networks in promoting high achievement (Pusztai 2009). In the world of higher education identification with the institution's value system and objectives is a complicated issue. Partly because the dominating world view of higher education institutions, especially in our region, is secular, or rather anti-religious

(Berger 1999, Geiger 1985), and partly because unlike in primary and secondary education, where the teacher plays a greater role in manifesting the culture of the institution, a higher education student encounters it mainly in the interpretations offered by fellow-students. Given that until very recently the topic of religion was considered taboo in personal relationships with faculty –another typical feature of our region–, students have been driven by their need to discuss spiritual issues towards informal relationship networks, either inside or outside the institution. Meanwhile, as theories of higher education involvement and integration point out, they may become distanced from the majority of the student society, the dominant behaviour patterns of which are probably not fully acceptable to a religious young person. The distance can be further increased by different forms of time management and use of space. In this way, non-traditional students' integration and access to important academic information and assistance can be hindered (Mahaffey –Smith 2009).

As regards relational embeddedness, these students' systems of ties are multiplied by ties to a religious community or circle of friends. Membership of a religious community or denomination serves as a basis for a large number of friendships, which makes it possible for relationships to be grounded on the voluntariness of co-membership rather than institutional rationality. The probability that relationships will be organised along these lines is supported by the fact that religious students consider religious homophily very important not only in their earlier friendships but also in the ones they form during their university years (Stark et al. 1996). According to earlier research findings, the higher education embeddedness of students attached to religious communities can be classified into three types. The first type includes those who are helped by their embeddedness in a religious community to achieve academic success and are therefore respected by their fellow students; the second group cannot reconcile their views with the dominant culture of the academic and social milieu of the institution, therefore they become isolated and sooner or later they find they do not belong anywhere. The third type consists of students who belong to intolerant religious communities; they are usually very much excluded from student society (Sherkat 2007).

Some studies investigating the system of correlations between religiosity and integration into higher education examine church-run universities and colleges and introduce the dimension of spiritual integration alongside the social and academic aspects (Morris et al. 2003). Students are spiritually integrated if they perceive that the institution contributes to their spiritual fulfilment, they can discuss ideological issues with their peers and lecturers, and their spiritual and academic development, scientific way of thinking and professional anticipations form a harmonious whole (Schreiner 2000,

Morris et al. 2003). Since during our research over the past few years we have found that the higher educational integration of students belonging to religion-based communities produced special features such as a stronger attachment to traditional academic values, in the present study we will try to find out to what extent religious students' social status and extra-institutional relationships influence their integration into higher education and academic advancement.

Integration into the Interpretive Communities of Higher Education

We interpreted the question of students' institutional embeddedness on the basis of the constructivist interpretation of community and Coleman's theory of social capital. We set out from a previous research finding, namely that an individual's school career is significantly influenced by the relationship network structures of student communities, the content of the information, values and norms conveyed by the networks and the relationship of that content to institutional goals. Both Coleman and Tinto concluded that the most efficient institutions are the ones that rely on cultural communities that are closed both formally and in content (Coleman 1988, Tinto 1993). Obviously, this does not apply to the world of higher education; yet student relationship networks play an outstandingly important role. After the constructivist turn, which made social sciences re-interpret the old concept of community, attention has been centred, on the basis of the intersubjective nature of knowledge, around members' joint creation of meaning and, moreover, the individual construction of the community's boundaries (Berger–Luckmann 1966). Cohesion within interpretive communities, which come into being as products of organisational homophily and professional socialisation, is provided by the network of meanings (Becher 1989, Fish 1980, Geertz 1973).

In our interpretation, students' relationships form a network that surrounds the individual and creates and uses more or less congruent meanings. The most suitable concept to represent this network is one used in other disciplines as well, namely the interpretive community. We wanted to know whether there are any differences between student groups with strong outside ties in terms of how much their integration into higher education, interpretation of academic goals and employment are helped or hindered by their surrounding interpretive communities (Pusztai 2011). Although voluntary membership in organisations and religious circles are usually described as social capital enhancing the chances of success and resources of communal supportive power (Coleman–Hoffer 1987), students belonging to minority religious groups or denominations still count as endangered regarding social integration into the campus (Mahaffey–Smith 2009). It was students with non-Judeo-Christian religious roots who have drawn attention to religious diversity among students.

Recently, surveys have produced three essential results. Firstly, the student population has been showing an increasing interest in spirituality; secondly, growing religious diversity has been also characteristic of higher education together with its various combinations with ethnic multiplicity, and thirdly, isolation for religious reasons is quite common in higher education (Astin et al. 2003, Mahaffey–Smith 2009).

Data and Variables

Our present analysis is based on the empirical results of the survey conducted among the first students pursuing their bachelor and master studies after the organisational restructuring of higher education.[32] Our data was collected in Hungarian-language institutions in the border region of Hungary, Romania and Ukraine in 2008. A representative sample of third-year bachelor students was taken at each faculty of the following institutions: the University of Debrecen, the College of Nyíregyháza, Ferenc Kölcsey Teacher Training College of the Reformed Church, Partium Christian University, the University of Oradea, the Satu Mare Extension of Babes-Bolyai University (both in Romania) and the Ferenc Rákóczi II. Transcarpathian Institute in Berehove, Ukraine. The sample size was proportionate to the number of students at each faculty. As we did not have a complete list of final-year bachelor students, we used group sampling, surveying randomly chosen seminar groups (N=1399). In spring 2010 we surveyed students starting their master's studies in the same institutions. According to the data provided by the institutions, the full population was about 900 students, and with the sample covering two thirds of the target population the final sample size was 602. In order for the sample to be representative by faculties we used weighting. Our research team has presented the overall goals and partial results in several studies (Kozma–Ceglédi 2010, Pusztai 2011). Our research has shown that although the surveyed area crosses borders, its higher education constitutes a unified system as regards student advancement in the multi-cycle system of higher education. Free movement across borders has allowed centuries-long traditions to revive.

The measurement of religiosity is precise only if it reflects its multidimensional character. The trends of the past decades have shown that the intensity of religiosity can be entirely different in the different dimensions. It is difficult to compare the importance of the various dimensions, but there is

---

32 The Impact of Tertiary Education on Regional Development survey was supported by OTKA T-69160.

no doubt that owing to the individualisation of religion people create a kind of easy-to-use religiosity tailored to their personal needs, so personal religious practice seems to be a highly influential dimension. We also consider it vital to examine attachment to larger and smaller communities, because these indicators are sensitive to changing patterns in the embeddedness of relationships. According to our earlier research findings, having a religious circle of friends has proved to be a very efficient incentive to achievement, providing the individual with resources they would otherwise be lacking in.

We decided to examine the above factors because we wanted to know whether they promote students' relational (structural) and cultural embeddedness in the society of the institution. The details on the conceptualisation and operationalisation of the latter concepts were presented in our earlier work (Pusztai 2011). The concept of embeddedness, originating in the sociology of economics, is an important constituent of Coleman's (1988) theory of social capital. It denotes the extent and quality of the individual's involvement in their personal relationship networks and extended social milieu. Based on Granovetter's concept (1985), we examined students' relational embeddedness in several dimensions (the orientation and multiplexity of inter- and intragenerational relationships in HE, intra- and extra-institutional social activities), and, treating them as vectors of centrifugal or centripetal forces, we typified the connections of students' personal relationships and activities with the society of the institution (relational embeddedness). In addition, our research also focused on students' choices between dominant academic goals, value systems and behaviour patterns in their institutional environment (cultural embeddedness). This dimension is represented by two factors in the present analysis, namely academically valuable interpretation of higher education goals and willingness to do self-motivated extracurricular work.

The Confessional and Religious Landscape

Religiosity is a multidimensional phenomenon, and its thorough investigation is obviously important. Although we can differentiate five dimensions of religiosity (practice, ideology, knowledge, experience and consequences), we usually classify the types of religiosity only according to personal and community factors (Glock-Stark 1968). However, it is very interesting to compare the data measured in different religious dimensions, especially the first four dimensions, and everyday life behaviour. If we interpret voluntary actions as a potential consequential dimension of religiosity, consequences in day to day life can be strongly consequent or inconsequent with practice dimensions. Obviously, this depends on the cultural and contextual norms acquired both in the family and the wider community. In this paper we wish to investigate the association between religious practice and the voluntary work consequences of religiosity among Central and Eastern European students twenty years after the collapse of the communist states. Considering religious affiliation, the first issue is confessional identity. Based on the recent research on the sociology of religion we can state that Euro-secularism characterizes post-communist countries in a different way than western European societies (Zulehner et al. 2008). Some of them are considered the most religious countries in Europe, e.g. Romania. Researchers have found various alternative explanations for this situation, one of them based on the confessional landscape. There is no doubt that the fundamentally mono-confessional blocks of Europe have been replaced by the broadest and most manifold multi-confessional belt here: Catholics, Protestants, Orthodox believers and also southern Muslims live close to each other. Ethnic and confessional factors are interrelated in multi-confessional and multi-ethnic states and religiosity is stronger in those regions where confessional affiliation functions as a central component of identity. As for the confessional landscape of the Central Eastern European region, it is supposed to be an influential factor within the present religious setting. Secularization has been more intensive in partly mono-confessional Protestant countries, and the proportion of religious Protestants has declined. The most secularized culture is displayed in the former provinces of East Germany and in the Czech Republic. Although according to the supply-side theory, confessional pluralism stimulates religiosity, some researchers consider confessional diversity the weak point of resistance to state-facilitated secularization because in this situation the representatives of the state-party made effective use of "divide et impera" tactics. Indeed, this worked very efficiently in Hungary.

According to the latest international comparative studies, Romania is the most religious country in Europe. It is a multi-ethnic and multi-confessional state, but obviously the regional differences are very striking. Orthodoxy is very dominant in the eastern and southern part of country. Compared to western Christianity, Orthodox religiosity seems to be more stable and stronger in religious practice. The Orthodox churches have traditionally had stronger ties with the state than Roman Catholics and Protestants in central Europe, but we do not have enough research findings on their role during the communist period. The ideological dimension of Orthodox religiosity is more traditional, with established institutions of public religiosity. As for the balance of religious knowledge and experience, we can state, that the emotional dimension is more important in Orthodox communities than intellectual thought, suspicions and reflexive analysis as e.g. in some protestant confessions. As for the consequences, we have a limited amount of information in comparison, only Tomka revealed a lower level of satisfaction with political transformation and democracy (Tomka 2005). What seems to be a highly marked characteristic is the unity of the religious community in belonging to a church and a very strong homogeneous religious practice in all social strata and age groups (Tomka 2005). The north-western part of the country (including the region under investigation) is a multi-confessional and multi-ethnic region, and it seemed to be more religious than other Central European areas.

After the Communist takeover different world views and ways of thinking, in particular faith-based world views, were declared to be a dangerous enemy of communism in Hungary, too. Religious education went on within the parishes, but it could attract only very few children. People who were affiliated to any of the religious communities became stigmatized and a number of clergymen who attempted to organize activities for young people or small communities were harassed. While various forms of indoctrination and persecution continued until the 1990s, the so-called soft dictatorship brought about a much more substantial religious change in Hungary. It contributed to an unambiguous religious revival after 1978 (Tomka 1999), and paved the way for "a reflex-like crude individualism aiming at the accumulation of material wealth and survival" (Hankiss 1986). Recently, more than half of the Hungarian population can be described as religious in their own way, one sixth as strongly affiliated with churches, and another sixth as atheist. However, several studies have shown that the basic indicators of social status were very strongly and negatively interrelated with religiosity.

In the western part of Romania and Ukraine there have been compact indigenous Hungarian ethnic minorities since 1920. Although this region is characterized by a significant Protestantism among Hungarians there is a significant gap within levels of religiosity among ethnic Hungarians and those in the home-country. This can probably be explained by their plural religious context. Until recently, religion has been one of the pillars of ethnic Hungarians' national identity in the reviving Orthodox context in Romania and in Ukraine.

Essential Dimensions of Student Religiosity

In the particular tripartite structure of the religiosity of Hungarian society, church-going religiosity (people who practice their religion within a church) and non-religiosity are two smaller groups of about the same size. Almost every second person claims to be religious in their own way (Tomka 1991). Essentially the same classification applies to young people as well. Tomka observed that the basic indicators of social status are very strongly but negatively interrelated with religiosity; however, in recent years the tendency seems to have weakened with respect to the frequency of churchgoing. For example, the most highly qualified people (with university degrees) follow the same path as the least qualified people. Among young people, highly qualified parents are already over-represented at both ends of the scale, and practising young church members come from not only more educated but also economically higher-status backgrounds, especially in big cities (Rosta-Tomka 2010). Young people increasingly practice their religion in small communities, which often exceeds or even replaces their practice in the large community. All research done among young people unanimously suggests that religion-based voluntary membership is by far the most popular organized activity among young people, even more popular than sports activities (Pusztai 2009). There are considerable differences between ethnic Hungarian and within-Hungary religiosity, as more of those in the minority communities practice religiosity (Pusztai 2011).

Three quarters of the surveyed students claim to belong to a denomination. In comparison to national data this is a very characteristic feature, which, in the light of theories that tend to offer macro-level explanations, might also be attributed to denominational diversity, the free and conscious choices after the fall of the political system which forced a totalitarian ideology, or the superficial traditional cultural presence of socialist modernisation which left the deep structure of society untouched (Iannaccone 1991). In addition, because of the multi-ethnic political formations of the region, the functions of religious identity are extended by its relationship to national and religious identities (Titarenko 2007, Doktór 2007). However, we do not intend to take a stand on the plausibility of the above alternatives or simultaneously valid explanations in the present study.

As our earlier regional studies reveal, the region is in a peculiar position as far as its denominational composition is concerned, as it is one of the multiconfessional areas in Europe, a continent which is primarily made up of blocks dominated by a single confession. In the Hungarian-language sample the region's multi-confessional nature is reflected in the proportion of Greek Catholics and Protestants, which is higher than the average of the region's countries, and other denominations are also well represented among university students. Over one third of the student sample (using Hungarian as the language of education) presented here are Reformed and only slightly more than a fifth are Roman Catholic. Every sixth or seventh student belongs to some other denomination. The denominational composition of the region is markedly different from that of other regions. Given that this is a region traditionally dominated by the Reformed Church, it is not surprising that a large number of students belong to this denomination at the institutions in the catchment area of the Reformed College and the University of Debrecen, which was intended to have a definitely Reformed spirituality at the time of its foundation in the early 20th century. It is also widely known that this region is the stronghold of the Greek Catholic community. Further typical regional features are that, unlike elsewhere, denominational identity plays a major role in students' self-identification, and cultural diversity is one of the key factors strengthening the extraordinary multiplicity of student society (Jancsák 2012).

Table 33: Denominational distribution of students among bachelor and master students

	Bachelor studies (2008)	Master studies (2010)
Reformed	33.5%	35.4%
Roman Catholic	22.7%	22.3%
Greek Catholic	11.2%	8.0%
Lutheran	2.1%	1.7%
Other	2.4%	2.8%
Refused to answer	10.4%	8.8%
Does not belong to a denomination	17.6%	21.1%
N=	1211	602

Source: The Role of Tertiary Education in Social and Economic Transformation: Bachelor Students (2008) and Master Students (2010).

As far as students' self-categorisation is concerned, at least every second respondent claims to be religious in their own way and about 16–18% claim to be practising church members, which suggests a stronger religious affiliation than the results of recent surveys. Furthermore, the proportion of those who definitely claim to be non-religious is also below the national figure (Hámori-Rosta 2013). Taking various religiosity indicators into account, it is clear that students with a personal religious practice make up about 40% of the entire student population (43.3% in bachelor, 39% in master programmes), which indicates the existence of student groups with strong and stable spiritual needs. More than half of the bachelor students (25.1% of the entire student population) and three fourths of master students (31.3% of the entire student population) are regular churchgoers. Compared to the popularity of membership in other voluntary groups, it is notable that 17.3% of bachelor students and 25.5% of master students are involved in small communities.

It is noteworthy that when we compare the two phases of university studies, personal religious practice shows a slight decline, but membership in smaller or larger religious communities increases. Education researchers examining the impact of institutions and institutional context pay special

200

attention to the changes taking place during the years spent in higher education. In our sample, apart from religious practice in communities (small or large), the tendency to have one or more religious friends shows a significant growth (from 60% to 74%) as students study on master's courses. In accordance with international, national and earlier regional findings, growing into adulthood means growing religiosity in our sample as well (Tomka 2010, Hámori-Rosta 2013). The increasing proportion of regular churchgoers, small community members and students having religious friends leads us to the conclusion that in terms of relationship-dependent religiosity indicators there is a clear positive shift during the higher education years (Pusztai 2009).

Social Background and Religiosity

In the last quarter of the 20th century basic indicators of social status had a strong and negative correlation with religiosity, but this seems to have been losing significance among high-status young people in Hungary during the past decades (Tomka 2010, Rosta 2010). In our sample, which is composed of students whose social status is on the whole less favourable than the Hungarian average in higher education, both practising church members and those who are religious in their own way have a lower than average status. Whereas in the case of bachelor students both their personal and communal religious practice are in inverse proportion to their parents' level of education, in the case of master students there is a strong -but not linear correlation- only with respect to churchgoing: the least active are the children of parents with higher education degrees and the most active are the children of parents with a secondary education. As for other indicators, among bachelor students the number of those who define themselves as non-religious, do not pray and have parents with higher education degrees is higher than expected in a random distribution, while among master students it is those who have both personal and communal religious practice and parents with secondary education who stand out. Neither activity in small communities nor having religious friends shows any correlation with the level of parental education in either phase. However, there is a significant correlation between the type of settlement students come from and each indicator of religiosity: religiosity is the least frequent among students from big cities and the most frequent among students from small places. It is to be noted that in this region the settlement type of a student's permanent place of residence serves as a powerful indicator of family status, as the composition of the student population is not very heterogeneous in terms of the parents' level of education (multi-cycle institutions are particularly dominated by students whose parents have secondary education), therefore in this milieu the type of settlement is a more powerful factor of inequality.

As we can see, students who claim to be religious are under-represented among the children of highly qualified parents and residents of high-status settlements; nor did the analysis of further indicators of individual and communal religious practice contradict this empirical finding. That is to say, religious students can be regarded as a group whose status is lower than average and which is strongly attracted towards outside ties purely because of their attachment to religion-based small or large communities. In this sense, according to the theory of student integration, they count as a high-risk group regarding socialisation in higher education and academic achievement. We tried to find out whether religious students were really weakly integrated.

Relational Embeddedness

We established a set of categories to classify student's relational embeddedness. Moving from the highest level of intergenerational integration to the highest level of isolation we used the terms intergenerational, widely intragenerational, narrowly intragenerational and isolated for bachelor students and strongly intergenerational, autonomous intergenerational, widely intragenerational and isolated for master students (Pusztai 2011).

Looking at the correlation between religiosity and embeddedness, we found that in spite of their unfavourable social status and relationships outside the world of higher education religious students are one of the most integrated groups at both phases. In the bachelor phase, students regularly practising in a large community (i.e. going to church at least a few times a month) are over-represented among intergenerationally embedded students, who are linked to the society of the institution in the most numerous ways. The widely intragenerational type contains practising students in the same proportion as the full sample, whereas among students with limited or no ties to the society of higher education there are far fewer practising individuals. On the whole, belonging to an extra-campus relationship network does not weaken, but strengthens bachelor students' embeddedness in higher education.

Religiosity indicators show distinctive patterns among master students as well. Among students with communal religious practice, those who, both in the communal and individual dimensions of religious practice, are strongly and in numerous ways integrated into the intergenerational social milieu of the institution are over-represented. The more autonomous individuals, who maintain stable intergenerational relationships only in their academic and research tasks, practise religion more intensely than the average, and students with personal religious practice are even over-represented among them, but their communal religious activity does not stand out as much as that of the previous group. Narrowly intragenerational students, who organise themselves into very closed twos or threes, primarily in order to cope with their studies together, are not essentially religious either in the communal or the individual dimension. As for isolated students, not only are the majority far from being religious in any respect, most of them do not have religious friends, either.

Table 34: Students' embeddedness in campus society by various dimensions of religious practice among bachelor students, percentage

Embeddedness in campus community		Intergene-rationally embedded	Widely intragenera-tional	Narrowly intragenera-tional	Isolated
Religious practice in a local community	Yes	**33.4%*****	23.0%	14.0%	18.2%
	No	66.6%	77.0%	**86.0%*****	81.8%
Religious practice in a small community	Yes	**26.7%*****	19.2%	10.7%	12.8%
	No	73.3%	80.8%	**89.3%*****	87.2%
Personal religious practice	Yes	**53.4%*****	44.2%	37.0%	37.8%
	No	46.6%	55.8%	**63.0%*****	62.2%
Religious friend	Yes	**73.3%*****	65.3%	57.3%	33.1%
	No	22.8%	33.2%	40.0%	**56.3%*****
N=		265	341	457	148

Source: The Role of Tertiary Education in Social and Economic Transformation: Bachelor Students (2008). The underlined figures indicate that the percentage in the given cell is higher than expected in a random distribution. A cell is marked with asterisks where the correlation is significant. Level of significance: *** =0.000.

Table 35: Students' embeddedness in campus society by various dimensions of religious practice among Master students, percentage

Embeddedness in campus community		Strongly intergene-rational	Autono-mous intergene-rational	Widely intragene-rational	Isolated
Religious practice in a local community	Yes	**51.5%*****	28.8%	18.2%	17.7%
	No	48.5%	71.2%	**81.8%*****	**82.3%*****
Religious practice in a small community	Yes	**46.6%*****	24.9%	20.0%	8.5%
	No	53.4%	75.1%	**80.0%*****	**91.5%*****
Personal religious practice	Yes	**60.6%*****	**45.9%*****	27.1%	24.0%
	No	39.4%	54.1%	**72.9%*****	**76.0%*****

Embeddedness in campus community		Strongly intergene-rational	Autono-mous intergene-rational	Widely intragene-rational	Isolated
Religious friend	Yes	<u>94.7%</u>***	68.8%	74.0%	44.8%
	No	5.3%	31.2%	26.0%	<u>55.2%</u>***
N=		131	169	180	94

Source: The Role of Tertiary Education in Social and Economic Transformation: Master Students (2010). The underlined figures indicate that the percentage in the given cell is higher than expected in a random distribution. A cell is marked with asterisks where the correlation is significant. Level of significance: *** =.000.

Looking at the correlation between embeddedness in campus society and students' religiosity, we must underline that although religious students' social status is lower and their religious relationship networks tend to draw them out of the institution, they still seem to be able to integrate into the academic and social context of the institution even more than their peers who do not have personal or communal religious practice and religious friends. Everything suggests that religion-based relationship networks function as interpretive communities which, far from distancing students from the community of the institution, help them get closer to it.

Cultural Embeddedness in Higher Education

In this section we will be examining two factors of cultural embeddedness in terms of their relationship with religiosity, namely the interpretation of the goals of higher education and the attitude to self-motivated learning.

We tried to find a correlation between students' ideas of the goals of their higher education and the four surveyed dimensions of religiosity. During our earlier research, when searching for the main components of the motives of entering higher education, we found that in the bachelor phase the major factors are obtaining knowledge and prestige, the attraction of student life and the hope for the family's social advancement. In the master phase, besides the first three factors mentioned above there is a fourth one: searching for one's place as a goal of tertiary studies, trying to find out what one has a talent for.

The various factors in this research change together with various religiosity indicators to a great extent, especially among bachelor students. In the first phase of studies there is a strong and significant correlation between being religious (in terms of all dimensions of religiosity) and the wish to increase one's knowledge. This goal is markedly typical of students with communal religious practice. Among master students, learning and obtaining knowledge both play a greater role among practising students, but the difference between groups is no longer significant in every dimension. Still, it is noteworthy that it is students with personal religious practice for whom this motivation is the most popular. During their bachelor's studies, religious students are significantly less motivated by the prospect by postponing the start of their working lives and the attraction of student life, whereas during the master years there is not much difference in this respect. Finally, according to our data, students who are religious in the personal sense or practice religion in a small or a large community, do not differ from the average at either phase as to whether they pursue their studies in order to get a high-prestige job or to help the advancement of the family.

It may seem paradoxical that the vast majority of practising students identify with the traditionally acknowledged and manifest goals of higher education such as obtaining knowledge, as few of them have inherited any higher-education experience from previous generations. Still, we have already encountered the phenomenon that students who practise their religion hold school and academic work in higher esteem than the children of highly qualified parents (Pusztai 2009).The question of which dimension of religious practice has the most powerful impact on one's interpretation of higher education goals also deserves attention. The least influential dimension is having a religious friend, the distinguishing force of which is actually diminishing, implying that the power of a religious interpretive community exceeds the influence of one or two religious friends.

Belonging to a community, especially a small one, is what creates considerable differences among bachelor students, whereas in the master years the influence of the community decreases, with the influence of personal practice not only continuing to exist but also increasing. We can perhaps illustrate this with the model of the age-specific utilisation of the social capital typical of closed networks based on redundancy of values and norms (Burt 2000). This suggests that the dissemination of information in a closed relationship network has a stronger impact on younger age groups than older ones.

Table 36: Interpretation of the goals of higher education studies by the different dimensions of religious practice among bachelor students, averages of weighted factor scores

		pursuit of knowledge	student life	obtaining prestige	social advancement
Religious practice in a local community	Yes	**15.0***	-25.8	3.2	-2.6
	No	-8.4	**4.0****	0.8	-2.7
Religious practice in a small community	Yes	**27.0***	-20.5	2.6	-8.9
	No	-9.7	**1.2****	1.0	-1.4

		pursuit of knowledge	student life	obtaining prestige	social advancement
Personal religious practice	Yes	**5.7***	-12.4	0.8	-.2
	No	-10.1	**5.0***	1.7	-4.6
Religious friend	Yes	**3.5***	-3.7	-2.9	-9.4
	No	-13.8	-.8	8.0	**7.8****

Source: The Role of Tertiary Education in Social and Economic Transformation: Bachelor Students (2008). The underlined figures indicate that the percentage in the given cell is higher than expected in a random distribution. A cell is marked with asterisks where the correlation is significant. Level of significance: *** =.000, **< 0.03.

Table 37: Interpretation of the goals of higher education studies by the different dimensions of religious practice among master students, averages of weighted factor scores

		pursuit of knowledge	student life	obtaining prestige	social advancement
Religious practice in a local community	Yes	8.9	5.6	4.2	-2.3
	No	-3.5	-2.2	-1.6	0.9
Religious practice in a small community	Yes	2.1	7.5	-5.3	-3.3
	No	-1.0	-2.2	2.0	1.4
Personal religious practice	Yes	**13.6****	-5.2	1.4	-7.0
	No	-8.7	3.3	-.9	4.5
Religious friend	Yes	3.0	-3.2	1.9	-2.0
	No	-7.8	8.3	-4.8	5.1

Source: The Role of Tertiary Education in Social and Economic Transformation: Master Students (2010). The underlined figures indicate that the percentage in the given cell is higher than expected in a random distribution. A cell is marked with asterisks where the correlation is significant. Level of significance: *** =.000, **< 0.03.

Extracurricular Student Activity

Undertaking voluntary academic tasks is quite rare among students, as most of them think there is no use making any effort apart from compulsory profitable activities that are rewarded with credits or a student grant increase and are prescribed by the curriculum and exam regulations.

We distinguished between two essential types of non-compulsory work during our factor analysis on an item series of tasks. One includes activities that encourage students to compete with their peers and stand out from among them, whereas the other is based on cooperation with faculty. The voluntary activity type based on students' competition with one another in academic or research areas, so-called intragenerational competition, includes winning a Fellowship granted by the Republic, membership of special colleges or talent programmes and being appointed year or group representative. The term intergenerational cooperation implies intensive professional cooperation between students and faculty and indicates students' interest in academic organisational embeddedness. Activities include contribution to the research carried out in the department or institute, research team membership, participation in national or international research, writing student conference papers, publication and working as a teaching assistant.

When we tried to find out how low-status or middle-class students could be mobilised en masse to perform such tasks, the level of parents' education did not prove to be a clear determinant in relation to these large-scale extracurricular commitments. It was only in bachelor students' intragenerational competition-related activities that we detected slightly more significant activity among the children of highly educated parents. Otherwise, our data even revealed that during bachelor studies, commitment to voluntary tasks is more closely linked to low settlement status, but the correlation is no longer significant during master studies (Pusztai 2011, Fényes-Pusztai 2012).

Voluntary tasks related to intergenerational cooperation show no significant correlation with categories of religious self-identification in either phase of higher education. However, bachelor students' intragenerational competition does: the non-religious end of the scale is under-represented, while the others perform better. As for master students, it is practising church members who are the most active.

Regarding other dimensions of religious practice, they show an unambiguously strong correlation with self-imposed extracurricular work in the master's phase. As for the bachelor's phase, the correlation exists only in intragenerational competition. No dimension of religiosity helps or hinders the activities based on cooperation with faculty, but practising students do far better at tasks related to intragenerational competition. The difference is greater between the two opposite groups regarding personal religious practice, and membership of a small or large community also has a marked influence on the willingness to undertake extra work. The close connection between religiosity and extracurricular activity is a general phenomenon in the master phase, so it seems any indicator of religious practice can promote willingness to do extra work both among students competing with their contemporaries and those cooperating with their lecturers. Apart from there being a more balanced relationship between the two sets of extracurricular activities in master studies, membership in a community seems to be a more powerful separating factor than personal religious practice.

Table 38: Participation in voluntary student activities by the different dimensions of religious practice among bachelor and master students, averages of weighted factor scores

		Bachelor Studies (2008)		Master Studies (2010)	
		Intergenerational cooperation	*Intragenerational competition*	*Intergenerational cooperation*	*Intragenerational competition*
Religious practice in a local community	Yes	4.7	**<u>48.7</u>*****	**<u>12.3</u>****	**<u>17.7</u>****
	No	0.7	34.6	-10.5	-5.2
Religious practice in a small community	Yes	2.9	<u>47.7</u>**	**<u>13.1</u>****	**<u>21.6</u>****
	No	1.3	35.6	-10.0	-6.0
Personal religious practice	Yes	3.5	<u>44.2</u>***	**<u>6.1</u>***	**<u>11.6</u>***
	No	0.0	32.3	-10.5	-5.4
Religious friend	Yes	2.5	<u>40.3</u>*	-3.0	5.4
	No	0.2	33.4	-6.8	-9.4

Source: The Role of Tertiary Education in Social and Economic Transformation: Bachelor Students (2008), Master Students (2010). The underlined figures indicate that the percentage in the given cell is higher than expected in a random distribution. A cell is marked with asterisks where the correlation is significant. Level of significance: *** =.000, **< 0.03, **< 0.05.

Reasons for Doing Extracurricular Work

In the last section of our paper we attempt to compare demographic factors and indicators of family status with indicators of religiosity with respect to their impact on willingness to undertake extracurricular work. As we also wanted to know whether the inclusion of religiosity as a factor modifies the impact of the other factors, we created two-step models.

During our analysis we learnt that of the demographic and social status indicators it is mature student age and father's university degree that have the most important influence on bachelor students' extracurricular activities based on intragenerational competition. In the second step, after including various indicators of religiosity, we found that it is regular religious practice in a large community that has the most significant impact. It is remarkable that its appearance among the indicators reduces the influence of mature age; yet it does not reduce, in fact it even slightly increases, the influence of father with a degree. That leads us to the conclusion that the older students in our sample must practise their religion in larger numbers, unlike the children of highly qualified fathers, as the influence of that factor does not typically decrease. Therefore it is likely that one group of bachelor students doing competitive extra work has highly qualified fathers, whereas the other practises religion and has fathers without a degree. On the whole, willingness to do competitive extracurricular work is promoted by religious practice in a large community more significantly than by other indicators of religious practice.

As for bachelor students' extracurricular work based on intergenerational cooperation, in the first stage it was determined by a demographic factor: male students were definitely more motivated in this respect than female students. The inclusion of the indicator of communal religious practice reinforced the impact of sex even further, so it can be stated that neither social status nor religious practice enhance the chance of intergenerational cooperation. As we pointed out in another study, there are other elements of the institutional context that may have a major influence on extracurricular work based on intergenerational cooperation (Pusztai 2011).

Table 39: Comparison of demographic, status and religious factors supporting bachelor students' willingness to do extracurricular work, odds ratios (Exp (B) values)

	Intragenerational competition		Intergenerational cooperation	
	1	2	1	2
Male	.940	.979	1.343*	1.361**
Older student	1.950**	1.740*	.676	.650
Father with a degree	1.974**	1.986**	1.203	1.203
Mother with a degree	.873	.886	1.157	1.164
Residence in a city	1.004	1.047	.793	.803
Religious practice in community		1.797***		1.216
Constant	.536***	.457**	.652**	.620***
Reduction of -2LL	-1.6%	-2.6%	-0.9%	-1.1%

Source: The Role of Tertiary Education in Social and Economic Transformation: Bachelor Students (2008), Master Students (2010). The significance of Wald statistics ***: $p<0.001$, **: $p<0.01$, *: $p<0.05$. The fit of the models is indicated by the decrease of the -2*loglikelihood value in percentage terms.

In contrast, none of the demographic and status indicators show any correlation with competition-based voluntary work among master students. This may be due to the fact that the region's higher education is becoming more and more homogeneous with respect to social status, especially as we move upwards in the multi-cycle system. This is how the institutional selection that started with selective two-directional migration[33] will be completed

---

33 The phenomenon of two-directional selective migration was specified by our research team during the analysis of data from a regional university. We discovered

(Szemerszki 2010, Ceglédi-Nyüsti 2012). Personal religious practice has an even greater impact on undertaking competition-based extracurricular work than religious practice in a large community.

As regards cooperation with faculty, master students do not generally seem to gain any advantage from being male, older than average, or children of highly qualified fathers. Our detailed analysis proves that the chance of cooperation with faculty is greatly enhanced by regular religious practice in a large community, and even more so by personal religious practice, as was already suggested by the two-variable analysis. The conclusion is that the role of religion as a factor promoting extracurricular work is much more comprehensive and significant in the master than in the bachelor phase.

Table 40: Factors supporting master students' willingness to do extracurricular work, odds ratios (Exp (B) values)

	Intragenerational competition		Intergenerational cooperation	
	1	2	1	2
Male	1.097	1.168	1.189	1.218
Age	.930	.912	1.323	1.248
Father with a degree	1.409	1.404	1.342	1.366
Mother with a degree	.842	.874	.852	.887
Residence in a big city	.881	.918	.819	.890
Personal religious practice		1.572**		1.560**
Constant	.720**	.569***	.742*	.578**
Reduction of -2LL	-0.4%	-1.2%	-0.9%	-1.7%

Source: The Role of Tertiary Education in Social and Economic Transformation: Master Students (2010). The significance of Wald statistics ***: p<0.001, **: p<0.01, *: p<0.05. The fit of the models is indicated by the decrease of the -2*loglikelihood value in percentage terms.

By way of summary it can be stated that fathers' high qualifications have a strong impact on bachelor students' attitude to extra work in higher education. The analysis draws our attention to factors such as the various indicators of student religiosity, which in some cases have an impact approaching and in some cases surpassing that of parents' level of education. Although the explanatory power of our models is low, the aim of our analysis was not

---

that from the institution's catchment area upper-middle class young people go to universities in the capital, low-status students choose a college in the country, so the region's central university is left with quite a homogeneous (lower) middle class student population.

to improve it, as we had already pointed out that students' attitude towards extra work is influenced to a great extent by the social context of the institution and the behaviour patterns of the faculty (Pusztai 2011).

Conclusion

The purpose of our analysis was to investigate the contradictions in the picture of religious students given by the literature. Firstly, in spite of recent changes, what is still meant by the correlation between religiosity and social status is that practising students have low status, and secondly, because of their attachment to their religious communities, the international literature usually lists them among risk groups for low achievement and attrition.

Although the social position of religious students in Hungary has recently changed for the better, we have come to the conclusion that the multi-confessional student population we surveyed in the border region shows a trend towards increased religious practice, and a more marked spiritual orientation, but less favourable social status. Therefore, we considered it fully justified to examine their relational and cultural embeddedness in higher education in order to find out whether their academic careers are helped or hindered by the religious interpretive community.

Our analysis of relational embeddedness has led us to the conclusion that contrary to expectations, students belonging to religious communities are among the most strongly and intergenerationally integrated students; that is to say, their religion-based relationship networks do not draw them out of the institution, but instead, they are the most successful in integration into the academic and social community of the institution.

As for cultural embeddedness, religious students are highly committed to participating in higher education with the objective of enriching their knowledge, and this interpretation, which enhances achievement, is supported by all dimensions of religiosity. Community membership, especially membership of a small community, is a supporting factor mainly in the bachelor phase, whereas among master students the influence of communities decreases and that of personal religious practice increases. We found it useful to examine the impact of religiosity indicators not only in the interpretation of objectives but also in various extracurricular tasks undertaken by students. Among bachelor students, religiosity supported only one extracurricular activity, namely extra work based on competition with contemporaries, but among master students it seemed to support both types of extra student work.

As we were primarily interested in knowing whether any indicator of religious practice is capable of compensating for family status indicators, we constructed a multi-variable regression model to examine what factors promote extracurricular student work done in order to acquire knowledge. We came to the conclusion that religious factors do increase the chance of this happening at certain points. Among indicators of religious practice it is practice in a large community that acts as an impetus in most senses, since this is already able to help students to take part in competitive extracurricular activities in their bachelor years. Later, inspiration is generally provided by belonging to a community, and the chance of cooperating with faculty is enhanced even further by personal religious practice.

The diversity of campus environments

Abstract

The current trends in higher education largely consist of homogenization at both national and international levels, while at the same time we are also witnessing major structural, programme and reputational diversification (Hrubos 2012). The institutions themselves and their units are now largely different, but the system is not only arranged into a hierarchical order in terms of gradual differences, as the compilers of various lists of colleges and universities tend to believe, but also by serious nominal differences, which necessitate an urgent examination of regional and institutional differences. In our research we introduce the concept of social capital, which has enriched our knowledge related to the institutional diversity of higher education (Pusztai 2011). While previously we concentrated primarily on the heterogeneity of the relational and cultural integration of the students, in this project we discuss as factors those elements of the institutional environment that exert a more or less powerful attraction on the individual. We intend to find out where institutional effects are rooted and how they are measured most effectively. In the study an attempt is made to survey the roots of institutional effects and their dimensions. Subsequently, we examine how institutional effects influence students, and finally we provide a portrait of typical institution types in a cross-border higher educational region.

The Socialization of Students and Institutional Effects

The issue of how entering into higher education and obtaining a degree affects an individual's career is well researched. The experts on the question pointed out early on that intra-institutional effects play an important role in this process (Feldman-Newcomb 1973, Astin 1993, Tinto 1993). As a result, a rich international literature emerged, and efforts have been made to summarize and systematize it in encyclopaedia-style publications (Pascarella-Terenzini 1991, 2005). Whether the effects which influence the students concerned should be regarded as intervention from the institutional side, or whether we regard its results as the natural reaction and development of students to the environment depends upon what concept we have created of the socialization of students in their respective higher educational environment.

Basically, there can be two approaches to institutional effects. In one, the institutional contribution is understood as the success of the institution in integrating the student into the culture of higher education. The other examines how the institution is able to follow and meet the varied needs of the heterogeneous student community. A few decades ago most researches believed in a one-way and linear reconstructional model of the socialization of the students. In the structuralist-functionalist interpretation, socialization used to mean that the student learned to live within the framework offered and determined by the institution. In this model, the end result of the process of socialization is a student fully integrated into the world of higher education, and their behaviour is what is expected from students. This approach tends to look at organizational role acquisition as a predominantly one-way process, since the starting student is converted into a full-fledged student under the pressure of the active institutional norms and sanctions. Educational publications and works by experts dealing with the macro-level phenomena of higher education still use this schematic and simplified approach, working with a uni-dimensional image of the student. In this approach the student is a uniformally predictable end-product.

The other version of the reconstructional socialization model uses the student's reconstruction of the indelible culture brought with them from their family as a starting point. In this approach, higher education is a means used by the elite to legitimize their power. Maintaining the elite is carried out in a meritocratic disguise. The students identified as excellent by the system are those who are, through their social status, close to institutional habits (Reay et al. 2001, Thomas 2002). The concept of institutional habits, based upon Bourdieu's works on the sociology of higher education, includes the influence of the dominant social or cultural group, which permeates the entire organization. The influence is relayed to the students by the actors and curriculum content of the institution, thus affecting the students' careers (Bourdieu 1988, Berger 2000, Reay et al. 2001, Thomas 2002). The situation in which the objective social structure is in harmony with the incorporated structure is described by Bourdieu as "the situation of the fish in the water." An institution, which is the guardian of high culture, tends to benefit students of higher status through such things as the contents of the curriculum, teaching practice, the choreography of exams and the by-laws of the institution, among others. Students of a lower social background are therefore exposed to a culture shock, as they find themselves in an environment different from those they are used to in their families, and are like fish on the shore (Reay et al. 2001, Thomas 2002).

The constructivist model of the socialization of students is radically different from the reconstructional one. In the former, the culture of the students is continually built up in the course of the interaction between the students and the other actors of the higher educational organization (Kiss 2008). One pole within the constructivist concept is based upon the symbolic interactionist tradition. This approach focuses on the momentary nature and situativity of the process of social bargaining, i.e., the student's socialization

214

(Huber 1991). In this concept we talk about the individual effects of the of the institution. The effects are, however, difficult even to estimate, since the sample is so fragmented that it is empirically unmanageable.

The active and constructive participation of the individual, the process of the socialization of students, the interaction between the habitus of the students and the influences of the institution, the combination of intra- and extrainstitutional factors and the recognition of the operational mechanisms of reflexivity urge us to re-consider the theories of socialization in more detail and in a more subtle way. Our research findings suggest that another version of the constructivist socialization interpretation may be worthy of consideration. In that approach, the socialization of students is regarded as an individual process that takes place in an institution or one of its units as a cooperation between the students and the respective institution, and the result is the outcome of this joint process (Berger–Luckmann 1966, Tierney 2000, Pusztai 2011). It is, therefore, not really possible to talk about the culture of higher education as such, only that of individual campuses. This is logical, since a community living together in the framework of traditions and permanent interaction is able to create a culture, consisting of lasting social features and norms. In such a community a consensus emerges regarding values, norms and attitudes, even if there is a difference between the declared and actual values and norms. The participation of the individuals in joint activities ensures the continuity of campus culture. Shared life and shared activities are also supported by the coherence based upon the common subject matter among a group of students, in addition to their spatial-geographical location (Pusztai 2011). Our research findings underpin this broader, multi-actor socialization model involving a number of various interactions. In our project we did not only attempt to identify the dominant ideas and attitudes of students, but also wished to diagnose how well integrated students are into the society of the campus from a relational and cultural aspect (Pusztai 2011).

Models of Institutional Influence

A considerable advance in research into higher education is that experts, when wishing to explain the efficiency of students, do not restrict their observations to the social status of the family of a student. They pay increasing attention to the issue of institutional effects and influences. This, however, is not always easy since there are a number of phenomena included and mixed into the concept, so consequently it is difficult to agree on a standard term (Astin–Antonio 2011). It is useful to return to the Input-Environment-Output (IEO) model of higher education, which was originally designed and launched to identify those institutional resources which promote the development of students (Astin 1993). Despite the fact that the concept is based upon clear logic, it sometimes still occurs that researchers work with faulty or not fully logical models. Various factors which are not clearly defined and elaborated may cause problems for workers in the field. One such mistake is a confusion of cause and consequence. We accept the criticism that certain indicators[34], while they promise to measure environmental effects, in fact measure the progress of the student, replacing it with the complexity of environmental effects, thus blurring the borderline between cause and consequence (Astin-Antonio 2011). It is clear that we can only speak about serious research into environmental effects and influence if we identify the sources of such effects in the institutional environment.

One of several uncertain presuppositions is when researchers take into account some of the characteristic features of the institution in the course of an inter-institutional comparison, but believe that these are the only determining factors of the efficiency of students, and disregard the social and cultural differences within the society of students. These approaches usually lead to the fetishisation of one or more institutional characteristics, and do not take into consideration the indicators of the students when they enter higher education, the effects coming from the outside world and the extra-curricular effects of the institutional environment. Researchers must be aware that the progress of students in higher education does not exclusively depend on the time they spend in their respective institutions, as they are also exposed to external influences during those years.

Another, similarly erroneous presupposition is that positive influences helping students in achieving their educational goals can only come from within the institution. In our earlier research we dealt with the erroneous assumptions related to the exclusive origin of positive effects. We registered the significant positive influence of resources outside the institution, e. g. the positive effect of membership of voluntary groups (Pusztai 2011. As for the erroneous assumptions regarding institutional effects, it is easy to forget the fact that the quality of an institution and the way students perceive it are not necessarily the same thing. It is therefore important to consider what it is that becomes a universally approved fact within the society of an institution (Astin-Antonio 2011, Pusztai 2011). Another problem is that environmental effects and the intensity of the students' participation (Astin 1993) –in other words, integration– (Tinto 1993) are confused. One is a characteristic feature of the context, and the other is a feature of the individual; it is therefore advisable to treat the two separately. In this study, we process all available data, and clearly separate (1) the factors present when students enter higher

---

34 We regard the College Learning Effectiveness Inventory (CLEI) and Involvement
    with College Activity (ICA Scale) as such.

education (2) from those present during the integration/involvement of the students, and (3) the environmental factors emerging in the background of institutional effects.

What Lies Behind the Individual Characteristics of Students?

When the individual characteristics of students are examined, researchers usually concentrate on their social and cultural background. When we reached the point at which we decided to include membership of social networks in our research as an important individual characteristic feature in the analytical models, the next logical step was to consider the educational institutions as a major network of social connections. The joint experience of the students who study there is one of the main attributes of the institution itself. It became clear that we had to examine the effects of the institutional environment on the efficiency of the students, and these effects are not the same as the quality and intensity of the bonds linking the individual to the institution, since these bonds vary from individual to individual. One individual attribute of the students' belonging to the institution which we found during our observations is what we termed integration or embeddedness (Pusztai 2011). We further identified relational and cultural layers within this embeddedness. We examined the personal embeddedness of the students across several dimensions, in the context of inter- and intragenerational relations, concentrating on the direction, intensity and multiplexity of the integration, and the interrelation between the social activities within and outside the institution. We observed a powerful interrelation between relational and cultural embeddedness, i.e., the acceptance of predominant views and opinions in the community. We also found that a powerful embeddedness does not necessarily support the individual's learning efficiency. We explained this with the popularity of certain opinions that are disadvantageous for learning but that are present within the institution (Pusztai 2011, 2012).

We came to the conclusion that the institutional environment is an independent, contextual variable. In our earlier studies we discussed it as the subculture of an institutional unit, attempting to understand it as the various forms of local consensus that students wish to establish in connection with their studies (Pusztai 2011). We found it necessary, however, to systematically reconsider the most important characteristics of the institutional environment. In this study we first survey the various interpretations of the higher educational environment in the related international literature, then undertake to provide our own interpretation, based upon an international database, and to analyse its effects. We should point out that while we emphasize the influence and importance of the higher educational environment, we address some criticism of research projects that only use and analyse aggregate background data from students, thus partly avoiding the problem of dealing with individual variables. We do so despite the fact that we are fully aware of the ever-increasing difficulties involved in gathering and analysing individual data from students and of the limits of generalization from such data.

The Higher Educational Environment

Higher education institutions are well researched, with a number of leading international journals publishing studies on the topic. Previously, most research projects concentrated on one particular institution, and the methodology often included an analysis of the statistical indicators of the institution concerned, or made use of psychometric techniques. These psychological and education-political approaches were, however, not suitable for surveying the culture of the campus and the pressures of the social environment. Including more data from students makes it possible to use more and more colourful approaches. Earlier, standardized test were designed in order to grasp the personal development of students and the intensity[35] of their participation in the activities going on on campus, but surveying the experience of students has also seen considerable progress. Researchers make efforts to be more sensitive to the specialities of the culture existing at the various institutions, and to trace the factors affecting the life of students (Astin 1993, Hurtado 2007).

It is, naturally, necessary to clarify what exactly we mean by the context of students, i.e., what we mean when we talk about the influencing social environment around them. This is exactly what we wanted to survey in our previous work: how large the community surrounding the students is, and what is its nature. In earlier times, the size of the institution was important because it seemed that a substantial population is necessary to create common features in the community in order for it to be attractive. It was soon found out, however, that relatively small institutions also have a powerful, sometimes even more powerful, attraction for their students. Prominent researchers in the area came to the conclusion that the best context is the one that offers real points of contact. The student moves about in this context, and it is therefore necessary to take into account the characteristics of the various smaller and larger units of the institution (Pascarella-Terenzini 2005, Astin-Antonio 2011). As has been pointed out in our previous report, the dimensions of student context are not constant, either (Pusztai 2011). Developing

---

35 These include, among others, the Environment Assessment Technique, the Institutional Functioning Inventory, the Institutional Goals Inventory, the College Characteristic Index, the College and University Environmental Scale, and the College Students Experiences Scale (Astin-Antonio 2012).

standardized indicators to describe the environment is not easy, since the institutional effects and environment are just as multidimensional a terrain as the efficiency of the students (Pascarella 2006). The institutional environment is divided into objective factors, independent of the students, and subjective ones, which depend upon the judgment of the students. The objective elements include the features of the higher education institution, such as its size (number of students and staff), the type of the institution in terms of its educational mission and means of financing, and the position of the institution in the system of higher education. These features are best described by the selectivity of the institution. Researchers relying upon major databases have the opportunity (and data) to include the composition of the communities of students and staff in the objectively tangible factors. Some of the descriptors of the institutional environment are objective data derived from statistical or administrative data bases, while the subjective data should be aggregated from the individual reports that the researchers hear from the students. Some large-scale overseas research projects also use reports from the teachers as well, in order to obtain a complete image of the institutional environment. In this way, some research projects also include aggregate data from the professional results of the faculty (number of publications and awards), the commitment of the staff to teaching and research, and the degree of acceptance of students belonging to another culture (Astin 1993). Aggregating certain individual student data (e. g. commitment to learning, interactions within the institution) may serve as a good starting point for an analysis of the context. This process needs to be systematic, too.

Depending on where the researcher is situated among the various social paradigms, they will use different indicators in order to describe institutional characteristics. Some find it sufficient to use the organizational indicators available in the macro-level statistics of the institution concerned (size, type, etc.), while others are sensitive to the organizational culture and its distance from the culture of the students, and they tend to rely upon individual quantitative analysis or qualitative methods instead of pure statistical data.

The theories of institutional effects are based upon the conviction that the uniform institutional environment has a specific effect on the students, so attempts have been made to identify the most important elements of the environment. The most popular approaches identify learning dimensions, -both formal and informal-, or combine these (Tinto 1993, Astin 1993, Tierney 2000, Weidman et al. 2001, Kaufman–Feldman 2004, Astin–Antonio 2011). Institutional characteristics such as faculty qualifications, the declared mission of the institution or department are located in the formal dimension of the structure of studies. An important element in the informal dimension of the structure of studies is the hidden curriculum of the institution, manifested in the messages carried in the context of the studies themselves.

The messages are relayed to the students by the faculty of the institution. Several researchers believe that the validating behaviour of the teachers[36] is the most important factor of the institutional environment. They test institutional practices which confirm students in their belief that they are competent and suited to their institution (Tinto 1993, Rendon et al. 2000, Tierney 2000).

The aspect of the environment which includes social relationships also has a formal dimension. It consists of the number and spatial arrangement of the individuals involved in the interaction. It is not only the population of a campus which is important, but also the proximity of the students, which is influenced by the proportion of those living on the campus and those commuting from other places. An entire complexity of various features of contemporary culture can be condensed into the social informal dimension, and exerts a normative pressure on the individuals.

Others identify four independent dimensions: the physical, the compositional, the organizational and the cultural layers (Strange 2001, Strange-Bannings 2003). In this model the physical environment does not only include the infrastructure and milieu necessary for learning and student life, but the location and internal spaces of the campus, and the message carried by its symbols, which have an effect similar to that of the hidden curriculum (Strange 2003). In this concept, the composition of the population of students is listed as the second dimension of the institutional environment. The population of students today very rarely shows any degree of homogeneity. The diversity in terms of age, gender, nationality, and cultural and religious background is now an important characteristic feature of institutions (Rendon et al. 2000, Forray 2003, Hurtado 2007, Harper-Quaye 2009, Engler 2013). Sensitive analyses take into account the diversity of the faculty in addition to the social status of the community of students (Hanushek et al. 2003, Winston–Zimmermann 2004).

The third dimension of the institutional environment is the one that contains the organizational features. It is possible to describe an organization's attitude to students in several ways, with complexity, formality and the openness towards activities being the most appropriate (Strange 2003). The fourth dimension contains the effects of the environmental culture on the students, emphasizing the constructed nature of that culture (Strange–Banning 2001, Strange 2003). The features of this dimension are similar to what we identified as determining the faculty community in our previous research project. At that time we discussed educational orientation, acceptable

---

36 Rendon emphasizes that this does not imply some sort of a superior or lenient attitude on the part of the teacher, but an effort to assist students in the construction of new knowledge.

working morale, reliable organizational partners and the dominant ideas regarding extra work under this heading (Pusztai 2011), but other researchers also include here the nature of interpersonal relations, and the subculture and traditions characteristic of the institution or unit (Strange 2003).

Questions and Data for Analysis

In our study we intend to contribute to the clarification of the concept of institutional environment through the operationalization of the four-dimensional concept described above in order to find out how the specific layers of the institution affect the efficiency of the students. Then, using the most characteristic dimensions, we describe the types of environment in the region concerned. In order to examine the institutional effects by taking into account the characteristics of the students when they enter higher education, we control the interrelations for the most important status indicator, the education of the parents. In our hypothesis the factors of the institutional environment are able to modify the efficiency which would be expected to derive from the individual background.

For the analysis, we used the international data base of the research project entitled "Higher Education for Social Cohesion Cooperative Research and Development in a Cross-border Area."[37] The research was conducted in the higher education institutions of Hungary, Romania and the Ukraine[38] in

---

37 The research was conducted with the support of the EU and Hungary, co-financed with EszA, within the grant application no. TÁMOP 4.2.4.A/2-11-1-2012-0001 "National Excellence Programme – Domestic Research Support Convergence Programme."

38 Institutions involved in the research project: University of Debrecen (Hungary), University of Protestant Theology, Debrecen (Hungary), the College of Nyíregyháza (Hungar), Ferenc Rákóczi II College of Subcarpathia (Beregszász – Berehovo, Ukraine), the Hungarian Faculty of Arts, State University of the Ukraine in Munkács (Uzhorod, Ukraine), the Partium Christian University (Nagyvárad – Oradea, Romania), the State University of Nagyvárad (Oradea, Romania), Szatmárnémeti College Faculty of Babes-Bolyai University (Szatmárnémeti – Satu Mare, Romania) and the Emanuel University (Nagyvárad – Oradea, Romania). First and third year undergraduate day students and first year postgraduate students were involved in the sample. Sampling was proportional among the faculties, and randomly selected sample seminar groups were requested to answer our inventories. In the Romanian sample, groups were formed according to the faculties, course cycles and forms of financing. No mean average was formed. While the Romanian sample is multi-ethnic, in the Ukrainian one only students from the Hungarian minority are represented. A mean average was formed in some places as a result of the varying willingness of students to answer our inventory.

2012. (N=2,728). For the present analysis we used representative data from the institution network of Hungary and Romania.

The dependent variables are in each case individual efficiency indicators, created as a result of the dichotomization of a multi-dimensional efficiency index in order to identify those who perform above the average. They included unbroken progress, belief in the benefits of learning, self-confidence in meeting the study requirements, curricular and extra-curricular activities, active participation in studying, the acceptance of the norms of higher education, the possession of work experience, and the willingness of the individual to continue their studies.

In this analysis we identified the dimensions of the institutional environment, and attached indicators to them. Analyses of institutional environment often use means of calculating aggregate averages that they then dichotomize. They also rely on the comparison of individual and faculty characteristics with the help of multi-dimensional contingency tables and regression models[39]. The majority of the environmental factors have been created by the formation of aggregated variables of individual data in this essay, too, so as to make a summary of individual perceptions of the individual environment, the "environment they themselves created" (Astin -Antonio 2011:91).

Individual as well as environmental factors have also been included in the analysis, primarily in order to provide a control for the interrelationships. Regression analysis has been used for a comparison of the individual and environmental effects, and multi-variable contingency tables have been applied to reveal the differential effects. A cluster analysis has been conducted in order to define the environment types.

Physical Dimensions of the Institutional Environment

The first of the four dimensions of the students' institutional environment is the physical environment. In international literature it is emphasized that satisfactory information about this environment may primarily be obtained on location, as a number of the elements of the natural and built environment of the campus and the way students use that space all belong here. Qualitative work on location is required to survey all of this. An outsider will compare what they observe with their experience of other higher education institutions, and not with the expectations of the students; we therefore cannot rely on the observations of external spectators. In our search for the

---

39 In addition to simple or graded multi-variable regression, multi-level and multi-variable analyses have alse been carried out. In order to test the complicated Tinto-model, structural equations were used by Cabrera et al. (1993), while Halpin (1990) used a multilevel method.

effects of the physical environment which influences the progress of students, our database proved useful primarily in mapping the infrastructure helping students in organizing their daily life and work. We are aware that the students' judgement of this dimension is subjective, as it largely depends upon their social status and expectations. From another perspective, it would be valuable data, enriching our knowledge of the individual characteristics of the students. In this case, however, we intend to understand the attributes of the institutional environment, so the opinions of the students belonging to the same institutional units are quantified at context level. This dimension of the institutional effects has been made up of two components: first, the way students tend to use the important elements of the infrastructure, and second, their satisfaction with the institutional infrastructure. The two sets of variables constituting the dimensions were first examined at individual level, then separately subjected to main component analysis. Then, the level of satisfaction with the use of the infrastructure by faculties[40] was aggregated. We then identified the main components which represented the chief indicators of the faculties. After the dichotomization of the components, weaker and stronger groups of students in terms of the use of the infrastructure were identified.

Since an international sample was used, we had an opportunity to observe that the students in Romanian-language institutions in Romania found the infrastructure of their respective institutions much better. We wanted to know what these institutions were like from a structural point of view. Although the majority of the faculties are financed by the state and they provide integrated master courses, the students usually find the infrastructure of the faculties and institutions owned and financed by various churches which provide integrated master courses much better. Faculties and institutions that used to be state-run universities are also better provided for in the students' opinion.

As we first intended to find out how the physical factors of the institutional environment influence the performance of the students, we compared the performances of students of infrastructurally richer and poorer institutions. At the infrastructurally richer faculties, the numbers of library goers, and users of sports- and eating facilities were found to be considerably higher. The factors listed with infrastructure in this study in themselves support the good performance of students (in the two environments, the proportion of students above the average is 50.1% and 44.5%, and the proportions of excellent students are 20% and 13.5% respectively). Given the diversity of students, however,

---

40 Institutional infrastructure includes the library, eating- and sports facilities and accommodation. We examined the satisfaction of students with the infrasructure, but we found that it does not support efficiency to any considerable degree.

we need to examine how these effects appear in various segments, and what other factors there may be behind the interrelationships.

In order to control for this interrelationship, we included further variables in the analysis. Recent research into higher education has confirmed that, similarly to public education, in higher education the social status of the family is a powerful factor. The parents' level of education is one of the most important factors that we take into account when students enter into higher education. Students coming from different social backgrounds receive different help from their parents from intellectual, financial, aspirational and procedural perspectives. This is why we examined the positive effects of an infrastructurally rich environment when controlled for the educational level of the parents. A multi-variable regression analysis of the infrastructure and the parents' educational level revealed that the father having at least a secondary education plays an important role in a student's being above averagely successful ($\beta=0.066$, $P=0.003$), while the effects of the infrastructure are, though still significant, more moderate ($\beta=0.052$, $P=0.007$). As for becoming an excellent student, the father having at least a secondary education ($\beta=0.082$, $P=0.000$) and an extensive use of the infrastructure ($\beta=0.083$, $P=0.000$) are almost equally important. The educational level of the mother did not prove to be significant in our analyses.

The advantages afforded by the advanced level education of the parents are present when the students concerned are at a relatively poor infrastructural environment. Rich infrastructure appears to support the children of parents with a secondary education in helping them to be better than the average. Under similar circumstances, the children of parents with an advanced education tend to progress towards excellence. At campuses with a rich infrastructure the disadvantage of students from a lower social background, though still tangible, does not significantly hinder them compared to children of parents with higher educational levels. The positive effects of the advantages offered by the physical environment are clear, but they do not affect the various groups of students with the same intensity.

Table 41: _Interrelations between the institutional infrastructure and the efficiency of students with parents of different educational levels_

Context	Poor infrastructure			Rich infrastructure		
	qualification of parents			qualification of parents		
Student	Primary	Secondary	Higher education	Primary	Secondary	Higher education
Successful	43.7%	44.0%	51.1%	44.9%	51.2%	53.4%
Average or poorer	56.3%	56.0%	48.9%	55.1%	48.8%	46.6%

Context	Poor infrastructure			Rich infrastructure		
	qualification of parents			qualification of parents		
Student	Primary	Secondary	Higher education	Primary	Secondary	Higher education
Excellent	12.2%	12.9%	<u>18.0%</u>*	13.7%	20.0%	<u>24.7%</u>**
Not excellent	87.8%	87.1%	82.0%	<u>86.3%</u>	80.0%	75.3%
N=	222	657	417	205	574	373

Source: Higher Education for Social Cohesion – Cooperative Research and Development in a Cross-border area 2012. The underlined figures indicate that the percentage in the given cell is higher than expected in a random distribution. A cell is marked with asterisks where the correlation is significant. Level of significance: *** =.000, **< 0.03, *< 0.01.

The Institutional Composition as the Second Dimension of the Environment

Although the infrastructural facilities of the campus seem to be an element of the complexity of institutional effects, our earlier research findings make us aware that the social context of the institution is even more important. The most elaborate institutional effect models suggest that it is advisable to break the phenomenon up into the various effects of the composition, i.e. into formal and informal social interactions.

Composition is the indicator of the homogeneity or heterogeneity of the population of students within the sub-units of the institutional environment. Researchers have followed with intense interest the effects of the composition of students according to their social status. We also used this as a starting point, and first wished to approach the education level of students' parents. The educational averages of the parents of students of various faculties were compared, and the faculties where students had parents with lower or higher educational levels than the average of the sample were separated.

The compositional differences are dramatic in the categories of the statistical-administrative institutional typologies. There are considerable international differences in the educational levels of students' parents. In Hungary, students have parents with a higher level of education on average than the students in the two neighbouring countries. Students in state-owned institutions also tend to have parents with higher educational levels than those in the denominational and minority institutions. At the institutions providing two stage courses we find groups of students with parents with homogeneously high educational levels.

The regression analyses suggest that at the institutions where students have parents with higher educational levels, the effects of the institutional environment are negligible. The above average proportion of fathers with a secondary education means they are able to contribute to their children's progress to excellence ($\beta=0.071$, $P=0.004$), and at an individual level this effects also remains significant ($\beta=0.081$, $P=0.000$).

Table 42: *Interrelations between the level of education of parents and the efficiency of students with parents of different educational levels*

Context	Proportion of fathers with elementary education above the average			Proportion of fathers with elementary education above the average		
	qualification of parents			qualification of parents		
Student	Primary	Secondary	Higher education	Elementary	Secondary	Higher education
Successful	43.7%	43.6%	49.7%	44.9%	51.7%	53.9%
Average or poorer	56.3%	56.4%	50.3%	54.7%	48.3%	46.1%
Excellent	14.4%	13.9%	17.3%	10.0%	19.0%	23.9%**
Not excellent	85.6%	86.1%	82.7%	90.0%	81.0%	76.1%
N=	277	656	330	150	575	460

Source: Higher Education for Social Cohesion – Cooperative Research and Development in a Cross-border area 2012. The underlined figures indicate that the percentage in the given cell is higher than expected in a random distribution. A cell is marked with asterisks where the correlation is significant. Level of significance: *** =0.000, **< 0.03, *< 0.01.

In a unit where the proportion of fathers with higher qualifications is high, the proportion of successful and efficient students is also significantly higher. When conducting contingency analysis, which is able to reveal more subtle details, we found that an environment rich in the children of fathers with a college or university degree only supports the excellence of students with such fathers. The effect is not extended to the children of fathers with a secondary or elementary qualification. The table also confirms that the number of students with fathers with secondary qualifications is high, and this encourages students to perform well. On the other hand, students of parents with elementary education have limited chances to become excellent. In other words, the composition with a high number of parents with high qualifications does not affect the efficiency of all the students in the sample in an equal way. A reason for this may be the great difference between the institutional habitus and the habitus of the students coming from families where the qualifications of the parents are low. They bring with them from their family background all the most important objective factors shaping their performance, aspirations, movement within the institution, and decisions. Their difficulties in adapting to their environment are caused by the lack of harmony between the external structures and their original attitudes, and this finally confirms their feeling of incompetence. In our earlier research projects we pointed out several times that of the characteristics of an institution's social composition it is not only the educational level of parents that deserves attention. In the higher educational region in this study students' parents have predominantly secondary qualifications (fathers: 43%, mothers: 45%). The proportion of parents with elementary and those with advanced qualifications is balanced[41], so it is further background factors that make the scene complicated. As the type of the settlement where the students come from may represent advantages in one's school career, we formulated a question of whether the individual performance of students is influenced if certain settlement types are over-represented in the sample.

At the statistical-administrative institutions the composition of settlements shows a characteristic pattern. At the institutions in Hungary the overwhelming majority of students come from small towns, whereas in Romania the students come from big cities and larger villages. At the denominational and minority institutions students mostly come from villages. On undergraduate courses the majority of students come from villages, while on postgraduate ones most of the students come from cities, and on the full courses students tend to come from small towns.

With the comparison of the variables by regression analysis, it is clear that the contextual dominance of students from cities has a significantly positive influence among the good ($\beta=0.062$, $P=0.002$) and the excellent ($\beta=0.07$, $P=0.000$) students. The advantage does not match the individual advantages derived from the high educational level of the father (good students: $\beta=0.063$, $P=0.004$; excellent students $\beta=0.083$, $P=0.000$). In the status groups at the various institutional contexts it is clear that the proportion of good (46%) and excellent students (16%) is lower among those who come from small settlements. The respective figures for towns and cities are (52% and 20%). The efficiency advantage of students with elementary and advanced qualifications is much larger in contexts where most students come from towns and cities. Although the advantage enjoyed by children of parents with elementary qualifications exists in an environment which varies according to the home settlement type, it is not as great. It should be noted that both the regression analysis and the table analysis verify that the dominance of villages among the home settlements of students does not afford any advantage over small towns.

---

41 Among the fathers those with elementary qualifications outnumber mothers with these qualifications by 32% to 27%.

Table 43: *Interrelations between the home settlement type and the efficiency of students with parents of different educational levels*

Context	Composition with a majority of small settlements			Composition with urban environment		
	qualification of parents			qualification of parents		
Student	Primary	Secondary	Higher education	Primary	Secondary	Higher education
Successful	41.0%	46.5%	49.4%	44.1%	52.3%	54.9%
Average or poorer	59.0%	53.5%	50.6%	55.9%	47.7%	45.1%
Excellent	12.4%	15.4%	19.44%	14.3%	18.8%	24.7%**
Not excellent	87.6%	84.6%	80.6%	85.7.0%	81.2%	75.3%
N=	266	667	324	161	547	368

Source: Higher Education for Social Cohesion – Cooperative Research and Development in a Cross-border area 2012. The underlined figures indicate that the percentage in the given cell is higher than expected in a random distribution. A cell is marked with asterisks where the correlation is significant. Level of significance: *** =0.000, **< 0.03, *< 0.01.

As regards gender composition, at one quarter of the faculties men outnumbered women (these are primarily technical and IT faculties, but there was a faculty of arts and a theological faculty as well). The gender proportions significantly determine the image of the institutions and their units in the region concerned (Fényes 2014). In state-owned institutions and at postgraduate levels, men outnumber women. The regression analysis, controlled for parental qualifications indicate that the higher number of men is a factor impeding students in becoming excellent, though the same does not apply to students' performing better than the average.

Previously, the social networks prevailing at a faculty were identified as a major feature of the composition. We examined the dominant types of social networks at the institutions and their units, and we named them according to their dominant type of network. At the faculties in Hungary, units were characterized by powerful inter- and intragenerational networks. In Romania, the networks are more fragmented. At state universities and (ethnically) majority institutions as well as those providing full courses we find close intragenerational networks.

A parallel examination of the structural patterns and efficiency indicators appears to reveal that at the faculties characterized by broad inner and outer intragenerational networks, the number of excellent students and those above the average is lower. At faculties characterized primarily by intergenerational networks the proportion of such students is outstandingly high. The performance at faculties dominated by connection networks consisting of smaller and tighter cells is slightly behind this (47%, 16%), but is still higher than the performance observable at faculties where isolated or very broad intragenerational networks are in operation.

Regression analyses indicate that powerful intergenerational networks have a significantly positive effect on excellence (β=0.07, P=0.000) and above average performance (β=0.061, P=0.002). The other three types of connection structures do not seem to promote learning efficiency. The dominance of broader intragenerational networks appears to be independent of learning efficiency, while the dominance of close and tight intragenerational networks (β=0.067, P=0.01; β=0.058, P=0.003) and isolated ones (β=0.061, P=0.002; β=0.050, P=0.01) tend to adversely affect learning efficiency. Fathers' education seems to be the most powerful influencing factor in the broad intragenerational networks (β=0.091, P=0.000) and the least powerful is in intergenerational connections (β=0.059, P=0.009). It is not surprising that inner networks do not constitute a strongly influencing factor for the institutional environment. We find it important that maintaining large networks that are otherwise useful resources is not very profitable in this environment. On the other hand, operating the intergenerational network is highly useful for students at a context level, as it tends to compensate for the disadvantages caused by the different educational levels of the parents.

Table 44: Interrelations between the relationship composition of the unit concerned and the efficiency of students with parents of different educational levels

Context	Environment rich in intergenerational relations			Environment poor in intergenerational relations		
	qualification of parents			qualification of parents		
Student	Primary	Secondary	Higher education	Primary	Secondary	Higher education
Successful	46.2%	52.9%	52.8%	42.5%	42.3%	51.7%
Average or poorer	53.9%	47.1%	47.2%	57.5%	57.7%	48.3%
Excellent	13.1%	21.1%	23.3%	12.7%	11.7%	19.7%
Not excellent	86.9%	78.9%	76.7%	87.3%	88.3%	80.3%
N=	206	592	322	221	639	468

Source: Higher Education for Social Cohesion – Cooperative Research and Development in a Cross-border area 2012. The underlined figures indicate that the percentage in the given cell is higher than expected in a random distribution. A cell is marked with asterisks where the correlation is significant. Level of significance: *** =.000, **< 0.03, *< 0.01.

When students with an intergenerational embeddedness are in the majority at a faculty, the proportion of excellent students and those above the average is higher. The multi-variable contingency analysis related to the differentiated effects confirms the assumptions that emerged from the results of the regression analysis. It is noteworthy that those students whose parents have a secondary education are the major beneficiaries of the student-teacher relationship. Among those who are successful they are followed by the children of parents with elementary qualifications. Students whose parents have advanced qualifications tend to progress to excellence in greater numbers than others.

Organizational Characteristics as Influencing Factors of the Institutional Environment

Of the factors available with the help of the database related to the organizational characteristics of an institution, a special mission, selectivity and the level of confidence in the institution are the ones we intend to deal with. With a special mission, denominational institutions and those maintained by national minorities play an important role in the region. The data indicate that selectivity is more powerful at institutions in Hungary, and the explanation for this may be that the institutions in Romania tend to admit applicants at their first attempt. It is a general belief at the denominational and ethnic minority institutions, and is in accordance with our earlier findings, that these schools are not very selective, and almost all their students are admitted at the first attempt (Pusztai 2009). Institutions offering two stage courses are believed to be strongly selective. Faculties doing undergraduate training have a high number of students who are admitted at the first attempt. Participating in the mission of a denominational or ethnic minority school has a slightly negative effect on the performance of students, which is in accordance with their socially inclusive, expansional function. At the denominational schools the significant interrelation with the educational level of the parents is not tangible. At the ethnic institutions, however, learning at an advanced level in the mother tongue requires considerable extra energy from both teachers and learners, as the negative effect remains there even after the educational level of the parents is included in the analysis ($\beta=0.124$, $P=0.000$; $\beta=0.091$, $P=0.000$).

We intended to survey the meritocratic character of the institutional environment when we separated the perceptions of selective enrolment and admittance at the first attempt. Both have a significantly positive influence on the success of students in themselves, but when the variable of the parents' educational level is added, this positive influence immediately vanishes. From this, we can conclude that the meritocratic self-image of a unit of a higher education institution in itself does not spur students to higher performance (β=0.43, P=0.02; β=0.056, P=0.004).

Confidence in the institution is an outstandingly important factor in research into public education, and several projects have attempted to identify its sources (Bryk et al. 2002). In our research we did not seek to identify its components, we only wished to register its presence and survey its effects.

The community at the institutions in Hungary tend to trust the dean, whereas the students at the institutions in Romania trust the teaching staff and the administrative personnel. At the denominational and ethnic institutions the students place their confidence in the members of the organization. At the institutions offering two stage courses students often trust the teachers and the heads of units.

The various actors in the organizations are judged differently. A comparison of the levels of confidence was intended to find out whether students find the decision makers reliable and trustworthy, or a threat to the organization. The heads of the faculties and other units, the administrative personnel and the teachers are considered trustworthy in different communities. Of these, only the confidence in the teachers was found to be a positive influence on the performance of the students, controlled for the educational level of the parents. (β=–0.053, P=0.007).

Table 45: _Interrelations between the intergenerational confidence and the efficiency of students with parents of different educational levels_

Context	Low level or organizational trust			High level of organizational trust		
	qualification of parents			qualification of parents		
Student	Primary	Secondary	Higher education	Primary	Secondary	Higher education
Successful	42.3%	44.9%	50.3%**	46.2%	50.4%	54.8%
Average or poorer	57.6%	55.1%	49.7%	53.8%	49.6%	45.2%
Excellent	13.8%	13.6%	21.4%**	11.9%	19.5%	20.7%
Not excellent	86.2%	86.4%	78.6%	88.1%**	80.5%	79.3%
N=	217	671	467	210	560	323

Source: Higher Education for Social Cohesion – Cooperative Research and Development in a Cross-border area 2012. The underlined figures indicate that the percentage in the given cell is higher than expected in a random distribution. A cell is marked with asterisks where the correlation is significant. Level of significance: *** =.000, **< 0.03, *< 0.01.

Intergenerational trust, dominating the institution or its unit, has a generally positive effect, experienced at every group of the parental educational level. It appears to support excellence only in the case of parents with advanced qualifications, otherwise its benevolent effects only act to take individuals somewhat higher than the average. It is particularly effective in the case of children of parents with secondary qualifications. The similarities of the institutional habituses is again an explanation for the different effects. The question arises whether confidence in peers is able to compensate for this phenomenon?

When examining the relational structures, we noticed that the campus environments permeated by broad intragenerational networks have a neutral or even negative effect on students' performance. Although international research projects have identified the power of student communities as an important supportive factor (Astin 1993, Tinto 1993), our data do not confirm that the organizational actors of peers (i.e. an interest negotiating organization), cooperation with peers and the value harmony of the community of the students are directly related to performance[42]. We do not find this surprising, since in the course of an international research project into domestic and foreign Hungarian higher education institutions we pointed out that closer relational embeddedness does not necessarily support efficiency. We also drew the attention of the reader to occasional effects that may crop up at the campus (Pusztai 2011).

Table 46: *Interrelations between the intragenerational value orientation and the efficiency of students with parents of different educational levels*

Context	Powerful value diversity			Powerful value homogeneity		
	qualification of parents			qualification of parents		
Student	Primary	Secondary	Higher education	Primary	Secondary	Higher education
Successful	45.5%	49.3%	52.2%	42.7%	45.0%	51.0%
Average or poorer	54.5%	50.7%	47.8%	57.3%	55.0%	48.0%
Excellent	15.3%	16.9%	22.0%*	9.9%	15.5%	19.7%

42 At denominational institutions faculties are characetrized by cooperation and a harmony of values. At ethnic minority institutions faculties which enjoy a harmony of values are those providing undergrtaduate training. (Ethnic) Majority institutions and those offering full courses are more powerfully characterized by peer cooperation. In Hungary, cooperation, in Romania value harmony is predominant.

Context	Powerful value diversity			Powerful value homogeneity		
	qualification of parents			qualification of parents		
Student	Primary	Secondary	Higher education	Primary	Secondary	Higher education
Not excellent	84.7%	83.1%	78.0%	90.1%	84.5%	80.3%
N=	235	676	490	192	555	300

Source: Higher Education for Social Cohesion – Cooperative Research and Development in a Cross-border area 2012. The underlined figures indicate that the percentage in the given cell is higher than expected in a random distribution. A cell is marked with asterisks where the correlation is significant. Level of significance: *** =.000, **< 0.03, *< 0.01.

At the institutional units where the value system of the students is not diverse, the efficiency of individuals tends to be weaker, and the proportion of above average and excellent students is lower in each group when dividing students according to the educational level of the parents. In search of an explanation for this, we turned to the fourth dimension of the institutional environment, so as to examine the value orientations common at the institutional units. We believe that value orientation, norms and values exert a pressure on the individual.

The Pressure of the Environmental Culture

When we examined the special influence of contemporary culture, out of the general value orientations[43] we registered the significantly positive effects of the now common post-material value orientation (appreciating family, friends, happiness, safety and pleasant experiences) in the students' becoming more successful than the average ($\beta=0.043$, P=0.027). We also observed the benevolent effects of traditional value orientation (seeking peace, stability, patriotic, religious and traditional value system) in the students' becoming excellent in their studies ($\beta=0.047$, P=0.015) controlled for the educational levels of the parents. The so-called new materialistic views, preferring power

---

43 As a result of the longitudinal data gathering, stable patterns of ideas regarding values and future career plans were identified in the region (Bocsi-Szabó 2013). In the Romanian contexts, traditional and new materialistic ideas dominate, whereas in Hungary post-materialistic views prevail. At state and majority institutions post-material concepts dominate students' ideas, while at ethnic minority schools new materialistic views are common, and at the denominational institutions we find traditional ideas. At undergraduate level the value orientation of the students is new materialistic, while at postgraduate level and in two stage courses post-material ideas dominate.

and material wealth, do not support students in their efforts to be efficient and successful (β=0.044, P=0.025).

Institutional culture appears to be strongly determined by views related to the ideal job prevalent at the faculty. The views of the students regarding their ideal job were largely similar to the findings of our previous projects, although this time the sample of students involved in the research was international. The latent variables related to the values attached to a job were mapped with factor analysis. The types were aggregated by institutional units in order to learn how common an image of a job at a faculty is. Finally, we separated the units where a certain image of a job was much more common than at other units. The dominance of altruistic career views at a faculty meant to us that the desire of the students was to find a job in which they could be useful for society, and deal with people in a friendly environment. All in all, they wanted a job with responsibility, in which they had a chance to help other people. In the present sample, with the other career type, the idea of a successful career and the desire to find security seemed to merge into one. Progress in one's career, and the need to earn enough featured here, together with the security of the job and its compatibility with a family. The popular image of a job is the one where the individual is able to implement their ideas at a high prestige workplace, full of challenges, and is ideal for an individual with a powerful professional identity. Ideas focusing on independence involve flexitime work for individuals who do not dream of excessive workloads.

At institutions in Romania, independence dominates, whereas in Hungary students dream of a safe career. At the denominational institutions altruistic ideas are popular. At minority schools, students also have altruistic ideas, but they also long for independence and flexible working hours. At the state universities and ethnic majority universities and colleges, students want a chance for self-realization in a stable career.

After surveying the ideas of students regarding their future career at various institutions, we wanted to learn whether the dominant ideas promote or impede students' success and efficiency, regardless of their family background. Both the regression analysis and the contingency table analysis indicate that it is only the ideas featuring challenge, self-realization and the importance of performance which urge students to be more efficient (β=0.105, P=0.000; β=0.103, P=0.000).

Table 47: Interrelations between ideas regarding students' future career and the efficiency of students with parents of different educational levels

Context	Self-realization unimportant			Self-realization important		
	qualification of parents			qualification of parents		
Student	Primary	Secondary	Higher education	Primary	Secondary	Higher education
Successful	37.6%	41.9%	51.0%**	55.8.%	55.2%	53.8%
Average or poorer	62.4%	58.1%	49.0%	44.2%	44.8%	46.2%
Excellent	11.1%	12.3%	17.9%**	16.0%	21.9%	25.7%*
Not excellent	88.9%	87.7%	82.1%	84.0%	78.1%	79.3%
N=	271	724	463	156	507	327

Source: Higher Education for Social Cohesion – Cooperative Research and Development in a Cross-border area 2012. The underlined figures indicate that the percentage in the given cell is higher than expected in a random distribution. A cell is marked with asterisks where the correlation is significant. Level of significance: *** =.000, **< 0.03, *< 001.

Types of Environment

After studying the environment dimensions, we continued by attempting to examine the characteristic types of institutional environment in the region. One of our questions was whether there is any significant interrelation between the institutional environment and the financing sector, the mother nation, and profile and form of the course.

Five basic types of institutional environment have been identified. At the environment with a meritocratic elite identity, students are proud that they were admitted after a strong selection procedure, and there are also strict inner filters. Hard work is welcome, diligent preparation for the entrance examination is replaced by daily hard work within the university. The organizational environment is characterized by general trust in the role partner, students find the leaders of the faculty and the interest negotiating organizations trustworthy, and the general idea is that both the teaching staff and administrative personnel assist students in every way they can. These educational environments are provided with all the facilities necessary for smooth work. The composition of the institutional units is dominated by students coming from an urban environment and educated families. As for connection structures, close friendships are more common than extensive communities. Individuals are rarely isolated. The prevailing value orientation is post-materialistic, obtaining power and wealth as an objective in life is here the lowest on the priority list. An altruistic and stable career is the most common goal.

In a permissive, receptive environment students believe that they are studying in the most easily accessible form of education. Low selectivity at enrolment goes hand in hand with not particularly strict inner filters, but often the expectations of the students in terms of their progress remain unfulfilled. They tend to respond with lower levels of trust in the authorities of the institution. They do not find their role partners very trustworthy, and they are also dissatisfied with the infrastructure of their institution. There is, however, a wide range of rich interactions with the teachers inside and outside the institution. That is probably why the students participate in study clubs and circles in higher numbers than average, although they do not seem to prefer research-oriented training. In these environments the students come from families with low qualifications.

These students come from cities and villages, and they are strongly integrated into their families even after starting their studies. They often work at the family farm or business. They actively participate in free time activities (and often not only with their fellow students). Among students arranged into intergenerational or broad community networks there are two basic value orientations: traditional and materialistic, and they long for a flexible job or one that offers challenges.

At a disillusioned environment, the general impression of the students is that although preparation for the entrance exam was tough, and they underwent a strict selection procedure, it was replaced with a lower workload inside the institution. Though the environment necessary for studying is provided, and they may win more scholarships than average, it is not fashionable to be involved in research work. What is more, they reject it, so it is not surprising that the number of regular grants based upon performance is the lowest here. This may be a consequence of the fact that the connections between students and teachers are the poorest here. A sign of disillusionment is that students have high aspirations, but fear that their studies will not contribute to the realization of their ideas, and they will not find a job. They are therefore dissatisfied with their learning environment, and do not trust the actors of the organization. Students' organizations and the teaching staff have a poor reputation, and the social networks are underdeveloped. The efforts of the leadership of the faculty are only partly able to counterbalance the consequences of the general dissatisfaction. The education of the parents of these students is above the average, but most of the students come from small towns rather than cities. As far as the social networks are concerned, these environments tend to be at the bottom of the list. These communities are characterized by close friendships, and a relatively high number of isolated individuals. They have post-material values and long for stable and predictable careers. Environments relying on external stimuli and encouragement are characterized by medium selection, but this is not the most important feature. Interestingly, although they have poor and often inadequate infrastructure, students still trust the role partners, especially the teaching staff and administrative personnel. The connections with the teachers, however, remain traditionally in the classroom. Investing in private tuition before the entrance examination is a common practice, especially among ethnic minority students and, although the workload at the institution appears to be lower, they apply for and win study and other scholarships in outstandingly high numbers. This is perhaps also the reason why these students are so keenly interested in research, as a result of which attending conferences and publishing essays are popular activities, though the institution is sometimes unable to provide them with sufficient opportunities to do this. This kind of environment is common at ethnic minority schools, where commitment and hard work are part of the basic values of the institution. Most students come from villages and small towns, and their parents usually have secondary qualifications. Apart from students isolated as a result of commuting from home, most students have close friends. Similarly, membership in religious communities is also high. In these campus societies altruistic ideas about a future career and post-material values are common.

In a friendly environment students are aware that they were admitted after a relatively weak admittance procedure, but the internal filters are stricter. These students are more satisfied than the average with the contribution of the institution to their personal development. Though their workload is also above the average, they participate in voluntary organizations and voluntary work in high numbers. The composition of students is dominated by the children of parents with low qualifications. The students mostly come from villages. They trust all the representatives of the institution, especially the students' elected representatives. The norms of the institution allow multiplex connections between the students and the teachers, which may include discussions about scholarly and other topics, and plans for the future, and the students often receive personal attention from their teachers. There is a great demand for the institutional infrastructure, and the students make use of it, e. g. the proportion of those who live in the dorms is high. The cohesion of the community is the highest, and there is a harmony of values. Traditional and post-materialistic value orientation are common. Solidarity and integrity are powerful, and ideas about a future career are clearly altruistic.

A meritocratic elite, the disillusioned environment type and the type relying on external stimuli are characteristic of Hungary, with the permissive-receptive and the friendly types more common in Romania (P=0,000). The friendly and permissive-receptive types appear in the denominational institutions, while the others are found in the state sector (P=0,000). In terms of training profiles, a meritocratic environment is typical at medical schools and art schools, the permissive-receptive type is common at agricultural, IT and technical institutions, the disillusioned type is typical at faculties of law, arts and business. The environment that tends to rely on external encouragement and input is found at agricultural and teacher training institutions, especially at those for ethnic minorities. A friendly environment is what we find at theological seminaries, and with science and social studies (P=0,000). Undergraduate courses tend to be friendly and permissive-receptive, disillusionment characterises the environment of a number of postgraduate courses, where we also find environments relying on external inputs. We often find a meritocratic environment on two stage courses (P=0,000).

Naturally, different environments have different effects on students, depending upon their demographic and social characteristics, their previous studies, and their level of integration into their institutions, and the complexity of these relations requires further research. When controlled for the educational level of the parents it is clear that the effects of the meritocratic environment are more positive than those of the others. With certain groups of students, a permissive-receptive environment may have a positive effect, while a friendly one may have a negative effect on their performance and efficiency.

Conclusions

Although the related literature regards the higher education environment as an important influencing factor, there is no consensus in the interpretation and evaluation of the concept. Apart from the fact that very often the cause and consequence of the effect are confused in the professional discourse, the situation is made difficult by a shift from a static model of the socialization of students to a dynamic, constructivist one. Also, macro-level statistical-administrative data are sometimes replaced with measured information, exchanging aggregated perceptual data for non-contextual data, while individual proximity indicators further complicate the picture. In our present study, after surveying related international work, we made an attempt at the operationalization of a four-dimensional concept of institutional environment, based upon an available international database from 2012. Subsequently, the general and differentiated effects of the environment types on the individual efficiency and success of students were analysed. So as to understand individual efficiency, after the dichotomization of multi-dimensional efficiency index, we established two variables, in order to be able to identify those groups of students who are above average and who are excellent in their studies. The effects of the specific dimensions of the environment (physical, compositional, organizational and cultural) on efficiency were examined one by one, and we monitored the specific effects of the institutions on the status groups of students. Eventually, five environment types emerged from the major features of the environmental dimensions in the higher education region under investigation.

238

Conclusions

In our research we intended to survey the role played by social connections when students make use of the expanding opportunities offered by contemporary higher education. The contribution of institutions as chains of social relationships to students' progress was examined from an educational-sociological perspective. Our volume of studies consists of three parts, each part containing three studies. As a summary of the most important findings of our research, we first present our most important observations related to the region concerned. We then follow with the results, which led us to the conclusion that the resources provided by higher education institutions, usually referred to as campuses, may be termed social capital. In the third chapter, we publish our conclusions related to the success and efficiency of students.

The region involved in our research

This research is justified because in Central and Eastern European countries social interest in higher education increased dramatically after the collapse of the communist regimes. As a consequence, the horizontal and vertical expansion of the system took place much more rapidly in these countries than in the Western European nations. At the same time, the number of potential students diminished, generating a competition among higher education institutions. For institutions in underdeveloped regions and those that have a recruitment basis smaller than the average, the changes meant that the number of students coming from families of lower social status has increased. Students with parents with low qualifications, those who study in vocational secondary schools and grammal schools in small towns, those commuting from small villages, and members of national and ethnic minorities began to appear in high numbers at these colleges and universities.

Our research concentrated on the higher education institutions in the border zone of three countries. The presentation of our findings is meant to be an awareness raising initiative, since in spite of the fact that higher education is becoming increasingly international, most research projects work with data gathered at national level. We, on the other hand, focused on a region on the periphery of three countries. This area is often ignored by researchers conducting national surveys, since the centres of higher education are usually in the capitals of the countries concerned. The area in the border zone of Hungary, Romania and the Ukraine is an example of how international regions of higher educations emerge. The territory that is today shared by three states used to constitute one single region and, after a long, forced pause in the twentieth century, it is now being resurrected as a region with a cohesive identity. After the downfall of the dictatorships and the evaporation of the state borders, initially the gaps in the incomplete systems of public- and higher education became obvious. Following this, students gradually became more mobile. As a result of this mobility, a system of multi-level higher education came into being in the multi-ethnic region. In the border region several institutions used to be run down and untended; these colleges and universities were rapidly refurbished and remodelled, although often financial support from the state was not available. In those cases, non-governmental organizations, for example churches, played an active role. Private and church institutions, although often not receiving any support from the government, play a pioneering role in the broader social integration of students in the region. As a result, in their institutions student society is more heterogeneous than in the public sector, where students tend to form internal castes. After the change of political system, an intensive expansion of the institutional network started, but even the 2012 statistics suggest that in these regions access to higher education is still very difficult, and young people are more pessimistic about getting a degree and finding a job than in other parts of the country.

A peculiarity of the region concerned is that it is on the easternmost border of the European Union; in fact, it stretches beyond the easternmost borders. This means that higher education is based upon different structures in the different countries, and also that the expansion of the institutional system took place at different speeds and under different controls. In the countries concerned, education in the language of the ethnic minorities is not provided equally, so students belonging to such minorities have access only to certain institutions, and not to the entire spectrum of higher education. The problem is particularly acute, not just in higher education, but also in vocational training. For students coming from countries outside the European Union, the possibilities for mobility and for the acceptance of their degrees earned in another country are not equally available. Despite these difficulties, there is intensive student mobility in the region.

The students involved in our research live in an area characterized by a belated social transformation and a geographically peripheral situation. Although demographic trends are also negative in these areas, the problem is not as grave as it is elsewhere, due to a higher number of children born in families with parents with low qualifications. As a result, there seems to be a pool of replacement for higher education institutions. This is certainly a challenge for the institutions in the region. In addition to colleges and universities, some new boarding institutions, and communities for living and learning welcome gifted students from ethnic minorities.

Students recruited at higher education institutions show regional characteristics, and one of the permanent features is the narrow catchment area.

The proportion of students from families of lower social status – parents with low qualifications, and unemployed parents – gradually increases within the entire student population of the institutions in the region concerned. There are special directions of student mobility in the border region: the higher the family status of a student, the more likely it is that they will move towards the centre of the region or to one of the national centres of higher education.

Since the introduction of multi-cycle training, students entering postgraduate or doctoral courses must face a new social selection procedure. Social differences have increased not only in the process of earning a degree, but also in finding a good job. The progress of students coming from underprivileged families is not unbroken, since we encounter fewer of them at the higher years and at postgraduate level than at the lower years and on undergraduate courses. Migration from the region is significant, due to the shortage of jobs; the loss of human resources is therefore a considerable problem.

An important finding of our research is that despite the indicators mentioned previously, there are considerable differences between the institutions and campuses. The differences are observed in the social composition of the students at the colleges and universities, the structure of their connections, the integrating potentials of the community and the most important features of their internal institutional culture. In other words, the area only appears to be uniform from the outside, as new centre-periphery relationships, and a special hierarchy of the institutions and their units, have emerged in the area. All of this warns us not to make schematic and simplified observations, despite the national and international homogenization of higher education, since the functions undertaken and those actually accomplished have extended considerably, and the world of higher education has become incredibly colourful even within a relatively small geographical territory.

The social network as a resource on campuses

Social inequalities, cultural diversity, regional differences, cultural differences and a general lack of trust, hamper the people of Central- and Europe in fully utilizing the advantages offered by the European Union. This is particularly true for the region included in our observations. In an increasingly complex society, forces splitting and dividing the members of that society can only be counterbalanced by social cohesion, conscious cooperation between individuals, groups and organizations, the recognition of interdependence and an ability to rise above short-term, selfish interests. A redefinition of the functions of higher education may play an important role in this process, since the dual and closely interconnected roles of colleges and universities are to promote individual and social progress and welfare. It is possible to

241

evaluate this system of objectives through its social embeddedness and the effective and adequate answers it provides to the problems of society. In our opinion, it is necessary to reveal the system of the resources as they are manifest in the web of connections of the institution so as to see and understand how the objectives are reached.

When studying the restructuring of higher education, researchers face problems similar to those encountered in elementary and secondary education. Students' careers are explained with several major paradigms. In the dominant paradigm of educational-sociological research projects dealing with the social mobility of students, individuals are the units of analysis, and attention is exclusively focused on the typical demographic and status factors shaping students' careers. This approach still prevails in European educational-sociological work. In our opinion, a shortcoming of this approach is that it is only suitable for explaining behaviour in the sense used by Weber; it disregards the intentional orientations of the individual, and pays little attention to revaling the ways in which the intentions and objectives of the individual are arranged into a series of purposeful activities. The reason for this is that the conflict theory paradigm rests on the idea that social status determines the situation of the individual, and the decisions of the person are unimportant. Furthermore, the influence of the specific social connection systems on the decisions of the individual is entirely disregarded.

In the rational decision paradigm, which concentrates strongly on the calculations made by the individual, the person chooses from among alternative actions according to their specific interests, aiming to find the best achievable solution. Educational studies produced following this approach consider students as consumers who, in their career in higher education, always make pragmatic decisions. Students, however, may be largely influenced by social context, the embeddedness of the individual in specific personal connections and in the entire system of social connections. In network analysis theory, based upon sociometric traditions, behaviour is interpreted as a category of forces induced by the network of connections of the individual, and concentrates on interpersonal connections, and not so much on the categories or characteristic features of the person concerned. As a result of the efforts aimed at reaching a synthesis, social capital theory now incorporates the principles of rational and purposeful action and the influencing and distorting effects of the specific social environment as well. In social capital theory it is often emphasized that activities aimed at satisfying individual needs are realized in the environment of the person concerned. The theory in this way uses and amalgamates the elements of several others, and offers explanations not only for individual actions, but also for changes in the social structure. We used that theory for an analysis of the processes taking place in higher education.

242

The influence of resources on students' progress in higher education was revealed through an examination of the differing achievements and performance of students studying in various sectors of higher education. Of the components of social capital within the institution, the stability of intergenerational relations, and the density of networks with higher closure were found to be more effective than extracurricular activities which complement the studies of the individuals concerned. Our analysis suggests that strongly explanatory, popular theories have a restricted responding capacity, and we were led to the conclusion that social capital is in itself able to support efficiency in higher education, and to reduce the class-determinism of the reproduction of cultural capital. The dominance of stable, cohesive connections, supporting the safety of norms, is capable of compensating for the inequalities among students which are rooted in their social differences. In such an environment, students coming from underprivileged families are able to perform better. This observation is similar to the findings of Coleman and his students, which suggest that the preference of students in choosing schools and their study performance are not only the products of their positions in the vertical structure of society and their own rational decisions. These are strongly influenced by the effects of social capital on the decisions of the individual. Social capital consists of the person's specific norms and network of connections at school, in the community and during free-time activities.

In our work we analyse the question of students' institutional integration by using the conclusions of socialization theories and efficiency models of higher education, and the ideas of a constructivist community interpretation, as well as Coleman's social capital theory. We learn from Coleman's theory that the behaviour of students is largely influenced by the structure of social networks of the schools concerned, the information, values and norms relayed through that social network, and the relationship of the shared understanding of goals to the goals of the organization. Coleman believes that the most effective institutions are those that rest upon functional communities, where the community of the school constitutes a closed network both from a formal perspective and in terms of its content. It is clear that the world of higher education is more open, but we assumed that the social networks of students still had a highly important role. After the constructivist turn, as a result of which social sciences re-interpreted the old concept of communities, the starting point was the inter-subjective nature of knowledge, and the joint meaning-forming ability of those connected; what is more, the individual construction of the boundaries of the community became the focus of observations. The concept of a locally well-defined community was re-defined under the influence of Cohen's theory of symbolic communities. The concept, searching for an interpretation of the culture which binds the members of a community together, reached beyond the formal issues involving the individuals connected to each other through various relationships. Using all these preliminaries considerations, we formulated our idea that it is the network of meanings used jointly that binds the communities together – the interpreting communities that emerge as a result of homophily, and disciplinary and professional socialization. We therefore interpreted the communities of students as a network that surrounds the individuals. That network creates and uses largely uniform meanings, and is best described by Fish's concept of the "interpreting community."

For a systematic examination of students' institutional connections, we introduced the term academic embeddedness or integration. In our view, a number of activities of students entering higher education, such as the creation of attitudes to the norms of the institution concerned, their learning, extra work, their sense of security and their efficiency, largely depend upon the connections and discourses they are embedded in. Embeddedness, a concept originally used in socio-economics, is now an important building block of Coleman's theory on social capital. It refers to the degree and quality of the individual's integration into their own network of personal connections and broader social relations. Using Granovetter's concept of embeddedness, we examined the students' personal connections (relational embeddedness), the structure of the network of connections surrounding them (structural context), and the explanatory effects of dominant values and norms (cultural embeddedness).

In our opinion, a conceptual value of social capital is that it expands the space and possibilities – as well as the responsibilities – of the staff and students working together in a college or university, and concentrates on the educational contribution, rather than on an acceptance of the old reproduction mechanisms of society and attempts to try to avoid educational laws and regulations.

Roads leading to success

Educational researchers have long debated how it is possible to define the entirety of the skills and competences to be achieved by students by the end of their studies in higher education. The question is whether what is defined is universal, or only applicable at national, regional or institutional level(s). It is justified to argue that it is only possible to conceptualize student efficiency with the utmost care, and on condition of the acceptance of certain value generating premises. The operationalization of the concept is an extremely complex procedure. As there is no professional concensus on the interpretation of the efficiency of students, we summarised some of the possible dimensions and indicators. While in Europe these research projects are necessitated by the need to compare employees who earn a degree in the national higher education systems, in America researchers concentrate on the effects of the institutions on the progress of the students, and compare the efficiency of the various institutions. Related to the idea of the accountability of higher education which emerged in the 1990s, a need emerged for identifying statistical data suitable for measuring the progress of students during their years in the system. Researchers find the measurable value added by colleges and universities to the progress of students a more reliable indicator than the lists of excellence of institutions, since these lists often distort reality.

In the course of the debates dealing with the efficiency of students in higher education, concepts introduced more recently suggest that a constructive, interpretive process of studying in good 'company', that is, a good social environment, is more important than learning specific facts and practising mechanical skills. In accordance with this, the definition of efficiency has also shifted towards a context-dependent, complex, holistic image of the individual. Recent research projects have again dealt with the question of how various institutions shape the value system and attitudes of students, and how classroom- and extra-curricular experience influence them. A comparison of the status indicators and resources of students (demographic and social attributes) upon entering higher education and the same indicators at their graduation will show that there are considerable differences between institutions in terms of their contribution to the development and progress of their students. Our major indicators include the major milestones in students' educational career, a transfer from one level to the next, and we also think in terms of the holistic efficiency indicators of higher education. In the course of our project we made efforts to create extended and long-term and complex efficiency indicators.

Our results indicate that in addition to the student's original resources (demographic, social, cultural and regional), there is another set of resources that is created as a result of the years spent in higher education through the individual's connections with peers and interaction with the main agents of socialization. These factors appear to be appropriate for the independent measurement of students' progress in their respective institutions. We included the features of embeddedness among students' major attributes, and pointed out the presence and multitude of non-traditional student groups. We argue that a considerable segment of the effects of the institutions is certainly tangible through an analysis of the inter- and intragenerational embeddedness of the students. Our overall experience is that the process through which students are embedded in their respective academic communities takes place in parallel with their integration into their networks of connections. A student embedded to a larger extent is closer to the dominant positions in the institution or unit. The effect of this embeddedness is more powerful than the composition of values which include the parental cultural capital. It is to be noted, however, that these effects are not in harmony; intergenerational embeddedness always has a powerful positive influence, whereas the effects of bonds in the intragenerational network are not always explicitly positive. A multi-aspect embeddedness in the institution usually has a positive effect, and extra-curricular and voluntary activities promote the success of students, but when an individual shares all the views of the society of students (peers) this may also have hampering effects.

Multi-variable analyses direct our attention primarily to the informal aspect of student-teacher relationships. Trust in the teachers over other actors in university life has a definite advantage, and the mentoring effect of a teacher is even more obviously positive. The most important element of this phenomenon is the perception of the student that their career at the institution is monitored and followed by at least one teacher. Our research was not extended to the relationships between students and teachers within the classroom, and it is clear that the effectiveness of the roles of educators within and outside the classroom should receive more attention in future researech projects.

We believe that another important finding of our research is the fact that we questioned Tinto and Astin's integration hypothesis, according to which the links binding the student to the educational and social systems of their institutions, and the culture relayed through these links, are to be sharply differentiated from the connections outside the institution, as the latter are negative and seriously jeopardize the success of the student. The changes in the culture of the student society is not primarily caused by the increase in the number of non-traditional students, but rather by the mutual influence of the traditional and non-traditional groups. When studying the various traditional and non-traditional groups of students we found that the increasingly pluralistic academic culture, manifested in smaller and larger institutional communities, did not always provide values, norms and behaviour patterns that supported extra performance and excellence in studies. There are, at the same time, groups that benefit from intra-institutional networks and gain inspiration for further or continued studies, and they channel this culture into the life of students. It is possible to find independent and positive effects of certain communities outside the institution, which improve students' perception of reality outside. Belonging to national minorities, religious communities or NGOs, and – to a certain extent – the community of the student hostels, having a family background committed to education, and having close friends are all sources from which students are able to bring inspiration to improve their academic performance. The effects

246

of students' belonging to ethnic minorities, religions communities or NGOs requires further attention, and specific, fine-tuned research.

We believe that the most important theoretical finding of our research is that we created an independent image of the young people involved in our observations, and the image matches the concepts of education sociology and the current images of students which usually appear in similar research projects. Furthermore, with the help of the socialization models of students, the effects of the campus and the concept of social capital, we highlighted the importance of the social networks of students in the changing world of higher education. In the course of our work, we looked upon the social environment of higher education as an influential and far-reaching element of the institutional culture. This is a feature of the institutional culture which has a determining importance and for us it is essential to study its character and system of interrelations for the purposes of creating and shaping institutional policies. It is our conviction that the importance of our results reaches beyond the social networks and embeddedness of those students learning in the colleges and universities of the specific region we studied and the influence of the network recources on the efficiency of the students of the area. We intended to offer an aspect of analysis for the educational research community which enriches the literature related to students and the institutional environment with an entirely new dimension.

References

Ainsworth, J. W. (2002). "Why does it take the Village? The Mediation of Neighborhood Effects on Educational Achievement". *Social Forces.* Vol. 81. No. 1. 117–152.

Albert, F., B. Dávid (1999). "A bizalmas kapcsolatokról" [The trustfully relations] In: Szívós, P., I. Gy. Tóth eds. *Monitor.* Budapest: TÁRKI. 218–230.

Albert, F., B. Dávid (2007). *Embert barátjáról. A barátság szociológiája.* [Sociology of friendships] Budapest: Századvég.

Algan, Y., P. Cahuc, A. Shleifer (2013): "Teaching practices and social capital". American Economic Journal: Applied Economics. Vol. 5. No. 3. 189–210.

Altbach, P. G. (2009): "Introduction". In: Ludeman, R. B., Osfield, K. J. eds. *Student Affairs and Services in Higher Education: Global Foundation Issues and Best Practices.* International Association of Student Affairs and Services (IASAS) XIII–XIV.

Amaral, A. (2008). "The emergence of neo-liberalism and the alteration of evaluation systems' objectives". In: *Innovation and Quality in the University.* 529–581.

Angelusz, R., R. Tardos eds. (1991). Társadalmak rejtett hálózata. [Hidden netwoks in society] Budapest: Magyar Közvéleménykutató Intézet.

Angelusz, R., R. Tardos (2001). "Change and Stability in Social Network Resources: the Case of Hungary under Transformation". In: Lin, N., R. Burt, L. Cook eds. *Social Capital: Theory and Research.* New York: Aldine de Gruyter. 297–323.

Antrop-González, R., W. Vélez, T. Garret (2003). *Where are the academically successful Puerto Rican students?* Five Success Factors of High Achieving Puerto Rican High School Students. Working Paper No. 61. http://files.eric.ed.gov/fulltext/ED502158.pdf.

Arcidiacono, P., S. Nicholson (2005). "Peer effects in medical school". *Journal of Public Economic.* Vol. 89. No. 2–3. 327–350.

Arum, R., J. Roska (2011). *Academically Adrift*: Limited Learning on College Campuses. Chicago: University of Chicago Press 54–57.

Astin, A. W. (1973): "Measurement and determinants of the outputs of higher education". In: Solmon, L., P. Taubman eds. *Does college matter? Some evidence on the impacts of higher education.* New York: Academic Press.

Astin, A. W. (1993). *What Matters in College: Four Critical Years Revisited.* San Francisco, CA: Jossey-Bass.

Astin, A. W., H. S. Astin, J. A. Lindholm (2003): "Assessing students' spiritual and religious qualities". *Journal of College Student Development.* Vol. 30. No. 1. 41–61.

Astin, A. W., A. L. Antonio (2011). *Assesment For Excellence.* New York: Rowman and Littlefield.

Astin, A. W., H. S. Astin, J. A. Lindholm (2011). *Cultivating the Spirit: How College Can Enhance Students' Inner Lives.* San Francisco: Jossey-Bass.

Astone, N. M., S. McLanah (1991). "Family Structure, Parental Practices, and High School Completion". *American Sociological Review.* Vol. 56. No. 3. 309–320.

Astone, N. M., C. Nathanson, R. Schoen, J. K. Young (1999). "Family Demography, Social *Theory, and Investment in Social Capital" Population and Development Review.* Vol. 25. No. 1. 1–31.

Azzi, C., R. G. Ehrenberg (1975). "Household Allocation of Time and Church Attendance". *The Journal of Political Economy.* Vol. 83. No. 1. 27–56.

Bacskai, K. (2008). "Református iskolák tanárai". *Magyar Pedagógia,* Vol. 108. No. 4. 359–378.

Bacskai, K. (2013). *Mit ér (el) a tanár, ha közép-európai? Alacsony státusú diákokat tanító eredményes tanárok két közép-európai országban.* [Central European teachers' efficiency. Teachers of low-status students in two Central European countries] PhD thesis. Debrecen: University of Debrecen https://dea.lib.unideb.hu/(15. 12. 2014).

Bagley, C. (2009). "Professionals, people and power: sourcing social capital on an early years education and health care programme". In: Allan, J., J. Ozga, G. Smyth eds. (2009). *Social Capital, Professionalism and Diversity.* Boston Sense Publishers. 107–123.

Banta, T. W., G. R. Pike (2007). "Revisiting the blind alley of value-added". *Assessment Update.* Vol. 19. No. 1. 1–15.

Bean, J. P., B. S. Metzner (1985). "A conceptual model of nontraditional undergraduate student attrition". *Review of Educational Research.* Vol. 55. No. 4. 485–540.

Bean, J. P., R. K. Bradley (1986). "Untangling the satisfaction performance relationship for college students." *Journal of Higher Education.* Vol. 57. No. 4. 393–412.

Bean, J. P. (2005). "Nine Themes of College Student Retention". In: Seidman, A. ed. *College student retention: formula for student success*. Westpont: Praeger Publishers. 215–245.

Becher, T. *(1989). Academic Tribes and Territories: intellectual inquiry across the disciplines*. Bristol: Open University Press.

Beck, U. (2001). *The brave new world of work*. Cambridge: Polity Press.

Becker, G. S. (1994). "Human Capital and the Rise and Fall of Families". In: Becker, G. S. *Human Capital: A Theoretical and Empirical Analysis with Special Reference to Education*. Chicago: The University of Chicago Press. 257–298.

Berardo, K. (2005). *Intercultural competence: A synthesis and discussion of current research and theories*. An Area Studies Project. University of Luton.

Berger, J. P. (2000). "Optimizing Capital Optimizing Capital, Social Reproduction, and Undergraduate Persistence". In: Braxton, J. M. ed. *Reworking the student departure puzzle*. Nashville: Vanderbilt University Press. 95–124.

Berger, P. L. (1999). "The Desecularization of the World-. A Global Overview". In: Berger, P. ed. *The desecularization of the world: resurgent religion and world politics*. Washington: Ethics and Public Policy Center. 1–19.

Berger, P. L., T. Luckmann (1966). *The social construction of reality; a treatise in the sociology of knowledge*. Garden City, N.Y., Doubleday.

Bernstein, B. (1971). *Class, Codes and Control*. London: Routledge & Kegan Paul.

Blau, P. M., O. D. Duncan (1998). "A rétegződés folyamata". [The process of stratification] In: Róbert, P. ed. *Társadalmi mobilitás: hagyományos és új megközelítések*. [Social mobility: traditional and new approaches] Budapest: Új Mandátum. 130–141.

Bloch, R. (2008). "Researching study reforms and students". *Reflecting Education*. Vol. 4. No. 2. 39–50.

Bocsi, V., D Szabó (2013). "Examination of students' labour market attitudes reflected in a regional study". Angyalosi, G., Á. Münnich, G. Pusztai eds. *Interdisciplinary Research in Humanities*. Nitra: CPUN, Faculty of Central European Studies. 195–210.

Bolivar, J., J. H. Chrispeels (2010). "Enhancing parent leadership through building social and intellectual capital". *American Journal of Educational Research Journal*. Vol. 48. No. 1. 4–38.

Bordás, A. (2012). "Pedagógusok szakmai tanuló közösségei szociokulturális konstruktivista megközelítésben". [Professional and learning communities of teachers in a constructivist approach] In: Pusztai, G., I. Fenyő, Á. Engler eds. *A tanárok tanárának lenni. Tanulmányok Szabó László Tamás 70. születésnapjára.* [The teacher of the teachers. Festschrift in honor of Tamás László Szabó] Debrecen: Center for Higher Education Research and Development. 226–246.

Bourdieu, P., J. C. Passeron (1977). *Reproduction in education, society and culture.* London: Sage.

Bourdieu, P. (1986). "The forms of capital". In: Richardson, J. ed. *Handbook of theory and research for the sociology of education.* Westport: Greenwood. 241–258.

Bourdieu, P. (1988): *Homo Academicus.* Stanford: Stanford University Press.

Bögre, Zs. (2004). *Vallásosság és identitás. Élettörténetek a diktatúrában (1948–1964).* [Religiosity and identity. Biographies during the dictatorship] Budapest-Pécs: Studia Sociologica, Dialóg Campus.

Bray, M. (2007). *The Shadow Education System: Private Tutoring and Its Implications for Planners.* Párizs: Unesco IIEP

Breugel, I. (2009). "Children's friendships and social cohesion in the diverse and competitive world of english schools". In: Allan, J., J. Ozga, G. Smyth eds. *Social Capital, Professionalism and Diversity.* Boston Sense Publishers. 139–157.

Brundsen, V., M. Davis, M. Shevlin, M. Bracken (2000). "Why do Higher Education Students Drop Out? A test of Tinto's model". *Journal of Further and Higher Education.* Vol. 24. No. 3. 301–310.

Bryk, A., V. E. Lee, P. B. Holland (1992). *Catholic Schools and the Common Good.* Cambridge: Harvard University Press.

Bryk, A., E. Camburn, K. L. Seashore (1999): "Professional community in Chicago elementary scools: Facilitating factors and organizational consequences". *Educational Administration Quarterly.* Vol. 35. No. 5. 751–781.

Bryk, A., B. Schneider (2002). *Trust in Schools: a core resource for Improvement.* New York: Rusell Sage Foundation.

Bryk, A., P. Bender-Sebring, E. Allensworth, S. Lupescu, J. Easton (2010). *Organizing schools for improvement: Lessons from Chicago.* Chicago: University of Chicago Press.

Buhrmester, D., W. Furman, M. T. Wittenberg, H. T. Reis (1988). "Five Domains of Interpersonal Competence in Peer Relationships". *Journal of Personality and Social Psychology*. Vol. 55. No. 6. 991–1008.

Bukodi, E. (2002): "Társadalmi mobilitás Magyarországon, 1983–2000". [Social mobility in Hungary 1983–2000] In: Kolosi, T., I. Gy. Tóth, Gy. Vukovich eds. *Társadalmi riport*. [Report on society] Budapest: TÁRKI. 193–206.

Bunderson, S. J., J. A. Thompson (2009). "The Call of the Wild: Zookeepers, Callings and the Double-Edged Sword of Deeply Meaningful Work." Administrative Science Quarterly. Vol. 54. No. 1. 32–57.

Burr, V. (1995). *An Introduction to Social Constructionism*. London: Routledge.

Burt, R. S. (2000). *Structural Holes versus Network Closure as Social Capital*. http://www.sfu.ca/~scolr/pdf-readings/Burt_Ronald.pdf (10. 04. 2006).

Burt, R. S. (2000). "The network structure of social capital". In: Staw, B. M., R. I. Sutton ed. *Research in Organisational Behavior*. Amsterdam; London and New York: Elsevier Science JAI. 345–423.

Cabrera, A., F., A. Nora, M. B. Castañeda (1993). "College persistence". *Journal of Higher Education*. Vol. 64. No. 2. 123–139.

Camara, W. J., E. W. Kimmel eds. (2005). *Choosing students. Higher education admissions tools for the 21st century*. London: Lawrence Erlbaum Associates.

Campbell, C. (2009). "Social capital in practice in schools". In: Allan, J., J. Ozga, G. Smyth eds. *Social Capital, Professionalism and Diversity*. Boston Sense Publishers. 51–63.

Carbonaro, W. J. (1998). "A Little Help from My Friends' Parents: Intergenerational Closure and Educational Outcomes". *Sociology of Education*. Vol. 71. No. 4. 295–313.

Carbonaro, W. J. (1999). "Opening the Debate on Closure and Schooling Outcomes". *American Sociological Review* Vol. 64. 682–686.

Carini, R. M., G. D. Kuh, S. P. Klein (2006). "Student engagement and student learning: Testing the linkages". *Research in Higher Education*. Vol. 47. No. 1. 1–32.

Ceglédi, T., Sz. Nyüsti (2012). "A jók mennek el?" Szelektív elvándorlás Hajdú-Bihar megye felvételizői körében". [Migration of eminent students from the Hajdú-Bihar county] *Felsőoktatási Műhely*. Vol. 5. No. 4. 95–117.

Chen, T.-M., G. A. Barnett (2000): "Research of international student flows from a macro perspective: A network analysis of 1985, 1989 and 1995". *Higher Education*. Vol. 39. No. 4. 435–453.

Chickering, A. W., J. Kytle (1999): "The collegiate ideal in the twenty-first century". In: Toma, J. D., A. J. Kezar eds. *Reconceptualizing the collegiate ideal*. New Directions for Post-secondary education. No. 105. San Francisco: Jossey-Bass. 109–120.

Clark, B. R., M. Trow (1966): "The Organizational Context". In: Newcombe, T. M., E. K. Wilson eds. *College Peer Groups*. Chicago: Aldine. 17–70.

Clark, B. R. (1983): The Higher Education System: Academic Organization in Cross-National Perspective. Berkeley, CA: University of California Press.

Clark, A., O. Lelkes (2005). Deliver us from *evil: religion as insurance*. Paris – Jourdan Sciences Economiques PSE Working Papers 2005–43, PSE.

Cohen, M. D., J. G. March, J. P. Olsen (1972). "A Garbage Can Model of Organizational Choice". *Administrative Science Quarterly*. Vol. 17. No. 1. 1–25.

Coleman, J. S. (1961). *The Adolescens Society*. New York: The Free Press of Glencoe.

Coleman, J. (1966). *Equality of Educational Oppurtunity*. Washington: U.S. Government Printing Office http://mailer.fsu.edu/~ldsmith/garnet-ldsmith/Coleman%20Report.pdf

Coleman, J. S., T. Hoffer, S. Kilgore (1982). *High School Achievement: Public, Catholic and Private Schools Compared*. New York: Basic Books.

Coleman, J. S., T. Hoffer (1987). *Public and private high schools. The Impact of Communities*. New York: Basic Books.

Coleman, J. S. (1988). "Social Capital in the Creation of Human Capital". *American Journal of Sociology*. Vol. 94. S. 95–120.

Coleman, J. S. (1990). *Foundations of Social Theory*. Cambridge: Harvard University Press.

Coleman, J. S. (1997). "Family, school, and social capital". In: Saha, L. J. ed. *International Encyclopedia of the Sociology of Education*. Oxford: Pergamon. 623–625.

Corten, R., J. Dronkers (2006). "School Achievement of students From the Lower Strata in Public, Private Government-Dependent and Private, Government-Independent Schools: A cross-national test of the

Coleman-Hoffer thesis". *Educational Research and Evaluation*. Vol. 12. No. 2. 179–208.

Cotton, K. (1996). *School Size, School Climate, and Student Performance. School Improvement Research Series.* Portland: Northwestern Regional Educational Laboratory.

Cuyck van, A., J. Dronkers (1990). Catholic and Protestant Schools, a Better Choice in the Netherlands? *School Effectiveness and School Improvement*. Vol. 1. No. 3. 211–220.

Davie, G. (2002). "Praying alone? Church-going in Britain and social capital: a reply to Steve Bruce". *Journal of Contemporary Religion*. Vol. 17. No. 3. 329–34.

Darnell, A., D. E. Sherkat (1997). "The Impact of Conservative Protestant Fundamentalism on Educational Attainment". *American Sociological Review*. Vol. 62. No. 2. 306–315.

Deardorff, D. K. (2006). "The identification and assessment of intercultural competence as a student outcome of internationalization at institutions of higher education in the United States". *Journal of Studies in International Education* Vol. 10. No.10. 241–266.

Derényi, A. (2010). "A felsőoktatás és a foglalkoztathatóság kapcsolatának értelmezései". [Interpretation of the association between higher education and employability] *Educatio*. Vol. 18. No. 3. 361–369.

De Witte, K., S. Cabus (2013). "Dropout Prevention Measures in the Netherlands, an Evaluation". *Educational Review*. Vol. 65. No. 2. 155–176.

Dijkstra, A. B. (2006). *Private Delivery and Central Regulation.* The Dutch System of Choice. PIIRS Conference Paper. http://www.princeton.edu/~piirs/projects/Dijkstra%20paper_Mar31.doc (14. 01. 2007).

DiMaggio, P., J. W. Mohr (1985). "Cultural Capital, Educational Attainment and Marital Selection". *American Journal of Sociology*. Vol. 90. No. 6. 1231–1261.

Diósi, P. (2000). *Tarisznyaleltár. Budapesti fiatalok társas kapcsolataikról és generációjuk gondjairól.* Budapest: Fővárosi Pedagógiai Intézet.

Doktór, T. (2007). "Religion and National Identity in Eastern Europe". In: Révay, E., M. Tomka eds. *Church and Religious Life in Post-Communist Society.* Budapest–Piliscsaba: Loisir. 299–315.

Dronkers, J. (1995). "The Existence of Parental Choice in the Netherlands". Educational Policy. Vol. 9. No. 3. 227–243.

Dronkers, J., J. Baumert, K. Schwippert (1999). *Are German Non-Public Secondary Schools More Effective in Reaching Cognitive and Non-Cognitive Educational Goals?* Berlin: Max-Planck Institut.

Dronkers, J., P. Róbert (2004). "Has educational sector any impact on school effectiviness in Hungary? A comparison on the public and the newly established religious grammar schools". *European Societies.* Vol. 6. No. 2. 205–236.

Dronkers, J. (2004). *Do Public and Religious Schools Really Differ?* Assessing the European Evidence. http://www.iue.it/Personal/Dronkers / *articles/brookings11.pdf* (10. 01. 2007)

Dronkers, J., P. Róbert (2005). "A különböző fenntartású iskolák hatékonysága". [Efficiency of the schools of different maintainers] *Educatio.* Vol. 14. No. 3. 519–537.

Durkheim, É. (1997). *Suicide.* New York: Free Press.

Durkheim, É. (2014). *The Division of Labor in Society.* New York: Free Press.

Engler, Á. (2013). "Career Path and Private Life in the Context of Lifelong Learning" In: Angyalosi, G., Á. Münnich, G. Pusztai eds. *Interdisciplinary Research in Humanities.* Nitra: CPUN, Faculty of Central European Studies. 119–133.

Engler, Á. (2014). "The attitude of students to lifelong learning from gender perspective". In *Conference proceedings. The future of education.* Florence: Libreria universitaria. 462–464.

Evans, W., R. M. Schwab (1995). "Finishing High School and Starting College. Do Catholic School Make Difference?" *Quaterly Journal of Economics.* Vol. 110. No. 4. 941–974.

Fehérvári, A. (2014). *Szakmai képzés és társadalmi átalakulás.* [Vocational education and social transformation] Budapest: Új Mandátum.

Feldman, K. A., T. M. Newcomb (1969). *The impact of college on students.* San Francisco: Jossey-Bass.

Fényes, H., G. Pusztai (2006). "Férfiak hátránya a felsőoktatásban egy regionális minta tükrében". [The Disadvantages of Men in Higher Education] *Szociológiai Szemle.* Vol. 16. No. 1. 40–59.

Fényes, H. (2014). "Gender Role Attitudes among Higher Education Students in a Borderland Central-Eastern- European Region called 'Partium'" *CEPS Journal* Vol 4. No. 2. 49–70.

Fényes, H., G. Pusztai (2012). "Volunteering among Higher Education Students, Focusing on the Micro-level Effects on Volunteering". *Journal of Social Research and Policy*. Vol. 3. No. 1. 73–97.

Fenzel, M. L., R. H. Monteith (2008): "Successful Alternative Middle Schools for Urban Minority Children". *Journal of Education for Students Placed at Risk*. Vol. 13. No. 4. 381–401.

Fenzel, M. L. (2013). "Achievement in Faith-Based Schools". In. Hattie, J., E. M. Anderman *International Guide to Student Achievement*. London: Routledge. 128–131.

Field, J. (2005). *Social capital and lifelong learning*. Bristol: Policy Press.

Field, J. (2009). "A social capital toolkit for schols? Organisational perspectives on current social capital research". In: Allan, J., J. Ozga, G. Smyth eds. *Social Capital, Professionalism and Diversity*. Boston Sense Publishers. 21–37.

Finke, R. (2003). *Spiritual Capital: Definitions, Applications, and New Frontiers.* http://www.metanexus.net/spiritual_capital/pdf/finke.pdf (12.01.2007.).

Fish, S. (1980). *Is There a Text in This Class?* Cambridge: Harvard University Press.

Fónai, M., S. Márton, T. Ceglédi (2011). "Recruitment and Professional Image of Students at one of the Regional Universities in Hungary". *Journal of Social Research and Policy*. Vol. 2. No. 1. 53–65.

Fonyó, I. (1970) "Társas kapcsolatok elemzése kontaktometriai módszerrel". [The analysis of social relationships with the contactometric method] *Magyar Pszichológiai Szemle*. Vol. 27. No. 3. 422–437.

Forray R., K. (2003). "Roma/cigány diákok a felsőoktatásban". [Roma/Gypsy students in higher education] *Educatio*. Vol. 12. No. 2. 253–264.

Forray, R. K., T. Kozma (2013). "Social Equality versus Cultural Identity: Government Policies and Roma Education in East-Central Europe". In: Napier, D. B., S. Majhanovich eds. *Education, Dominance and Identity*. Rotterdam: Sense. 65 -83.

Freeman, R. B. (1986). "Who Escapes? The Relation of Churchgoing and Other Background Factors to the Socioeconomic Performance of Black Male Youths from Inner-city Tracts". In: Freeman, R. B., H. J. Holzer eds. *The Black Youth employment Crisis*. Chicago –London: University of Chicago Press. 353–376.

Frits, P., C. Leana (2009). "Applying Organizational Research to Public School Reform". *The Academy of Management Journal*. Vol. 52. No. 1. 101–124.

Fullan, M. (2014). *The principal: Maximizing impact.* San Francisco: Jossey-Bass.

Gamarnikow, E., A. Green (2009). "Social capitalism for linking professionalism and social justice in education 1–21". In: Allan, J., J. Ozga, G. Smyth eds. *Social Capital, Professionalism and Diversity.* Boston Sense Publishers.

Gamoran, A. (1992). "The Variable Effects of High School Tracking". *American Sociological Review.* Vol. 57. No. 6. 812–828.

Garami, E. (2013). *Kistérségi jellemzők együttes hatása az oktatás eredményességére és a* továbbtanulási döntésekre. [Combined effect of school districts on educational achievement and study plans] PhD thesis. University of Debrecen. https://dea.lib.unideb.hu/dea/(15. 12. 2014).

Gáti, A., P. Róbert (2013). "Employment during studies – a necessity or an investment?" In: Garai, O., Zs. Veroszta eds. *Hungarian graduates 2011.* Educatio Public Services Non-profit LLC. 93–111.

Gautier, M. L., J. Singelmann (1997). "Children's religious affiliation in Eastern Germany". *Journal of Contemporary Religion.* Vol. 12. No. 1. 5–15.

Geertz, C. (1973). "Thick description: toward an interpretive theory of culture". In: *The interpretation of cultures: selected essays.* New-York: Basic Books. 3–30.

Geiger, R., (1985). "The Private Alternative in Higher Education". *European Journal of Education.* Vol. 20. No. 4. 385–398.

Gereben, F. (2009). "Olvasás, művelődési szokások és a vallásosság". [Reading, cultural habits and religiosity] In: *Vallásosság és kultúra.* [Religiosity and culture] Budapest: Faludi Ferenc Academy. 73–96.

Goddard, Y., R. D. Goddard, M. Tschannen-Moran (2007): "A theoretical and empirical investigation of teacher collaboration for school improvement and student achievement in public elementary schools". *Teachers College Record.* Vol. 109. No. 4. 877–896.

Goldring, E. B., K. Phillips (2008). "Parent preferences and parent choices: the public-private decision about school choice". *Journal of Education Policy.* Vol. 23. No. 3. 209–230.

Goldthorpe, J., R. Erikson (2002). "Intergenerational Inequality: A Sociological Perspective". *Journal of Economic Perspectives.* Vol. 16. No. 3. 31–44.

Gordos, Á. (2000). "A kulturális és a társadalmi tőke szerepe az általános iskolás cigány gyermekek iskolai előmenetelében". [The role of cultural and social capital in school career of Gypsy students in primary school] *Új pedagógiai szemle*. Vol. 50. No. 7–8. 93–101.

Görgőy, R. (2001). "Vallásosság és karrier a kommunizmus alatti Magyarországon". [Religiosity and career during the communist period in Hungary] *Valóság*, Vol. 49. No. 7. 31–48.

Granovetter, M. (1973). "The strength of weak ties". *The American Journal of Sociology*. Vol. 78. No. 6. 1360–1380.

Granovetter, M. (1983). "The strength of weak ties: a network theory revisited". *Sociological Theory*. Vol. 1. No. 1. 201–233.

Granovetter, M. (1985). "Economic action and social structure: the problem of embeddedness". *American Journal of Sociology* Vol. 91. No 3. 481–510.

Greeley, A., P. Rossi (1966) *The education of Catholic Americans*. Chicago: Aldine.

Green, T. F. (1980). *Predicting the Behavior of the Educational System*. Syracuse: Syracuse University Press.

Greenbank, P. (2009). "Re-evaluating the Role of Social Capital in the Career Decision-making Behaviour of Working-class Students". *Research in Post-Compulsory Education*. Vol. 14. No. 2. 157–170.

Grogger, J., D. Neal (2000). "Further Evidence on the Effects of Catholic Secondary Schooling". In: Gale, W. G., J. R. Pach eds. *Brookings-Wharton Papers on Urban Affairs*. Washington Brookings Institution. 151–198.

Györgyi, Z. (2008). "Back to school: The KID programme in Hungary". *The Australian Journal of Vocational Education and Training in School*. Vol. 7. No. 7. 81–86.

Halász, G., J. Lannert (2003) *Jelentés a magyar közoktatásról 2003. [Report on Hungarian Public Education]* Budapest: National Institute of Public Education.

Hallinan, M., W. Kubitschek (2012). "A Comparison of Academic Achievement and Adherence to the Common School Ideal in Public and Catholic Schools". *Sociology of Education*. Vol. 85. No. 1. 1–22.

Halpin, R. L. (1990). "An Application of the Tinto Model to the Analysis of Freshman Persistence in a Community College". *Community College Review*. Vol. 17. No. 4. 22–32.

Hámori, Á., G. Rosta (2013). "Youth, Religion, Socialization. Changes in youth religiosity and its relationship to denominational education in Hungary". *Hungarian Educational Research Journal* Vol. 2. No.3. 1–16.

Hanifan, L. J. (1916). "The rural school and community center". *Annals of the American Academy of Political and Social Science*. Vol. 67. No. 1. 130–138.

Hanushek, E. A., J. F. Kain, J. M. Markham, S. G. Rivkin (2003). "Does Peer Ability Affect Student Achievement?" *Journal of Applied Econometrics*. Vol. 18. No. 5. 527–544.

Hargreaves, A., M. Fullan (2012). *Professional capital: Transforming teaching in every school*. New York: Teachers College Press.

Harper, S. R., S. J. Quaye eds. (2009). *Student Engagement in Higher Education*. New York and London: Routledge.

Harris, F.. J. Lester (2009). "Development among Undergraduate Women and Men". In: Harper, S. R., S. J. Quaye eds. (2009). *Student Engagement in Higher Education*. New York-London: Routledge. 99–117.

Harsányi, G., Sz. Vincze (2012). "Hungarian higher education and its international comparison." Farkas, B., J. Mező eds. *Crisis Aftermath: Economic policy changes in the EU and its Member States*. Szeged: University of Szeged 496–513.

Hatos, A., G. Pusztai, H. Fényes (2010). "Are factors of social capital able to modify social reproduction effects?" *Studia Universitatis Babes-Bolyai Sociologia*. Vol. 1. No. 55. 117–136.

Hegedűs, R. (2002). "Religiosity and social position – its association and development". In: Borowik, I., M. Tomka eds. *Religion and Social Change in Central and Eastern Europe*. Cracow: Nomos. 111–123.

Heuser, B. L. (2007). "Academic social cohesion within higher education". *Prospects*. Vol. 37 No. 3. 293–303.

Hirschi, A., S. Fischer (2013). "Work Values as a Predictors of Enterpreunerial Career Intentions: A Longitudinal Analysis of Gender Effect". *Career Development International*. Vol. 18. No. 3. 216–231.

Homans G. C. (1958). "Social Behavior as Exchange". *American Journal of Sociology*. Vol. 63. No. 2. 597–606.

Hrubos, I. (2009). "Az értékekről". [Values] In: Pusztai, G., M. Rébay eds. *Kié az oktatáskutatás? Tanulmányok Kozma Tamás 70 születésnapjára.* [Who responsible for the educational research? Festschrift in honor of Tamás Kozma] Debrecen: Csokonai 229–239.

Hrubos, I. (2010). "A foglalkoztathatóság kérdése az Európai Felsőoktatási Térségben". [The question of employability in the European Higher Education] *Educatio*. Vol. 19. No. 3. 347–360.

Hrubos, I. ed. (2012). *Elefántcsonttoronyból világítótorony. A felsőoktatási intézmények misszióinak bővülése, átalakulása.* [From the ivory tower to pharos. The expending and changing mission of higher education] Budapest: Aula.

Hrubos, I. (2014). "Horizontal Diversity of Higher Education Institutions" *Journal of the European Higher Education Area.* Vol. 4: No. 2. 75–94.

Huber, L. (1991). "Sozialisation in der Hochschule". In: Hurrelmann, K., D. Ulich eds. *Neues Handbuch der Sozialisationsforschung.* Weinheim/Basel: Beltz Verlag S. 417–441.

Humke, C., C. Schaffer (1995). "Relocation: A review of the effect of residential mobility on children and adolescents". *Psychology.* Vol. 32. No. 1. 16–24.

Humes, W. (2009). "The social capital agenda and teacher professionalism". In: Allan, J., J. Ozga, G. Smyth eds. *Social Capital, Professionalism and Diversity.* Boston Sense Publishers. 63–77.

Hurtado, S. (2007). "The Study of College Impact". In: Gumport, P. J. ed. *Sociology of Higher Education: Contributions and their Contexts.* Baltimore: Johns Hopkins University Press. 94–113.

Husen, T. (1990). *Education and the global concern.* Oxford: Pergamon.

Iannaccone, L. R. (1991). "The Consequences of Religious Market Structure". *Rationality and Society.* Vol. 3. No. 2. 156–177.

Iannaccone, L. R. (1998). "Introduction to the Economics of Religion". *Journal of Economic Literature.* Vol. 36. No. 3. 1465–1496.

Imre, A. (2008). "School Atmosphere, School Policies and Social Capital". In: Pusztai, G. ed. *Religion and Values in Education in Central and Eastern Europe.* Debrecen: Center for Higher Education Research and Development. 277–298.

Jancsák, Cs. (2012). "A tanárképzésben részt vevő hallgatók formálódó világa". [Changing society of teacher education students] In: Ercsei, K., Cs. Jancsák ed. *Tanárképzős hallgatók a bolognai folyamatban.* [Teacher education students in Bologna process]. Budpest: Hungarian Institute for Educational Research and Development 27–53.

Jensen, G. F. (1986). "Explaining Differences in Academic Behaviour between Public-School and Catholic-School Students: A Quantitative Case Study". *Sociology of Education.* Vol. 59. No. 1. 32–41.

Jeynes, W. H. (2002). "Meta-Analysis of the Effects of Attending Religious Schools and Religiosity on Black and Hispanic Academic Achievement". *Education and Urban Society.* Vol. 35. No. 1. 27–49.

261

Jeynes, W. H. (2007). "The Relationship between parental Involvement and urban secondary school student academic achievement". *Urban Education*. Vol. 42. No. 1. 82–102.

Jimerson, S., E. Carlson, M. Rotert, B. Egeland, A. L. Sroufe (1997). "Grade retention and school performance: An extended investigation". *Journal of School Psychology*. Vol. 34. 325–353.

Kálmán, G., Cs. Jancsák eds. (2006). *Ifjúsági korszakváltás*. [New era of youth] Szeged: Belvedere Meridionale.

Kálmán, O. (2012). "Az egyetem mint új tanulási környezet" [University as a new learning environment] In: Németh A. ed. *A Neveléstudományi Doktori Iskola programjai*: Tudományos arculat, kutatási eredmények [Projects in Doctoral School of Education: scientific feature, research results] Budapest: ELTE Eötvös 126–135.

Kardos, S. M., Johnson, S. Moore, H. G. Peske, D. Kauffman, E. Liu (2001): "Counting on Colleagues: New Teachers Encounter the Professional Cultures of Their Schools". *Educational Administration Quarterly*. Vol. 37. No. 2. 250–290.

Kaufman, P., K. A. Feldman (2004): "Forming Identities in College: A Sociological Approach." *Research in Higher Education*. Vol. 45. No. 5. 463–496.

Kim, D. H., B. Schneider (2005). "Social Capital in Action: Alignment of Parental Support in Adolescents' Transition to Postsecondary Education". *Social Forces*. Vol. 84. No. 2. 1181–1206.

Kiss, G. (2008). "The Relationship between the New Trends of Socialization and the Results of Differentiated (Educational) Tasks of Educational Institutions." In: Pusztai, G. ed. *Religion and Values in Education in Central and Eastern Europe*. Debrecen: Center for Higher Education Research and Development. 91–105.

Kiss, L. (2013). "'Low-status' bachelor programmes". In: Garai, O., Zs. Veroszta eds. *Hungarian graduates, 2011*. Budapest: Educatio Public Services Non-profit LLC. 67–93.

Kiss, P. (2010). Kompetenciamérés a felsőoktatásban. [Assessment student competences in higher education] Budapest: Educatio Public Services Non-profit LLC.

Kiss, P. (2011). "Kompetenciák a felsőoktatás hírvivői." [Student competences messengers of higher education] In: *Felsőoktatási Műhely* Vol. 4. No. 4. 11–16.

Kiss, P. (2013). "Graduates' job satisfaction". In: Garai, O., Zs. Veroszta eds. *Hugarian graduates 2011.* Educatio Public Services Non-profit LLC. 261–287.

Kiss, Zs. (2014). "A foglalkoztathatóság kérdései a University of Debrecenen". [Employability of graduates from the University of Debrecen] In: Juhász, E., T. Kozma eds. *Oktatáskutatás határon innen és túl.* [Educational research in a boarder region] Szeged: Belvedere Meridionale.

Kivinen, O., J. Nurmi, R. Salminiitty (2000). "Higher Education and Graduate Employment in Finland". *European Journal of Education.* Vol. 35. No. 2. 165–177.

Klein, S. P., G. D. Kuh, M. Chun, L. S. Hamilton, R. J. Shavelson (2005). "An Approach to Measuring Cognitive Outcomes Across Higher Education Institutions". *Journal of Higher Education.* Vol. 46. No. 3. 251–276.

Klein, S., R. Benjamin, R. Shavelson, R. Bolus (2007). The collegiate learning assessment: Facts and fantasies. *Evaluation Review.* Vol. 31. No. 5. 415–440.

Knight, P., M. Yorke (2006). *Embedding employability into the curriculum.* Learning and Employability 1. Leeds: The Higher Education Academy.

Knox, W. E., P. Lindsay, M. N. Kolb (1993) Does college make a difference? Long-term changes in activities and attitudes. Westport, CT: Greenwood Press.

Koltói, L., P. Kiss (2011). "Értelmiségi-utánpótlás. Politikai jártasság és végzettség összefüggése a fiatal felnőttek között". [Association between political expertise and graduation] In: *Felsőoktatási Műhely.* Vol. 4. No. 4. 81–94.

Kopp, M., Á. Skrabski (2003). "Vallásosság és lelki egészség". [Religiosity and health] *Távlatok.* Vol. 13. No. 1. 8–17.

Kovács, K. (2014). "The impact of sports on above-the-average and high-performing students' achievements in Hungarian and Romanian higher education institutions." *Journal of Social Sciences Research.* Vol. 5. No. 3. 794–802.

Kozma, T. (2004). *Kié az egyetem? A felsőoktatás nevelésszociológiája.* [Sociology of higher education] Budapest: Új Mandátum.

Kozma, T., G. Pusztai, K. Torkos (2005). "Roma Childhood in Eastern Europe". In: Yeakey, C. C., J. Richardson, J. Brooks-Buck eds. *Suffer the Little Children.* National and International Dimensions of Child Poverty and Public Policy. Oxford: Elsevier. 73–96.

Kozma, T., G. Pusztai (2006). "Hallgatók a határon. Észak-alföldi, kárpátaljai és partiumi főiskolások továbbtanulási igényeinek összehasonlító vizsgálata". [Analysis of students' further study plans in the border region of three countries] In: Kelemen, E., I. Falus eds. *Tanulmányok a neveléstudomány köréből*. [Research papers in educational science] Budapest: Műszaki Press 423–453.

Kozma, T. (2008). "Political Transformations and Higher Education Reforms". *European Education*. Vol. 40. No. 2. 29–46.

Kozma, T., T. Ceglédi ed. (2010). *Régió és oktatás: a Partium esete*. [Region and education: the case of Partium] Debrecen: Center for Higher Education Research and Development.

Kozma, T. (2010). "Expanzió. 2006–2010" [Expansion 2006–2010] *Educatio*. Vol. 19. No. 1. 7–18.

Kozma, T., K. Teperics, Z. Tőzsér, E. Kovács (2012). "Lifelong Learning in a Cross – Border Setting: the Case of Hungary and Romania". *Hungarian Educational Research Journal*. Vol. 2. No. 1. 163–179.

Kuh, G. D., J. Kinzie, J. H. Schuh, E. J. Whitt (2005). *Student success in college: Creating conditions that matter*. San Francisco: Jossey-Bass.

Kun, A. I. (2013). "Oktatási jelzés és szűrés a munkaerőpiacon". [Educational labelling and screening in labour market] *Competitio*. Vol. 12. No. 1. 39–60.

Kuzniewski, A. J. (1997). "Contending with Modernity: Catholic Higher Education in the Twentieth Century". *The American Historical Review*. Vol. 102. No. 4. 1246–1247.

Kwiek, M. (2013). "From System Expansion to System Contraction". In: Zgaga, P., U. Teichler, J. Brennan eds. *The Globalisation Challenge for European Higher Education*. Convergence and Diversity, Centres and Peripheries. Frankfurt am Main: Peter Lang.

Laarhoven, P., B. Bakker, J. Dronkers, H. Schijf (1990). "Achievement in Public and Private Secondary Education in the Netherlands". In: Anheiter, H. K., W. Seibel eds. *The Third Sector: Comparative Studies of Nonprofit Organisations*. Berlin: Walter de Gruyter. 165–182.

Ladányi, J. (1994). *Rétegződés és szelekció a felsőoktatásban*. [Stratification and selection in higher education] Budapest: Educatio.

Lannert, J. (2004). *Pályaválasztási aspirációk*. [Career aspirations of the young people in Hungaryion] PhD thesis. Budapest: University of Corvinus http://phd.lib.uni-corvinus.hu_sept_2006 (15. 12. 2012).

Lannert, J. (2006): "Az iskolaeredményességi kutatások nemzetközi tapasztalatai" [Conclusions of the research on school efficiency] In: Lannert, J., M. Nagy eds. *Az eredményes iskola.* [Efficiency of school] Budapest: NationalInstitute of Public Education.

Laarhoven van, P., B. Bakker, J. Dronkers, H. Schijf (1990). "Achievement in Public and Private Secondary Education in the Netherlands". In: Anheiter, H. K., W. Seibel eds. *The Third Sector: Comparative Studies of Non-profit Organisations.* Berlin: Walter de Gruyter.

Lauglo, J. (2010). *Do Private Schools Increase Social Class. Segregation in Basic Education Schools in Norway?* London Centre for Learning and Life Chances in Knowledge Economies and Societies.

Lawrence, B. S. (2006). "Organizational reference groups: A missing perspective on social context". *Organization Science.* Vol. 17. No. 1–2, 80–100.

Leana, C., P. Frits (2006). "Social Capital and Organizational Performance: Evidence from Urban Public Schools".*Organization Science.* Vol. 17. No. 3. 353–366.

Leana, C. (2010). "Social Capital: The Collective Component of Teaching Quality". *Voices in Urban Education.* Vol. 23. No. 27. 16–23.

Lee, V. E. (2002). "Catholic schools: private and social effects" William Sander. Boston: Kluwer Academic Publishers (book review). *Economics of Education Review.* Vol. 21. No. 5. 646–648.

Lehrer, E. L. (1999). "Religion as a Determinant of Educational Attainment: An Economic Perspective". *Social Science Research.* Vol. 28. No. 4. 358–379.

Lehrer, E. L. (2006). "Religion and high-school graduation: a comparative analysis of patterns for white and black young women". *Review of Economics of the Household.* Vol. 4. No. 3. 277–293.

Leithwood, K., K. L. Seashore, S. Anderson, K. Wahlstrom (2004). *How leadership influences student learning.* New York: The Wallace Foundation.

Leithwood, K., S. Anderson, B. Mascall, T. Strauss (2010). "School leaders' influence on student learning: The four paths". In: Bush, T., L. Bell, L. Middlewood eds. *The principles of educational leadership and management.* London: Sage.

Lenski, G. (1961). *The Religious Factor: A Sociological Study of Religion's Impact on Politics, Economics, and Family Life.* Garden City, NY: Doubleday.

Ligeti, Gy., I. Márton (2003). "A szülők és az iskola". [Parents and schools] *Új pedagógiai szemle*. Vol. 53. No. 4. 3–10.

Lin, N. (2001). *Social Capital: A Theory of Social Structure and Action.* Cambridge: Cambridge University Press.

Lin, N. (2005). "Social Capital". In: Beckert, J., M. Zagiroski eds. *Encyclopedia of Economic Sociology*. London: Routledge. 604–612.

Liu, W. C., C. K. J. Wang (2008): "Home environment and classroom climate: An investigation of their relation to student's academic self-concept in a streamed settings". *Current Psychology*. Vol. 27. No. 4. 242–256.

Loury, C. G. (1977). "A dynamic theory of racial income differences". In: Wallace, P., A. LaMond eds. *Women, Minorities and Employment Discrimination*. Lexington: Lexington Books 153–188.

Loury, L. D. (2004). "Does Church Attendance Really Increase Schooling?" *Journal for Scientific Studies of Religion*. Vol. 43. No. 1. 119–127.

Luyten, H., M. Hendriks, J. Scheerens eds. (2014). *School Size Effecrs Revisited. A qualitative and quantitative review of the research evidence in primary and secondary education.* Dordrecht, Springer.

Mahaffey, C. J., S. A. Smith (2009). "Creating welcoming campus environmets for students from Minority Religious Groups". In: Harper, S. R., S. J. Quaye eds. *Student Engagement in Higher Education*. New York-London: Routledge. 81–99.

Malone, R. (2009). "Building social capital, reconstructing habitus: addressing the problem of early school leaving in Ireland". In: Allan, J., J. Ozga, G. Smyth eds. *Social Capital, Professionalism and Diversity*. Boston Sense Publishers. 157–175.

Marginson, S., G. Rhoades (2002). "Beyond national states, markets, and systems of higher education: A glonacal agency heuristic". *Higher Education*. Vol. 43. No. 3. 281–309.

Martin, N. D., K. I. Spenner (2009). "Capital Conversion and Accumulation: Social Portrait of Legacies at on Elite University". *Research in Higher Education*. Vol. 50. No. 7. 623–648.

McDonald, L., S. Fitz Roy. I. Fuchs, I. Fooken, H. Klasen (2012). "Strategies for high retention rates of low-income families in FAST (Families and Schools Together): An evidence-based parenting programme in the USA, UK, Holland and Germany". *European Journal of Developmental Psychology*. Vol. 9. No. 1. 75–88.

McEwan, P. J. (2004). "The Potential Impact of Vouchers". *Peabody Journal of Education*. Vol. 79. No. 3. 57–80.

McNeal, R. B. Jr. (1999). "Parental Involvement as Social Capital: Differential Effectiviness on Science Achivement, Truancy and Dropping Out". *Social Forces*. Vol. 78. No. 1. 117–144.

McPherson, M. S., L. Smith-Lovin, J. M. Cook (2001). "Birds of a feather: homophily in social networks". *Annual Review of Sociology*. Vol. 27. No. 1. 415–444.

McQuaid, R., C. Lindsay (2005). "The Concept of Employability". *Urban Studies*. Vol. 42. No. 2. 197–219.

Meier, A. (1999). *Social Capital and School Achievement Among Adolescents* CDE *Working* Paper 1–53. http://www.ssc.wisc.edu/cde/cdewp/99-18.pdf (2006. 12. 12).

Minckler, C. H. (2011). *Teacher Social Capital: The Development of a Conceptual Model and Measurement Framework with Application to Educational Leadership and Teacher Efficacy*. University of Louisiana at Lafayette.

Minckler, C. H. (2013). "School Leadership That Builds Teacher Social Capital". *Educational Management Administration & Leadership* 12–17.

Montt, G. (2011). "Cross-national Differences in Educational Achievement Inequality". *Sociology of Education*. Vol. 84. No. 1. 49–68.

Morenoff, J. D., R. J. Sampson, F. Earls (1999). "Beyond Social Capital: Spatial Dynamics of Collective Efficancy for Children". *American Sociologocal Rewiew*. Vol. 64. october 633–661.

Morgan, D., A. Douane (1980). "When less is more: School size and social participation". *Social Psychology Quarterly*. 43. 241–252.

Morgan, S. L., A. B. Sorensen (1999). "Parental Networks, Social Clousure, and Mathematichs Learning: A Test of Coleman's Social Capital Explanation of School Effects". *American Sociologocal Rewiew*. Vol. 64. No. 5. 661–682.

Morris, J. M., A. B. Smith, B. M. Cejda (2003). "Spiritual integration as a predictor of persistence at a Christian institution of higher education". *Christian Higher Education*. Vol. 2. No. 4. 341–351.

Mullen, A. L., K. A. Goyette, J. A. Soares (2003). "Who goes to grad school? Social and academic correlates of educational continuation after college". *Sociology of Education*. Vol. 76. No. 2. 143–169.

Muller, C., C. G. Ellison (2001). "Religious Involvement, Social Capital and Academic Achievement: Evidence from the National Education Longitudinal Study of 1988". *Sociological Focus*. Vol. 34. No. 2. 155–183.

Neal, D. (1997). "The Effect of Catholic Secondary Schooling on Educational Achievement". Journal of Labour Economics. Vol. 15. No. 1. 98–123.

Neave, G. (1998): "The Evaluative State". Europen Journal of Education, Vol. 33. No. 3. 265–289.

Nye, B., S. Konstantopoulos, L. Hedges (2004): "How Large Are Teacher Effects?" Educational Evaluation and Policy Analysis. Vol. 26. No. 3. 237–57.

Nyüsti, Sz., T. Ceglédi (2013). "Migrating graduates, migrating for graduation – Patterns and underlying causes of migration for study and after graduation". In: Garai, O., Zs. Veroszta eds. Hungarian Graduates 2011. Educatio Public Services Non-profit LLC. 169–205.

Orbán, A., Z. Szántó (2005): "Társadalmi tőke". [Social capital] Erdélyi Társadalom. Vol. 3. No. 2. 55–70.

Otero, G., S. Chambers-Otero, R. Sparks, M. Sparks (2001): Relational Learning: Education for Mind, Body and Spirit. Melbourne: Hawker Brownlow Education.

Pace, C. R. (1984). Measuring the quality of college student experiences. Los Angeles: University of California, Center for the Study of Evaluation, Graduate School of Education.

Parcel, T., M. Dufur (2001): "Capital at Home and at School: Effects on Student Achievement". Social Forces. Vol. 79. No. 3. 881–911.

Pascarella, E. T., P. T. Terenzini (1991). How College Affects Students: Findings and Insights from Twenty Years of Research. San Francisco: Jossey-Bass.

Pascarella, E. T., P. T. Terenzini (2005). How College Affects Students. A Third decade of research. San Francisco: Jossey-Bass.

Pascarella, E. T. (2006). "How College Affects Students: Ten Directions for Future Research". Journal of College Student Development. Vol. 47. No. 5. 508–520.

Pasternack, P. (2005). Current and Future Trends in Higher Education. HoF Wittenberg and Institut für Hochschulforschung an der Martin-Luther-Universität Halle-Wittenberg. Wien: Federal Ministry for Education, Science and Culture.

Pataki, F. (2003). "Együttes élmény, kollektív emlékezet". [Common experience, collective memory] In: Pataki, F. Nevelés-ügyek. [Educational affairs] Budapest: Aula. 117–130.

Perna, L. W., M. A. Titus (2005). "The Relationship between Parental Involvement as Social Capital and College Enrollment: An Examination of Racial/Ethnic Group Differences". *The Journal of Higher Education.* Vol. 76. No. 5. 485–518.

Penuel, W. R., M. Riel, K. A. Frank, A. Krause (2009). "Analyzing teachers' professional interactions in a school as social capital: A social network approach". *Teachers College Record.* Vol. 11. No. 1. 124–163.

Polite, V. C. (1992)."Getting The Job Done Well: African American Students and Catholic Schools". *Journal of Negro Education.* Vol. 61. No. 2. 211–222.

Polónyi, I., J. Timár (2001) *Tudásgyár vagy papírgyár?* [Knowledge factories or diploma mills?] Budapest: Új Mandátum.

Polónyi, I. (2013). *Az aranykor vége – bezárnak-e a papírgyárak?* [The end of the gonden age: should diploma mills close down?] Budapest: Gondolat.

Polónyi, I., A. I. Kun eds. (2013). *Az Észak-alföldi régió oktatási helyzete – Képzés és munkaerőpiac.* [Educational conditions in North-Eastern Hungary: education and labour market] Budapest: Új Mandátum.

Polyák, I., G. Andrási, D. Kéry, K. Tardos (2012). Enhancing Intercultural Competence. http://dx.doi.org/10.2139/ssrn.2351881 (15. 12. 2013).

Portes, A., J. Sensenbrenner (1993). "Embeddedness and Immigration: Notes ont the Social Determinations of Economic Action". *American Journal of Sociology* Vol. 98. No. 6. 1320–50.

Portes, A., P. Landolt (1996). "The Downside of Social Capital". *The American Prospect.* Vol. 7. No. 26. 18–21.

Preuschoff, C., M. Weiß (2004). *Schulleistungen in staatlichen und privaten Schulen im Vergleich: eine Übersicht über neuere Forschungsergebnisse.* http://www.dipf.de/publikationen/tibi/tibi8 preuschof_weiss.pdf (15. 01. 2007).

Pusztai, G., E. Verdes (2002). "A társadalmi tőke hatása a felekezeti gimnazisták továbbtanulási terveire". [The effect of socialcapital on students' further study plans in church-run schools] *Szociológiai szemle.* Vol. 12. No. 1. 90–106.

Pusztai, G., J. Fináncz (2003). "A negyedik fokozat iránti társadalmi igény megjelenése". [The rise of demand on postgradual studies] *Educatio.* Vol. 13. No. 4. 618–634.

Pusztai, G. (2004). *Iskola és közösség*. Felekezeti középiskolások az ezred-fordulón. [Schools and communities. Church-run schools at the turn of the Millennium] Budapest: Gondolat.

Pusztai, G. (2004b). "Kapcsolat a jövő felé. Közösségi erőforrások szerepe roma/cigány diplomások iskolai pályafutásának alakulásában". [In connection with your future. The effect of network resources on school career of Roma/Gypsy graduates] *Valóság* Vol. 47. No. 5. 69–83.

Pusztai, G., É. Nagy (2005). "Tanulmányi célú mobilitás Magyarország keleti határvidékein". [Student mobility in Eastern border region of Hungary] *Educatio*. Vol. 14. No. 2. 360–384.

Pusztai, G. (2006). "Egy határmenti régió hallgatótársadalmának térszerkezete". [Spatial composition of student body in a border region] In: Juhász, E. ed. *A "Regionális egyetem" kutatás zárókonferenciájának tanulmánykötete*. [Final papers of "Regional University" research] 43–57.

Pusztai, G. (2006). "Community and Social Capital in Hungarian Denominational Schools Today". *Religion and Society in Central and Eastern Europe*. Vol. 1. No. 2. 1–15.

Pusztai, G. (2007) "Effect of Social Capital on Educational Achievement of Students in Denominational and Nondenominational School Sectors". In: Révay, E., M. Tomka eds. *Church and Religious Life in Post-Communist Societies*. Budapest: Loisir. 241–258.

Pusztai, G. (2007). "The long-term effects of denominational secondary schools". *European Journal of Mental Health*. Vol. 2. No. 1. 3–24.

Pusztai, G. Cs. Szabó (2008). "The Bologna Process as a Trojan Horse: Restructuring the Higher Education in Hungary". *European Education*. Vol. 40. No. 2. 85–103.

Pusztai, G. (2008). "Les bienfaits pedagogiques de la religiosité parmi les éleves hongrois de trois pays". *Social Compass*. Vol. 55. No. 4. 497–516.

Pusztai, G. (2009). *A társadalmi tőke és az iskola*. [Social capital in schools] Budapest: Új Mandátum.

Pusztai, G. (2011). *A láthatatlan kéztől a baráti kezekig. Hallgatói értelmező közösségek a felsőoktatásban*. [From the invisible hand to friendly hands. Interpretive communities of students in higher education] Budapest: Új Mandátum.

Pusztai, G., A. Hatos, T. Ceglédi eds. (2012). *Third Mission of Higher Education in a Cross-Border Region*. Debrecen: Center for Higher Education Research and Development.

Pusztai, G., K. Bacskai, K. Kardos (2012). "Vallásos közösségekhez tartozó hallgatók". [Students who belong to religious communities] In: Dusa, Á., K. Kovács eds. *Hallgatói élethelyzetek*. Debrecen: Debrecen University Press.

Pusztai, G. (2013). "A felsőoktatás munkára felkészítő szerepe a hallgatók értelmezésében". [Preparation for the labourmarket during the university studies] In: Kun, A. I., I. Polónyi eds. *Az Észak-Alföldi régió helyzete: Képzés és munkaerőpiac*. [Educational conditions in North-Eastern Hungary: education and labour market] Budapest: Új Mandátum. 9–29.

Pusztai, G. (2013). "Hallgatói vallásosság és felsőoktatási beágyazottság". [Students' religiosity and embeddedness in hgher education] *Confessio*. Vol. 37. No. 1. 26–44.

Pusztai, G. (2014). "Nem biztos csak a kétes a szememnek..." Hallgatói eredményességi koncepciók és mutatók a felsőoktatás-kutatásban. ["Nothing is sure for me but what's uncertain." Concepts and indicators of student success in higher education research] In: Nagy, P. T., Zs. Veroszta eds. (2014). *A felsőoktatás kutatása*. [The higher education research] Budapest: Új Mandátum. 123–145.

Putnam, R. D. (2004). *Education, Diversity, Social Cohesion and Social Capital*. Meeting of OECD Education Ministers. Dublin: OECD.

Rautopuro, J., P. Väisänen (2002). "The function of goal orientation and commitment to studies in different fields of university education". *The Finnish Journal of Education*. Kasvatus Vol. 33. No. 1. 6–20.

Reagans, R. E., E. W. Zuckerman (2001). "Networks, Diversity, and Performance: The Social Capital of Corporate R&D Units". *Organization Science*. Vol. 12. No. 4. 502–517.

Reay, D., G. Crozier, J. Clayton (2009). "Strangers in Paradise?: Working-class Students in Elite Universities". *Sociology*. Vol. 43. No. 6. 1103–1121.

Rechnitzer, J. (2009). "A felsőoktatás térszerkezetének változása és kapcsolata a regionális szerkezettel". *Educatio*. Vol. 18. No. 1. 50–63.

Regnerus, M. D. (2000). "Shaping Schooling Succes: Religious Sociaization and Educational Outcomes in Metropolitan Public Schools". *Journal For the Scientific Study of Religion*. Vol. 39. No. 3. 363–370.

Rendon, L. I., R. E. Jalomo, A. Nora (2000). "Theoretical considerations in the study of minority student retention in higher education". In: Braxton, J. ed. *Reworking the student departure puzzle*. Nashville: Vanderbilt University Press. 127–156.

Rendon, L., S. M. Munoz (2011). "Revisiting Validation Theory: Theoretical Foundations, Applications and Extensions". *Enrollment Management Journal*. Vol. 5. No. 2. 12–33.

Renn, K. A., K. D. Arnold (2003). "Reconceptualizing Research on College Student Peer Culture". *Journal of Higher Education*. Vol. 74. No. 3. 261–291.

Riesman, D. (1956). *The Lonely Crowd: A Study of the Changing American Character.* Doubleday Anchor Books.

Róbert, P. (1987). "Mobilitási és reprodukciós folyamatok a magyar társadalomban". [Social mobility and reproduction process in Hungarian society] In: Fokasz, N., A. Örkény eds. *Magyarország társadalomtörténete.* [The sociohistory of Hungary] Budapest: Új Mandátum. 193–206.

Róbert, P. (2000). "Bővülő felsőoktatás – ki jut be?" [Expension in higher education – who enters?] *Educatio*. Vol. 9. No. 1. 79–94.

Róbert, P. (2001). "Családösszetétel, társadalmi tőke és iskolai egyenlőtlenségek". [Family structure, social capital and educational inequalities] In: *Útközben*. Tanulmányok Somlai Péter 60. születésnapjára. [Under way. Festschrift in honor of Peter Somlai] Budapest: Új Mandátum.

Rodgers, T. (2007). "Measuring Value Added in Higher Education: A Proposed Methodology for Developing a Performance Indicator Based on the Economic Value Added to Graduates". *Education Economics*. Vol. 15. No. 1. 55–74.

Rodrigoa, M. J., A Almeidab, C. Spielc, W. Koops (2012). "Evidence-based parent education programmes to promote positive parenting". *European Journal of Developmental Psychology*. Vol. 9. No. 1. 2–10.

Rosta, G. (2010). "Vallásosság és politikai attitűdök az Európai Értékrend Vizsgálatban". [Religiosity and political attitudes in European Value Survey] In: Tomka, M., G. Rosta eds. *Mit értékelnek a magyarok?* [What are the value preferences of Hungarians?] Budapest: Faludi Ferenc Academy. 427–450.

Rumberger, R. W., T. L. Scott (2000). "The Distribution of Dropout and Turnover Rates among Urban and Suburban High Schools". *Sociology of Education*. Vol. 73. No. 1. 39–67.

Rychen, D., L. Salganik (2003). *Key competencies for a successful life and a well-functioning* society. Göttingen: Hogrefe & Huber.

Sacerdote, B. (2001). "Peer Effects with Random Assignment: Results for Dartmouth Room –mates". *Quarterly Journal of Economics.* Vol. 116. No. 2. 681–703.

Sandefur, R. L., E. O. Laumann (1998). "A Paradigm for Social Capital". Rationality and Society. Vol. 10. No. 4. 481–501.

Sanders, Jimy M. (2002): Ethnic boundaries and identity in plural societies. Annual Review of Sociology Vol. 28. No. 1. 327–357.

Schomburg, H., U. Teichler eds. (2011). *Employability and Mobility of Bachelor Graduates in Europe Key Results of the Bologna Process.* Rotterdam: Sense Publishers.

Schreiner, L. (2000). *Spiritual fit. Fund for improvement of postsecondary education: Through the eyes of retention.* Council for Christian Colleges and Universities.

Schultz, T. W. (1971). *Investment in human capital: the role of education and of research.* New York, N. Y.: Free Press,; London: Collier-Macmillan.

Scott, S., S. Kathy, C. Beckett, A. Kallitsoglou, M. Doolan, T. Ford (2012). "Should parenting programmes to improve children's life chances address child behaviour, reading skills, or both? Rationale for the Helping Children Achieve trial". *European Journal of Developmental Psychology.* Vol. 9. No. 1. 47–60.

Setényi, J. (1991). *Harc a középiskoláért. Kísérletek az egységes középiskola megteremtésére az 1945 utáni Európában.* [Struggle for the secondary school. Attempts to create a comprehensive secondary school in Europe after 1945] Budapest: Educatio.

Sewell, W. H., A. O. Haller, A Portes (1969). "The Educational and Early Occupational Attainment Process". *American Sociological Review.* Vol. 34. No. 1. 82–92.

S. Faragó M. (1986). *Beilleszkedés és szakmai szocializáció a felsőoktatásban.* [Adaptation and professional socialisation in higher education] Budapest: Tankönyvkiadó.

Shavelson, R. J. (2012). *Assessing College Learning: The Collegiate Learning Assessment.* University of Padernborn.

Sherkat, D. S. (2007). *Religion and Higher Education: The Good, the Bad and the Ugly.* Social Science Research Council. (http://religion.ssrc.org/reforum/Sherkat.pdf 2010. 07. 25.).

Sík, E. (2011). *A migráció szociológiája 2.* [Sociology of migration]Budapest: ELTE.

Siklós, B. (2006). "A munkáltatói oldal igényeit is figyelembe vevő felsőoktatási minőségbiztosítási rendszerek". [Higher education quality assurance systems with the point of view of employers] In: Bálint, J., I. Polónyi, B. Siklós eds. *A felsőoktatás minősége.* Budapest: Felsőoktatási Kutatóintézet.

Simmel, G (1949). "Sociology of sociability". *American Journal of Sociology.* Vol. 55. No. 3. 254–261.

Skrabski, Á., M. Kopp, I. Kawachi (2004). "Social capital and collective efficacy in Hungary: cross sectional associations with middle aged female and male mortality rates". *Journal of Epidemiol Community Health.* Vol. 58. No. 4. 340–345.

Smart, J. C., K. A. Feldman, C. A. Ethington (2000). *Academic disciplines: Holland's theory and the study of college students and faculty.* Nashville, TN: Vanderbilt University Press.

Spady, W. G. (1970). "Dropouts from higher education. An interdisciplinary review and synthesis". *Interchange.* Vol. 1. No. 1. 64–85.

Spitzberg, B. H., G. Changnon (2009). "Conceptualizing intercultural competence". In: Deardorff, D. K. ed. *The SAGE handbook of intercultural competence.* Thousand Oaks: Sage 2–52.

Standfest, C. (2005). *Erträge von Erziehungs- und Bildungsprozessen an Schulen in evangelischer Trägerschaft in Deutschland.* Nürnberg: Friedrich-Alexander-Universität, Erziehungswissenschaftlichen Fakultät.

Strange, C. C., J. H. Banning (2001). *Educating by Design: Creating Campus Learning Environments That Work.* San Francisco: Jossey-Bass.

Strange, C. C. (2003). "Dynamics of campus environments". In: Komives, S., D. B. Woodard eds. *Student services: A handbook for the profession.* San Francisco: Jossey-Bass. 297–316.

Stanton-Salazar, R. D., S. M. Dornbusch (1995). "Social capital and the reproduction of inequality: information networks among Mexican-origin high school students". *Sociology of Education.* Vol. 68. No. 2. 116–135.

Stewart, E. B. (2008). "School Stuctural characteristics, student effort, peer associations and parental involvement". *Education and Urban Society.* Vol. 40. No. 2. 179–204.

Stoll, L., K. L. Seashore (2007). "Professional learning communities: Elaborating new approaches". In: Stoll, L., K. L. Seashore eds. *Professional learning communities: Divergence, depth, and dilemmas.* Berkshire, England: Open University Press 1–14.

Szabó, I., A. Örkény (1997). "Középiskolások társadalmi cselekvési mintái". [Patterns of students involvement in public actions] *Iskolakultúra.* Vol. 7. No. 11. 39–58.

Szczepanski, J. (1969). *A felsőoktatás szociológiája.* [Sociology of higher education] Budapest: Felsőoktatási Pedagógiai Kutatóközpont.

Szemerszki, M. (2010). "Regionális eltérések a harmadfokú továbbtanulásban". [Regional differences of participation in tertiary level edcation] In: Kozma, T. T.Ceglédi eds. *Régió és oktatás. A Partium esete.* [Region and education: the case of Partium] Debrecen: Center for Higher Education Research and Development. 168–186.

Szemerszki, M. (2012). "A felsőfokú képzésbe belépők társadalmi háttere, iskolai életútja, a középfokú oktatás főbb sajátosságai". [The social background and previous school career of freshmen] In: Szemerszki, M. ed. *Az érettségitől a mesterképzésig. Továbbtanulás és szelekció.* [From the school leaving examination to the master studies. Tertiary education and selection.] Budapest: Hungarian Institute for Educational Research and Development. 113–140.

Szemerszki, M. (2013): "Tanulási utak és képzési tervek a felsőoktatásban". [Learning paths and educational plans in higher education] In: Garai, O., Zs. Veroszta eds. *Hungarian Graduates 2011.* Educatio Public Services Non-profit LLC. 37–67.

Szolár, É. (2010): The "Implementation of Two-Cycle Degree Structure in Hungary". *New Educational Review* Vol. 22. No. 3–4. 93–102.

Szolár, É. (2011): "The Bologna Process: the Reform of the European Higher Education Systems". *Romanian Journal of European Affairs* Vol. 11. No. 1. 81–100.

Teichler, U. ed. (2007). *Careers of University Graduates. Views and Experiences in Comparative Perspectives.* Dordrecht: Springer.

Teichler, U. (2008). "Diversification? Trends and Explanations of the Shape and Size of Higher Education". *Higher Education.* Vol. 56. No. 3. 349–379.

Teachman, J., K. Paasch, K. Carver (1996). "Social Capital and Dropping Out of School Early". *Journal of Marriage and the Family.* Vol. 58. No. 3. 773–783.

Thomas, S. L. (2000). "Ties that bind: A social network approach to understanding student integration and persistence". *The Journal of Higher Education.* Vol. 71. No. 5. 591–615.

Thomas, L. (2002). "Student Retention in Higher Education: the role of institutional habitus". *Journal of Education Policy.* Vol. 17. No. 4. 423–442.

Thomas, L., R. Jones (2007). *Embedding Employability in the Context of Widening Participation.* York: The Higher Education Academy.

Tierney, W. G. (2000). "Power, identity and dilemma of college student departure". In: Braxton, J. M. ed. *Reworking the student departure puzzle.* Nashville: Vanderbilt University Press. 213–235.

Tinto, V. (1993). *Leaving college. Rethinking the Causes ad Cures of Student Attrition.* Chicago-London: The University of Chicago Press.

Tinto, V. (2006). "Research and practice of student retention: What next?" *Journal of College Student Retention Research, Theory & Practice.* Vol. 8. No. 1. 1–19.

Titarenko, L. (2007). "Religion as an Indicator of Post-Soviet Transformation". In: Révay, E., M. Tomka eds. *Eastern European Religion.* Pázmány Társadalomtudomány 5. Budapest–Piliscsaba: Loisir. 33–51.

Tomka, M. (2010). "Vallási helyzetkép 2010". [The state of the religiosity] In: Rosta, G, M. Tomka eds. *Mit értékelnek a magyarok?* [What are the value preferences of Hungarians?] Budapest: Faludi Ferenc Academy. 401–426.

Tomka, M. (2011). *A vallás a modern világban.* [Religiosity in modernity] Budapest: Semmelweis University, Institute of Mental Health.

Tomusk, V. (1997): "Conflict and interaction in central and East European higher education: The triangle of red giants, white dwarfs and black holes". *Tertiary Education and Management.* Vol. 3. No. 3. 249–257.

Tornyi, Zs. Zs. (2009b). "Female Roles, Opportunities and Statuses among Female Professors and Researchers in Hungary". In: Adamiak, E., M. Chrząstowska, S. Sobkowiak, C. Methuen eds. *Gender and Religion in Central and Eastern Europe.* Poznan: Adam Mickiewicz University Press. 263–276.

Treiman, D. J. (1970): "Industrialization and social stratification." In: Laumann, E. ed. *Social stratification: research and theory for the 1970s.* Indianapolis: Bobbs-Merrill. 207–234.

Trow, M. (1974). *Problems in the transition from elite to mass higher education.* Paris: OECD.

Utasi, Á. (2002). "A társadalmi integráció és szolidaritás alapjai: a bizalmas kapcsolatok".[The foundations of social integration and solidarity: the confidential relations] *Századvég.* Vol. 24. No. 2. 3–26.

Utasi, Á. (2008). *Éltető kapcsolatok. A kapcsolatok hatása a szubjektív életminőségre.* [Invigorating relationships. The effect of the relationships on subjective well-being] Budapest: Új Mandátum.

Yorke, M. (2008). *Employability in higher education: what it is –what it is not.* Learning and Employability 1. Leeds: Higher Education Academy.

Youngs, P., M. B. King (2002). "Principal leadership for professional development to build school capacity". *Educational Administration Quarterly.* Vol. 38. No. 5. 643–670.

Vámos, Á. (2011). "Tanulási eredmények – szemlélet és gyakorlat összefüggése a felsőoktatásban". [Learning outcomes – the relationship between attitude and practice in higher education] In: *Felsőoktatási Műhely.* Vol. 4. No. 4. 33–48.

Van de Grift, W., T. Houtveen (1999). "Educational Leadership and Pupil Achievement in Primary Education". *School Effectiveness and School Improvement.* Vol. 10. No. 4. 373–390.

Varga, J. (2010). "Mennyit ér a diploma a kétezres években Magyarországon". [What is the value of the degree in Hungary] *Educatio.* Vol. 19. No. 3. 370–383.

Varga, J. (2013). "Labour market success of Hungarian higher education graduates in 2011" In: Garai, O., Zs. Veroszta eds. Hungarian Graduates 2011. Budapest: Educatio Public Services Non-profit LLC. 143–171.

Vastagh, Z. (2005). *Közös élmények fonalán.* [Linked by common experiences] Pécs: Argumentum.

Veroszta, Zs. (2010). *Felsőoktatási értékek – hallgatói szemmel. A felsőoktatás küldetésére vonatkozó hallgatói értékstruktúrák feltárása.* [Values in higher education from student perspective. Student interpretations of the mission of higher education.] Ph.D. thesis. Budapest: Corvinus University. http://phd.lib.uni-corvinus.hu/506/1/veroszta_zsuzsanna.pdf (03.01. 2014.).

Veroszta, Zs. (2010). "A foglalkoztathatósághoz kötődő hallgatói várakozások". [Expectations related to the employability of students] *Educatio.* Vol. 19. No. 3. 460–472.

Veroszta, Zs. (2012). "A felsőoktatás különböző szintjeire felvettek jellemzői". [Expectations related to the employability of students] In: Szemerszki, M. ed. *Az érettségitől a mesterképzésig. Továbbtanulás és szelekció.* [From the school leaving examination to the master studies. Tertiary education and selection.] Budapest: Hungarian Institute for Educational Research and Development. 51–82.

Veroszta, Zs. (2013). "The way to master programmes – an examination of the selection mechanisms in the bachelor/master transition in higher education". In: Garai, O., Zs. Veroszta eds. *Hungarian graduates 2011*. Budapest: Educatio Public Services Non-profit LLC. 9–37.

Vescio, V., D. Ross, A. Adams (2008). "A review of research on the impact of professional learning communities on teaching practice and student learning". *Teaching and Teacher Education*. Vol. 24. No. 1. 80–91.

Voas, D., A. Crockett (2005). "Religion in Britain: Neither Believing nor Belonging". *Sociology*. Vol. 39. No. 1. 11–28.

Weber, M. (2001). *The Protestant Ethic and the Spirit of Capitalism*. London: Routledge Classics.

Weidman, J. C., D: Twale, E.L. Stein (2001): *Socialization of Graduate and Professional Students in Higher Education: A Perilous Passage?* San Francisco: Jossey-Bass

Weininger, E. B., A. Lareau, (2003). "Translating Bourdieu into the American context: the question of social class and family-school relations". *Poetics*. Vol. 31. No. 5–6. 375–402.

Wellman, B. (1988). "Structural Analysis: From Method and Metaphor to Theory and Substance." In: Wellman, B., S. D. Berkowitz eds. *Social Structures: A Network Approach*. Cambridge: Cambridge University Press. 19–61.

Wellman, B. (1999). "The Network Community: An Introduction". In: Wellmann, B. ed. *Networks in the Global Village: Life in Contemporary Communities*. Boulder: Westview Press. 1–48.

Wigfield, A., S. R. Asher (2000). "Social ad motivational influences on reading". In: Kamil, M. L., P. B. Mosenthal, P. D. Pearson, R. Barr eds. *Handbook of Reading Research*. Mahwah: Lawrence Erlbaum Associates. 423–453.

Wilson, W. J. (1996). *When Work Disappears: The World of the New Urban Poor*. New York: Random House.

Winston, G., D. Zimmermann (2004). "Peer Effect in Higher Education". In: Hoxby, C. ed. *College Choices: The Economics of Where to Go, When to Go, and How to Pay For It?* University of Chicago Press. 395–423.

Zgaga, P., U. Teichler, J. Brennan eds. (2014). *The Globalisation Challenge for European Higher Education*. Convergence and Diversity, Centres and Peripheries. Frankfurt am Main: Peter Lang.